CLIFF ELLIS

The Winning Edge

by
Cliff Ellis with Phillip Marshall

SPORTS PUBLISHING INC.
WWW.SPORTSPUBLISHINGINC.COM

Director of Production, Book Design: Susan M. McKinney
Editor: Rob Rains
Cover design: Julie Denzer
Proofreader: David Hamburg
Production assistant: Crystal Gummere

ISBN: 1-58261-200-5

SPORTS PUBLISHING INC.
804 N. Neil
Champaign, IL 61820
www.sportspublishinginc.com

Printed in the United States.

This book is dedicated to all my children—those born to me: Chryssa, Clay, and Anna Catherine; and those who played for me.

Contents

Acknowledgments

I could not have created this book without enormous help from many people. Phillip Marshall and I spent many hours remembering, recording, and writing about the events of my life on the court. Carolyn and I spent days remembering and writing about the events of my life on and off the court.

And these words now are simply an emphasis of what I hope the entire book communicates; my family, my players, my coaches, my friends have made this biography a pleasure to live and compose.

To all the players who have played for me. They are the ones who have made my coaching career a happy and successful one. I wish them all success in life.

To all the assistant coaches and staff members who have worked with me, current and past. Thanks for your hard work and dedication.

To my loving wife, Carolyn, and to Phillip Marshall for so diligently working with me on this project and helping make it happen.

To the alumni of Ruckel Junior High, Niceville High, Ocala Vanguard High, Cumberland University, University of South Alabama, Clemson University, and Auburn University. I have been blessed to be a part of your family.

Foreword

---

by Dave Odom
Head Basketball Coach, Wake Forest University

Cliff Ellis is, above all else, a "lifer."

As basketball coaches, lifers live for the opportunity to teach, to compete, to enjoy relationships, and to share special memories. Cliff has lots of lasting relationships and memories—of his players and of his many friends who coach with him or against him.

I met Cliff shortly after he became head coach at Clemson. At that time, I was an assistant at the University of Virginia. We became instant friends. It's quite unusual for a head coach and an assistant to become good friends, but we did.

We have traveled together abroad on several occasions doing clinics for the armed services. That was really the springboard for our relationship.

Shared time with Cliff has taught me that the same qualities that make him a great coach also make him a great person.

Cliff is a genuine person. He cares deeply about his family, his friends, and his players. He is always loyal and expects loyalty in return.

He is fun-loving, almost never too serious. When needed most, he is always there.

Lose three or four games and Cliff will call and put things in perspective. Count on it! Ask anyone. Cliff Ellis is one of the top coaches in the country and very little has changed. He still coaches for the same reasons and treats others with dignity and respect.

Cliff has always performed well under pressure. He has great instincts and makes good spontaneous decisions. Because his players trust him, they always play well together. They play with a sense of confidence and they believe in their coach. They look and feel prepared. Their minds are not cluttered with meaningless details. They are given simple plans and execute them to perfection.

What Cliff has done as a coach is truly amazing. Some coaches, such as Dean Smith and John Wooden, remain at one school all of their working lives. Not Cliff. He is a mountain climber, a coach who takes on great challenges without fear.

He prefers the thrill of rebuilding or building—always doing what others choose never to attempt. There is no coach better at building a winner from scratch than Cliff Ellis.

He doesn't seek advantages; he creates them in the form of hard work and perseverance. There is no mountain too tall, no program too difficult for Cliff.

He is a lifer!

Introduction

by Phillip Marshall

Streamers were falling from the ceiling at Beard-Eaves Memorial Coliseum on the Auburn campus. The song "We Are the Champions" blared over the public address system. On the floor was a mass of humanity—students and businessmen, mothers and children, there to celebrate with Auburn's basketball team.

Auburn had won the 1999 Southeastern Conference championship.

Auburn has had outstanding basketball teams before. It even won an SEC championship, but that was in 1960 when the coach was Joel Eaves, and the offense was the Auburn Shuffle. It was a different game and a different time. For five straight seasons in the 1980s, Sonny Smith took Auburn to the NCAA Tournament. It got to the Elite Eight in 1986 and might have been as good at that point as any team in the country.

Charles Barkley and Chuck Person played at Auburn in those years on their way to the NBA. So did Chris Morris.

But even in those years, basketball was never the thing to do at Auburn. After Smith left, Auburn basketball went into a painful decline. There was talent, but not enough. There wasn't much accomplishment and nobody seemed to care.

That's the situation Cliff Ellis found when he arrived as head coach in 1994.

It was well known that he'd won championships at South Alabama and at Clemson. But win one at Auburn? There weren't many people who liked his chances. SEC basketball had taken off. It had become a dominant force in the NCAA Tournament. Arkansas and Kentucky had won national championships. Mississippi State and Florida had been in the Final Four. Auburn had been left behind.

So it was that it was all the more amazing on February 17, 1999. Auburn, which had gone 10 seasons without an NCAA Tournament bid, beat Vanderbilt 81-63 and won the SEC championship. Ellis became one of only two coaches to win championships in both the SEC and the ACC.

On the day Ellis accepted the Auburn head coaching job, he had a question, "If it can happen at Arkansas, why can't it happen at Auburn?" A lot of people were ready to give him a lot of reasons. Ellis wasn't ready to listen.

There were good times and bad, joys and disappointments. Then, in the remarkable season that was 1998-99, it all came together. Ellis had done it again, just like he did at Clemson, at South Alabama, and even at Cumberland College. He'd taken a program from the bottom to the top.

Ellis' story begins in the Florida panhandle. It's a story of determination and perseverance. It's a story of a man who has seen life from all sides. He's a husband, a father, a musician, an author, and a gourmet cook. He's even been an ostrich farmer.

But at the core of his soul, Cliff Ellis is a basketball coach. It's a calling he embraced as a teenager in Chipley, Florida. He didn't listen to those who said he should go in other directions.

Though he never played college basketball, Ellis studied the game. He learned from some of the best in the business. He embarked on a career that would lead him from the high schools of Florida to Lebanon, Tennessee, and finally to Auburn.

At every stop in his college career, he took over programs seemingly down and out and turned them not just into winners but into champions. He became renowned as a teacher of big men and for sending them on to the NBA. He did it all with a smile and dedication to hard work and determination that rubbed off on those around him.

As his players celebrated and the happy tears ran down his face on February 17, 1999, Ellis' thoughts went to all those who helped along the way. He thought about his family, about his parents, about the people who were willing to give opportunities to an ambitious young coach.

But mostly, he thought about his players, the men who took him again to the mountaintop of college basketball.

It was another remarkable chapter in a remarkable career.

CHAPTER ONE

Being a Winner

It really was amazing. The Auburn Tigers had won the 1999 regular-season SEC championship. Most people had thought that feat might never be accomplished. And then on Sunday, March 12, 2000, we were vying for another championship, this time the SEC tournament championship. Even though Auburn had not played in the championship game of the tournament many times in its history, most people had expected us to be right there in that situation. The truth is that our road to this game was traveled in ways that were totally unexpected.

In the fall of 1999, after our championship season, when we were chosen as *Sports Illustrated*'s preseason No. 1 pick and when Chris Porter was featured on the cover as the magazine's predicted player of the year, several people asked me if that bothered me. One thing these people were questioning was the *SI* cover jinx. Even some *SI* writers wondered if we had heard that being on the cover of their magazine would mean a sure loss. Others, especially some Auburn fans, worried that being picked high would create too much pressure, would paint too big a target on our backs.

My answer always was that being in everybody's preseason top five was an enormous compliment. These predictions are educated guesses based on past performance. They don't take into consideration the improvement of other teams, or the fact that an abundance of returning players can limit recruiting. Nevertheless, the predictions are high compliments. They provide great publicity for the basketball program and for the university. The good publicity can enhance recruiting. On the cover of *Sports Illustrated* is exactly where every athletic program in the United States wants to be.

A part of the preseason excitement was that, for the first time in Auburn history, all conference games were sold out. We had our first Midnight Mayhem basketball practice, and the coliseum was full. The SEC championship banner was displayed for the first time. The players sensed the love of the Auburn family and their appreciation.

The excitement, the anticipation, the expectations were growing. We were coming off the best season in basketball history, not only for Auburn University basketball, but also for collegiate basketball in the State of Alabama. Prior to the 1998-1999 season, we had not been mentioned in anybody's preseason poll but still had ended up as a No. 1 pick for the NCAA tournament. For everyone involved that year, each win was a gift, a thing to enjoy and savor. Fans, players, coaches, media were all surprised and therefore simply appreciative of the performance of that team.

During the following 1999-2000 season, the satisfaction of winning did seem to diminish for fans and media. We had four seniors back from a great team, including the phenomenally talented Chris Porter. Even with a 12-1 preseason run that included wins over Pepperdine, Penn, Southern Miss, and Florida State and a close loss to an eventual No. 1 Stanford, the excitement from outside the team was somewhat lessened.

Therefore, our theme for the year became "Concentrate on being true to yourself and being the best you can be." We had to forget about what others were saying—good and bad. We had to forget about high expectations and low satisfaction. Each player had to answer for himself whether he was giving his best effort, his best performance. Each player had to be his own evaluator and motivator.

Giving 150 percent is impossible; nobody is perfect or better than perfect. My questions for the team and for each player were "How close to perfect can you be?" and "Have you given your best effort?" For example, when we won against the University of Alabama–Birmingham for the first time in four tries in Auburn, we were pleased at having outscored our opponent, but we asked each player and each player asked himself, if he was true to himself and to his best effort. In our first loss, against Stanford, we were unhappy at the opponent's having outscored us, but we asked the same questions. Our evaluations of ourselves were more mature and more intrinsic.

We went into the season knowing that in every one of the 34 games we played, we would get everyone's best shot. Their motivation would come from playing a highly ranked team. Our motivation was always an individual and inner desire to give the best possible contribution to the team.

We also went into the season missing sophomore David Hamilton and two freshmen, Marquis Daniels and Jamison Brewer, who did not enter Auburn until the winter quarter.

David Hamilton's loss of his mother during the previous year, resulting in time away from Auburn, had naturally caused academic problems for him. He needed the summer and fall quarters to recover. David was ineligible to play games before December, but could practice. Marquis and Jamison were unavailable for practice and games before December. Preseason practice is vital for learning and teaching the fundamentals. Obviously, the absence of all these players affected their ability to mesh with the team. In fact, the staff coached three teams in the 1999-2000 season: the pre-December team without Hamilton, Daniels, and Brewer; the post-December team with all the players; and the final team without Chris Porter. With each team, the staff and players had to respond to changes in chemistry as well as changes in personnel contributions.

I knew going into the 2000 season that coaching this team would be another wonderful challenge, a time of responding to being on top at the same time that we were molding a new team. Coaching always requires the skills of psychologist, promoter, parent. This year would be no different. The 2000 season, like most seasons, was filled with some great victories and some difficult defeats.

The road we took to the title game of the SEC tournament and to the NCAA tournament was indeed not the one we were expected to follow. But the journey of 2000 with these young men on the team, with my staff, with Auburn University was a joy-filled and thrill-filled ride. Lots of people have described it as a roller-coaster ride. We did have highs that took my breath away; we did also have some stomach-wrenching lows. But none of it was boring.

In that 2000 season, as well as in most seasons of my life, I noticed that all of life is characterized by peaks and valleys, things to savor and things to regret, pulses akin to heartbeats. There are some days that I wish I could just live an even-keeled, peaceful journey on cruise control. Then I remember—that kind of life is akin to flatline, to death.

I am extremely fortunate that my whole life has been a great journey.

CHAPTER TWO

The Early Years

I was born in Marianna, Florida, on December 5, 1945, but my family moved before my first birthday to Chipley, Florida. Being raised in Chipley was a wonderful experience. Chipley is a small town—still only about 3,000 total population—in the panhandle of Florida. The people there, typical of small-town folk, knew everyone else's business and they cared about everybody, including me.

I started first grade at Chipley Elementary School, later named Kate Smith Elementary, when I was only five years old and quickly developed a love of sports. All my teachers would showcase me in the front of their classes because I could spell every major league baseball team. Miss Rosemary Cutts, Mrs. Ann Shuler, Mrs. Clarabelle Nelson, Miss Lola May were all impressed that I could spell Philadelphia and Cleveland when I was only six or seven.

My favorite reading material in elementary school was the sports page. I loved following major league baseball teams. My team was the Cleveland Indians. My favorite player was Al Rosen, the home run king and third baseman.

Baseball became my passion. What I wanted to be more than anything else at that time in my life was a major league third baseman. In the early fifties in small-town Chipley, I dreamed of going to one of those cities whose names I could only spell and wowing the thousands of people in the stands.

Another aspect of life in Chipley in the fifties was what my children think we lacked. We didn't have air conditioning. In spring and summer we entertained ourselves by cavorting in the water sprayed from the garden hose, swimming in Blue Pond, and playing a lot of baseball. I began playing when I was only seven with neighborhood guys who were much older—in the sixth grade. They would throw tennis balls with what I thought was real heat. They taught me to stay in the batter's box and not to back down.

Guys like Jimmy Parker, six years older and living four doors down from me; Freddie Hall, even older than Jimmy and living around the corner and across the railroad tracks; Billy McCormick, a great athlete living across the street; all these older guys paid attention to me, made sure I got into games, made me feel good about myself, gave me confidence.

They gave me experience that only older-brother kind of people could have given me. Freddie took me when I was only about nine years old to see Chipola Junior College basketball; I couldn't have been more excited to see the Boston Celtics. I knew all the stats about Chipola, including Bill Tuffli's scoring 55 points.

When I was about 11, Jimmy Parker asked me to go to his girlfriend's house with him—because she had a sister my age. I was as nervous as if it had been a real date. Mum deodorant used to be a cream, and I didn't know how to use it. I caked it under both armpits. When Jimmy picked me up, he wrinkled his nose and asked, "What in the world have you got on?" Jimmy and his girlfriend, Norma Harper, must have laughed at Nola and me. But I thought I was hot stuff. My flat-top was perfectly plastered with butch wax, and my perspiration was clearly under control.

There was a field on a lot behind my house where we played baseball. My friend Dale Bush and I, with our other friends, wanted to make sure it was a real baseball field, not just a field. Every spring, we would mow it and put down the base paths and pitching mound.

One year when I was about nine, we decided to sell season tickets to our games. We went through the neighborhood door-to-door promoting our team and selling the tickets. I had decided that we could do what the Graceville Oilers and the Pensacola Dons, local minor league baseball teams, were doing. We sold lemonade at the games. We put up a makeshift wooden fence. We thought we were in the big time. The people in the community got a kick out of it and still remember it today, over 40 years later. Early in life, I was already promoting, a skill that would stay with me when I got involved in music and when I started coaching.

My first taste of organized athletics occurred when I was eight and played in a farm league for the Chipley Little League. The coach—Philip Rountree, my mentor today—taught us everything—swimming, football, and baseball. I am very fortunate that I was growing up in Chipley when Coach Rountree was devoting his energies to helping kids like me. He taught us fundamental skills of sports and fundamental skills of living. He made us feel competent and confident by not focusing on our mistakes.

In this farm league, Coach Rountree was league organizer and facilitator of the coaches of the teams. One of my vivid memories of this time involved Tommy Hale, who was legally blind and played in the league, but not on my team. We were instructed to be very careful how we hit and threw to him. At the same time that Coach emphasized excellence in catching, hitting, and throwing, he also emphasized kindness and respect.

Late in one game when the outcome was fairly well determined, Coach Rountree put Tommy in to pitch. I am still moved by the memory of that ennobling act. Tommy Hale left Chipley to attend Florida School for the Deaf and Blind, but he took with him a strong belief in himself that is at least partly the result of playing with a coach and with players who affirmed him as a human being and avoided treating him as only a person with a disability. He eventually graduated from the University of Alabama, went to Atlanta to work for a government agency and to open his own business—a newsstand! He is retired and remains self-supporting and self-sufficient.

In the years when Coach Rountree was teaching me in Little League, he was also head football coach, head basketball coach, and head baseball coach.

There were many days that I would show up at the baseball field or the gym or the football field and stay long after the players had left practice so that I could have a few more catches or kicks or shots. Rather than running off what some varsity coaches would have considered a pest, Coach Rountree gave me pointers, made me feel special. Most of those days he would have to make me get on my bicycle to head home, guided and protected by the light from his headlights. He always made sure I got home safely.

Evidence that he was a good teacher is the success of his teams. He coached the 1954 Chipley Tigers to an undefeated football season. I remember thinking what a magical accomplishment that seemed to be. His basketball teams frequently went to the state playoffs. Several of his baseball players went on to earn scholarships to play college ball. In many ways, Philip Rountree was the coach I would eventually want to grow up to be like.

I remember sitting in Miss Ann Thaggard's eighth-grade classroom when I knew what I was going to do for the rest of my life. I wasn't sure that I would be the best high school baseball or basketball coach in the panhandle of Florida, but I knew that I would be happy working at it. And despite some frustrations I would experience as a player and despite my parents' hesitation at endorsing my decision and despite the appeal of some other possibilities, including music, I have never wavered in my belief that coaching is what I would be happy doing. I guess I am lucky that I had that focus so early in my life. I never had to wonder what I would be when I grew up.

With Coach Rountree's help, and because I had been playing baseball with all those older guys in the neighborhood, I was a fairly successful baseball player. I was the only nine-year-old to make Little League in that era and be a starter. I started at third base, where Al Rosen, my hero, had played. I made the all-star team when I was 10. I played Pony League when I was 12, an age when I should have actually still been playing Little League.

I thought I had a real future in baseball. I could hit; I couldn't hit the ball a long way, but I could place it anywhere I wanted to. I could run pretty well and I could play defense. I loved it.

I was devastated when Chipley High School dropped its baseball program just before I got there. A major frustration and disappointment of my young life was not getting to play baseball in high school, in college, and—I dreamed—in the major leagues. Of course, frustration and disappointment are not always bad things.

CHAPTER THREE

The Greatest Family

The two people who gave me the best training in handling frustration are my parents, Connie and Robert Ellis. They instilled in me what I have heard called the FIDO philosophy—"Forget It; Drive On." My brother Randy and sisters Carolyne and Teresa and I were not allowed to feel sorry for ourselves for any reason. If circumstances were not always what we wanted them to be, we were encouraged to make the best of the situation and "drive on."

On July 21, 1999, my dad died. I have always loved and appreciated what both my parents have done for me. However, after Dad had his stroke on Father's Day, and as my sisters, especially, and my brother and I cared for him in the hospital, rehab center, and then the nursing home—and subsequently, as we prepared to eulogize Dad after his death—I felt compelled even more to express what both my dad and my mom have meant to my life.

I am a baby boomer and have thought many times about how different and difficult life was for my parents' generation.

Coming of age at the end of the promising and roaring twenties, they were hit by the tough times of the Great Depression and then the horror of World War II. They came out of these experiences to create for us the comfortable lifestyle that we live. Tom Brokaw's *Greatest Generation* eloquently portrays the contributions of people like my mom and dad.

Dad graduated from Pensacola Tate High School in 1932 as valedictorian of his high school. He was offered a scholarship in math to Oglethorpe in Atlanta. Unfortunately, his family could not afford the living expenses for him to go. Instead he joined the Civilian Conservation Corps, a part of Roosevelt's New Deal, which provided people with a chance to work during the Depression. He did that for two or three years, sending his wages home to his family. After he left the CCC, he worked for the U.S. Geological Service, mapping territory from Foley, Alabama, to the Adirondacks, venturing with courage many miles from the sleepy towns of Northwest Florida where he had been born and raised.

At the same time my dad was making the most of a difficult situation, my mom was graduating from Marianna High School and coping with her own hard times. Her teachers in high school convinced her that taking business classes would be the best preparation for young women who could not afford college. And sure enough, that decision paid off; a local attorney who paid her sporadically the great wage of five dollars a week, hired her. Mom was willing to do this because she had the foresight to know that the experience would prove valuable. Soon her reputation for conscientious work earned her an offer from another law firm at the steady rate of 10 dollars a week. She continued to work hard, learning all she could on the job and taking civil service exams as those opportunities arose. Her determination and self-confidence are characteristics that I still admire in her and that my dad found attractive.

They met in 1940 and were together on December 7, 1941, when they heard Pearl Harbor had been bombed. Dad joined the army in 1942 and fought in the Battle of the Bulge, using his surveying skills to shoot the North Star and guide the aim of field artillery. Mom and Dad married and started their family just as the war was ending.

My sisters and brother and I are pretty much stairsteps. Carolyne and I are only 12 months apart in age. We became especially close during our teenage years, sharing the excitement and fears about relating to the opposite sex. I admired then and still admire her creativity and strength. Teresa, the baby of us, and I had the hardest time relating simply because of our age difference; six years is a long time in childhood. I don't know what I would do without her and Carolyne now. They are fun-loving, supportive, and amazing in their willingness to take care of family, especially our parents, as they have aged.

I don't know two brothers who are closer than Randy and I. We love to go fishing together, which means that we enjoy just being together. Fishing the rivers and ponds of Northwest Florida and Central Alabama is a sport that allows talking and sharing; we intensely enjoy this time together. It is amazing that we have gotten this close, because I was the proverbial abusive big brother. I quit wrestling with him only when he got big enough to beat me up.

One of the stories that always gets told at family reunions is indicative of how I used to try to take advantage of my little brother. One day I had come home from high school and ball practice without my books. I remembered just as I got to the house that my books were on the steps of the gym. In true Tom Sawyer fashion, I decided that there had to be a way to get my books without walking all the way—five blocks—back to school.

Randy was outside playing Roy Rogers, running around shooting the bad guys. I—as nonchalantly as I could—sat down on our front steps and asked Randy how fast he thought he could run. He, of course, thought he was a pretty speedy fellow. I pretended to question his quickness but told him that if he could run to the high school and back in 10 minutes, I would have to agree that he was sure enough fast. He assured me that he could accomplish that easily.

I prepared to time him, but then hesitated, worrying aloud that I wouldn't know if he went all the way to the school. We deliberated that problem for a few minutes, with Randy all the time wanting to prove himself, and assuring me he wouldn't cheat. Suddenly, I pretended to remember my books. "I know how you can prove you got to the school. My books are on the steps of the gym. If you get back here with my books in 10 minutes, I will agree that you are one fast kid."

When he came panting back home with my books in about 10 minutes, he wanted to know his time. I just said, "Thanks for getting my books." I like this story better than Randy does.

My parents' lives after the war were consumed by hard work and raising their children. My dad was the parts manager for a Ford dealership in Chipley, pretty much all of his adult life. Legend has it that the parts department did not need a parts manual when Robert Ellis was on duty; he knew the numbers and locations of all the parts!

My mom worked her way up to be secretary to the district engineer for the Department of Transportation office in Chipley. The district was afraid it might have to shut down when she retired at the age of 67.

Even though they worked hard, my parents never had a lot of money. Consequently, they taught us the value of the dollar. As late as the early sixties, when I wanted to go out on a date in high school, Dad would give me a dollar. That was enough to get in the movie and to buy popcorn and a drink. If I wanted anything extra, I could earn it—picking up pecans or loading watermelons.

The first real job I had was loading watermelons. It was a way to make a little extra money, and it was also incentive for me to do whatever it took to avoid that kind of work as a lifetime vocation. I rose at six in the morning and worked until six at night. We followed the tractors, breathing the diesel fumes and throwing five- to 10-pound watermelons to guys in the trailers. It was excruciatingly long and backbreaking work for which we were paid five dollars a day.

Even though everyone worked hard, our lives were anything but plain or deprived. Our parents sacrificed to give us happy times. They tried very hard to make our wishes come true on birthdays and at Christmas. I still get excited when I remember the thrill of getting my Roy Rogers hat, boots, and holster for Christmas. I didn't get Trigger, but my imagination was wild enough that I could do a very good imitation of galloping through the neighborhood. A few years later I remember becoming the envy of my buddies when I got for my birthday an authentic *indoor* basketball.

A very special part of my growing up was having my dreams actualized by parents who had to struggle to accomplish that.

I had great fun in my childhood. We played hard in the neighborhood. Every Saturday I got a quarter and went with my buddies to the double feature at the Vance Theater. It took 15 cents to see the movie, a nickel for a Coke, and a nickel for popcorn. We watched all of our cowboy heroes—Hopalong Cassady, Lash Larue, Tom Mix, Gene Autry, and my very favorite, Roy Rogers. I absolutely loved him and Dale and Trigger and Bullet and Pat Brady and Nellie Belle. I loved the stories of the good guys winning. For a couple of hours just about every Saturday of my childhood, I would immerse myself in the fantasy world of movies on the big screen where no conniving bad guy could whip any of my heroes—my guys.

I learned a lot from my parents. I learned to be respectful. We kids said, "Yes, ma'am" and "No, sir." We learned those rules of manners that were signs of respect, like taking our hats off indoors and holding doors for older people. I learned pride—pride in myself and in whom I represented. If I ever got my fanny whipped at school, that was the first of the whippings. When my dad told me to go to the bathroom and put my hands on the washing machine, I knew I was in trouble. My parents were my strongest advocates, and I knew their punishment was out of love for me and a desire that I make the best choices for my sake.

I learned that happiness depends on attitude and not circumstances. We did not have television for a long time; we were glad to listen to the radio. We had no air conditioning; we loved the attic fan. We did not get cars the day we turned 16; we were glad to get a ride.

I have a terrible habit of eating fast. It is the result of coming to a table loaded with the best food in the world. My mother can cook the best fried chicken, fresh corn and collards, creamed new potatoes, and biscuits a son could wish for—and pot roast, and fried fish, and caramel cake . . . the list is endless. The challenge when we sat down to eat was to see how fast we could finish the first helping and get first dibs on the second biscuit or fried chicken thigh. Despite our mother's admonitions, as soon as grace was said, Randy and I raced to get that second helping and often almost stabbed each other in the process.

Every Thursday night we had a fish fry, and sometimes we had fish more than once a week, because the one pastime that my father enjoyed was fishing. Dad worked about 55 hours a week, but he had Thursday afternoons off, and if the weather was good and the river was right, he was sculling his boat upstream and slinging his hook under the overhanging branches along the Choctawhatchee or Appalachicola rivers, loading the boat with bream or bass. When I got old enough, he would take me with him sometimes. I learned to love the peaceful beauty and the quiet challenge of fishing—and the joy of cleaning and scaling the fish just before they are mealed and fried. There's not much that is better.

One of the people who loved to go fishing with Dad was Preacher McDuffy. Our family attended the First Presbyterian Church of Chipley, attending Sunday school and worship every Sunday. Our favorite minister during my youth was Preacher McDuffy. He made our relationship to God and to people of God a joyful, comfortable experience. He wasn't just the preacher in church on Sunday; he was minister all week and frequently in the johnboat watching a cork attached to a cane pole.

My parents were not able to go to college themselves, but they made sure their four children all graduated. I graduated from Florida State. Carolyne graduated from Florida State also, in elementary education, and teaches school in Panama City Beach, Florida. Randy also graduated from Florida State, getting a degree in criminology, and he serves as probation and parole regional supervisor in the panhandle of Florida. Teresa finished school at the University of West Florida and works in Atlanta in communications and marketing.

Our parents instilled in us a healthy belief in ourselves and in right and honor and in service. The good that is in me I owe to my parents, Connie and Robert Ellis.

Chapter Four

The Greatest Extended Family

I had not only the family of small-town Chipley and the family of my parents and siblings to influence my development, I also had the advantage of a large and interested extended family.

Dad's mother, Gertrude Ellis, lived in Pensacola, Florida, with my Aunt Elizabeth Kaminski and my cousins, Joe and Jeanine. Randy and I would get on the L&N train in Chipley to go to visit them. We'd stop in DeFuniak Springs and pick up a cousin or two, usually Bobby Daughtry. We'd stop in Crestview and pick up Larry Ellis, another cousin. By the time we got to Gramma Ellis' we had a good basketball team and about half a baseball team.

One time when I was about 11 and visiting them, the Pensacola City Recreation Department had organized a summer baseball league. My cousin fibbed and told the league that I had just come to town to live with my grandmother. We helped our team win the league. Some people might say I was a ringer. I loved baseball so much and felt so natural in the game that I did about anything to get to play.

Gramma Ellis loved the Pensacola Dons minor league baseball team. She would take us all to as many games as we could find money to go to. I can still smell the popcorn and the cigars. I can breathe the dust that flew up when we scrambled to snag foul balls. The management wanted us to turn the balls in in exchange for a cheaper but autographed ball. I knew better than to give up a topflight minor league ball; one afternoon I ended up with three—all stuffed in Gramma Ellis' purse.

She took us all fishing in the bay right outside her back door. She would walk us two blocks to the bait house to pick out the shrimp bait and then back to the fishing spot to go over the safety rules. She wanted us to watch where we threw our lines; with so many cousins lined up on the shore, we had to make sure we didn't hook any ears. She wanted us to watch out for the alligator, too! Fortunately, I have no stories about seeing that alligator.

My favorite uncle is Gramma Ellis' youngest son, Bill. My Uncle Bill has been a major influence on my life. He has always encouraged and supported me, and in the 1999 season he did not miss a single home conference game, driving three and a half hours from DeFuniak Springs to Auburn and back after the game, even if it was a nine o'clock game!

When my friends or my son Clay's friends meet Uncle Bill, they become Uncle Bill's friends. Ben and Ginger Main and Jimmy and Sujane Weathers, my longtime friends, celebrated Uncle Bill's 74th birthday because now they love him, too. There is a spark in him that attracted us cousins when we were young and still attracts people of all ages.

When Uncle Bill turned 17, the United States had been fighting in World War II for over a year. He decided to lie about his age and join the navy. He became a gunner on a navy fighter plane in the Pacific campaign. At the same time that my dad was involved in the Battle of the Bulge, Uncle Bill was fighting in the Battle of Midway in one of the most precarious positions in which any of those young men found themselves. He had refused to fly again until 1999, over 50 years later, when he accompanied me to our game in Fayetteville against the University of Arkansas.

After the war, Uncle Bill played semipro baseball and was offered a contract to play with the Atlanta Crackers. He turned it down because he thought he deserved at least as much money as had been offered to another guy he had played service ball with. He knew he was better than the other player, and he had enough pride to refuse to play for less than he thought he deserved.

Instead he used his athletic prowess to organize his nephews into baseball games at family reunions, and in our competitions, outdid us all. He was a tremendous athlete, one of the fastest men I have ever seen run the bases. He instilled competitiveness in us. When any of us played games in high school, we could count on Uncle Bill being there to support us. And I can still count on him.

My other grandmother, Pauline Carlton, lived to be 102. I never, ever heard her offer anything but praise for her grandchildren. I knew that she would never believe that I could do wrong, and I tried very hard to live up to those expectations. She was always ready to listen and always had words of encouragement for whatever I was doing. It was very warm and enriching and empowering to have that unconditional love surrounding me and supporting me. Even though she was only about five feet tall, her grandchildren called her Big Mama—I guess because of her importance to us.

I was named after her husband, my grandfather, Clifford Carlton, who died in 1960. He and my Uncle Charlie brought the entire family from Perry, Florida, to Marianna in the thirties to escape the depression in the pulp wood business. They eventually opened OK Music Company, selling records, sheet music, radios, televisions, and record players. They also owned jukeboxes that they placed in what we called juke joints for both black and white clientele. Occasionally, I traveled with them on their routes to service the jukeboxes. I got to listen to all kinds of music, and I remember especially enjoying the rhythm and blues, blues, and jazz records. I am sure that early exposure to artists like Clyde McPhatter, Joe Turner, and LaVerne Baker is what influenced my eventual foray into the music business. I still love it! I have a great collection of 45s and albums, largely because we could visit OK Music Shop and get the used records from jukeboxes or discounted new records. I was one of the first kids in my neighborhood to have an Elvis Presley record.

Some of my favorite childhood memories are of Sunday dinners at Big Mama and Big Daddy's house. We would come out of church and jump into a hot car, trying to keep our skin from sticking to the scorching plastic seat covers. We would fight to sit by the window, and the lucky, forceful child would hang his head out the window all the way from Chipley to Marianna.

I loved walking through their front door, being engulfed by the smells of good food and by the warm greetings of aunts, uncles, cousins, and grandparents. Big Mama was the consummate homemaker and cook; Big Daddy was the eternal, consummate kid. His jukebox route took him into Alabama and Georgia, where he could buy fireworks. For special events he would treat his grandchildren with firecrackers over the protests of Big Mama and our mothers. Occasionally, he would whisper in my ear, "Now don't tell your mama about this," as he would hand me four or five nickels to go use on a pinball machine.

My childhood was fun and stable because I had a network of family at home and away that formed a safety net for me. I had too many people who cared about me for me to fail or make too many mistakes during that precarious time of most people's lives—adolescence.

CHAPTER FIVE

A Rough Time—Adolescence

I wonder sometimes what would have happened if Chipley High School had not dropped its baseball program. But unfortunately I could only play summer baseball after the sixth grade, and I did continue that until about the 11th grade.

Even though baseball was my first love and my best sport, I loved basketball, too. I was the only seventh-grade starter on the junior high team. In the first game, I was so nervous, I thought I was going to die. I had watched high school and junior high games, but now I was out on the floor playing, and I wanted very badly to succeed. And if I do say so myself, I tore it up. I was the go-to guy. I could shoot it! I still feel that I can shoot about as well as anyone, including my players. I haven't challenged Scott Pohlman yet, but whenever I have taken on our players in a game of horse, I have won.

A friend, George Watts, and I had made the junior varsity team as eighth graders, and we were both going to start the first game. A great disappointment to us was that the school athletic organization ruled us ineligible because we were in the eighth grade. Once again I was crushed by sports-related decisions beyond my control. Of course, I thought the authorities were using stupid reasoning.

In the ninth grade, I made the junior varsity teams and did well. Our varsity team finished second in the state tournament that year. I felt a part of a good program. In my sophomore year, I played with the varsity some and with the junior varsity some.

In my junior year at Chipley High, I faced frustration and disappointment again. For one thing, I was not as physically mature as the guys I was playing with or against. Since my birthday is in December and the cutoff day for school birthdays in Florida at that time was January 1, I was one of the youngest boys in my class all through school. My youthfulness became a problem in the 11th grade. Most guys had had their drivers' licenses for a year. I was a scrawny kid anyway, and being a year or two younger than some of the guys in my class made my slight stature even more noticeable. I weighed about 135 pounds and was about 5'8" in my junior and senior years. My size alone made it difficult to compete.

Another problem for me was the result of a coaching change. In my junior year, the basketball coach was an assistant football coach who instituted the rule that a player who participated in basketball had to have played football. I guess he wanted to make sure that the best athletes went out for football. I hated that rule. I loved sandlot football, but I wasn't big enough to play interscholastically. I started on the wrong foot with this basketball coach because I didn't play football.

I went through my final years of high school very disenchanted and discontented. I went from being a top athlete and student in grammar school and junior high to being a very average Joe in high school. I went from being an A student to doing just enough to get by. Stupidly, I tried my first cigarette. I went on a paper route with a friend, and he pulled out a Pall Mall. Fortunately, I went home and got sick. I have since become convinced that one of the craziest things a person can do is smoke. About that time a cousin gave me my first beer—in a milkshake cup. I thought I would gag; I think I described it as horse urine. During that stage in my life, I was definitely rebelling against what I considered a mismanaged establishment. My high school career was just somewhat of a stagnant period in my life.

I dated some in high school, but not much. I did not get my driver's license until I was a senior. My dilemma with girls is symbolized in my mind by an experience that seems pretty funny now, but was frustrating for a 14-year-old. A beautiful young girl from Louisiana about my age visited her grandmother in Chipley during the summer. I was stricken and would ride my bicycle around to her grandmother's to visit on the porch swing. I cherish the memory of stealing a kiss on her cheek and of her slowly turning toward me to say, "I'm glad you did that." I understand the metaphor of fireworks going off. Here was a gorgeous brunette from exotic Louisiana, happy that I was kissing her. The only trouble was that a high school senior also discovered this sweet young visitor. The next time I headed to the grandmother's house on my bicycle, he came riding by me in his souped-up hot rod and asked me where I was going. All I could do was answer, "I'm just heading to Euly Bass' store," and pedaled as hard as I could right on by that house.

I continued through high school to play basketball by agreeing to be a manager for the football team. I had a few good games, including a game against Florida School for Boys when I scored 18. We finished runner-up in our conference my senior year, and the next year I went to Chipola Junior College, the only place I could afford to go, hoping to perhaps develop physically and become a walk-on. I broke my ankle in a sandlot football game and ended up going in a different direction—the golf team.

A great man coached at Chipola for over 30 years—Milton Johnson. He won many state titles and took many teams to the national junior college tournament in Kansas. I never got to play for him, but he gave me attention and became a teacher and a colleague in coaching.

When Chipola decided in 1964 to have its first golf team, I said, "I can play golf." Somehow, despite all my frustrating experiences, I still had confidence in myself.

I had learned to play by just going out to a small nine-hole golf course in Chipley with three or four of my friends. My dad had bought an old, worn set of Bobby Jones clubs for me to use. Bob Deal, George Watts, Fred Peel, Dianne Laney (Yes, we let a girl play—even though she could beat the socks off us), and I would get our mothers to drop us off at the course, and we taught each other to play. Some of us had read about playing; we all would watch other trained players. That was my training for the Chipola golf team.

When I joined the golf team, my family didn't have enough money for me to get a good set of golf clubs. I played with clubs the students used in golf class. The clubs were all worn and old and of an assortment of brands and styles. That was all I had, so that's what I used.

I hit golf balls every day, bound and determined that I was going to compete, and we were going to win. In that short run in golf, I wanted to be the best that I could be. Playing No. 1 on that golf team that ended up second in our conference and being named MVP with those borrowed clubs is an accomplishment that I am still extremely proud of.

My toughest golf match at Chipola or anywhere occurred on a beautiful, sunny afternoon at Florida Caverns Country Club in Marianna, Florida. Our opponent was the Florida State freshman team. I wore shorts, rubbed in Coppertone suntan oil, and put on my Hush Puppy golf shoes, to which I had had the local shoe store add spikes.

The Florida State players drove up in their beautiful garnet-and-gold station wagon, driven by none other than the legendary Hugh Durham, FSU's basketball coach. The team stepped out of the fine vehicle dressed in their fine khaki pants, matching belts, and garnet-and-gold golf shirts.

At the tee box, I was introduced to my opponent for the day, Hubert Green, who would eventually win the PGA and is currently playing the Senior Tour. Trying to be a gentleman and since it was our home course, I described the first hole for our foursome. The drive was a blind shot over a hill, and due to the terrain of the course, players needed to keep their drives to the left. I parred the hole, and so did Hubert.

The second hole was a 310-yard par 4 with a wide and tall live oak tree 250 yards out that blocks the green. Describing the hole at the tee box, I said, "Gentlemen, you want to keep the ball left of the oak tree. Keep your driver in the bag and use an iron, playing to the left, and you'll have a 100-yard chip shot to the green." I teed off left and was in good position. Hubert paused for a minute, looked at that big oak tree, and took out his driver. The ball exploded off the tee, into the atmosphere. It easily sailed over the oak tree and landed on the green four feet from the hole for an eagle putt, which he would eventually sink. I turned to the group and stated, "Gentlemen, this match is over." I spent the rest of the day enjoying the beauty of the links and working on my tan. I was defeated soundly, never winning a hole.

This past summer at Hombre Golf Club in Panama City Beach, where Hubert is the tour club pro, I was able to share that story with Hubert along with friends Wes Burnham and Roy Centana.

Another significant person I met when I was at Chipola was a high school girl named Carolyn Ratzlaff. We met at a dance at Marianna Country Club. We danced and I called later to ask her out. She says that the first time she saw me was when she was serving punch at a college dance, and that I walked in with my nose in the air—that Carly Simon's "You're So Vain" was written about me. Despite that first impression, we developed a relationship that has lasted over 35 years.

We never went steady until we became engaged after I graduated from Florida State. Carolyn graduated from high school valedictorian of her class and received some academic scholarship money to attend Chipola and the University of West Florida. It was good for us to stay in contact but to go to different schools. She developed her interests in English, theater, and teaching. I went to Florida State with a renewed interest in doing well in school and developed an interest that started at Chipola and would pay for the rest of my education—singing in a rock-and-roll band.

CHAPTER SIX

The Villagers

I was at Chipola Junior College when my music career began. I'd been around music most of my life with my uncle and my family and in church, but I'd never really thought about being a singer.

At Chipola, there was a group of talented musicians who had formed a rock-and-roll band. Ironically, all of us had played basketball in high school against each other. These friends played at Malone High School, and we were conference rivals. My senior year in high school, Malone beat us in the finals of the Northwest Florida Conference Championship.

One evening, this group, which at the time was called the Uniques, was jamming in Marianna, Florida. One of the members asked if I would like to listen to the jam session. I was ecstatic, couldn't wait to get to the jam session. After a few numbers, I asked them if I could jam with them. They asked what song I would like to do. One of my favorite songs in the early '60s was a song called "You Can't Judge the Book by

Looking at Its Cover" by Bo Didley. I had played that 45-rpm record till the grooves wore out on the old Zenith record player at home. I knew every word.

When I grabbed the microphone, it was the same feeling I had felt playing basketball as a youngster; the same feeling when I walked on the basketball court as a coach for the first time—the same feeling I had trying to make the college golf team and the feeling was "this is me." There was electricity with the band and me. It was "tight," as musicians like to describe it. I was now a singer and could not let go. I had sung in the choir at church and with the high school glee club, but this was a different feeling. The Uniques asked me to join them at their next dance. This dance would follow a high school football game in Marianna.

I was nervous, but anxious. The band played a few numbers before I came up. The crowd was laid back, staying toward the back of the cafeteria where we were playing. Hardly anyone was dancing. Now it was my special moment with this band. I took the stage, grabbed the microphone, did a little dance called the James Brown, belted out the Bo Didley tune, and the crowd was all over the dance floor. I'll never forget the look on the faces of the other members of the band. This was a happening, and the Uniques were about to head in another direction.

The next dance was a homecoming dance at Sneads, Florida. We were paid the grand total of $50 for the dance. There were five of us. I said to myself, I actually get paid to do this—I would have done it for nothing at the time. After all, the girls liked it. If the girls liked it and I could get paid doing it, rock-n-roll singing was for me, Big Time. I was 18 at the time.

The band was very good for my coaching career in many ways. It taught me to be an entertainer, and that element has stayed with me in every coaching job I've had. Furthermore, I was basically a shy person in high school. I could not stand getting up in front of a classroom to give a report or anything like that. Holding the microphone as lead singer got me beyond that shyness. I could express myself, and as it turned out, I did it fairly well, as record sales and tours would show. We would eventually play in front of thousands, playing dance halls, auditoriums, National Guard armories, colleges, and the like.

Once in the Uniques as its lead singer, I had started something that was going to become a big part of my life over the next few years.

Soon after joining the band, we changed our name to The Villagers. We did this because another group called the Uniques produced a Top 10 hit called "All These Things."

When I joined the band, I dived into it headfirst. As with everything else I had tried, I wanted to be the best.

At that time, the Beatles were making an impact with their music in our country. I joined my band in 1964. In 1964 and 1965 we played throughout the Southeast. Often playing the various dances and concerts during this time, I was looking for the winning edge for our band. I made one long drive down to Panama City Beach, Florida, to listen to a group called the Swinging Medallions. The group was the classical "beach music" band. Everyone seemed to enjoy this group and their style.

At this same event were some of the guys from a group called the K-otics from Montgomery, Alabama. As we talked, the discussion came around to recordings. I felt in my own mind that for the Villagers to advance in the business, we needed to cut a record. Ed Sanford, who later on would record the national hit "Smoke from a Distant Fire" as part of Sanford and Townsend, was a member of the K-otics, and he told me that there was an excellent recording studio called Fame Recording Studio in Muscle Shoals, Alabama. The light came on in my head. The Villagers must find this place in Muscle Shoals, Alabama. I got the telephone number from directory assistance.

When I called Fame Recording Studio, a person by the name of Rick Hall answered the phone. Little did I or anyone else know at the time how powerful this man would become in the record business. I asked him if we could record at his studio. He said we could and set up a session on a Saturday in March 1966. He also stated that the session would be $55 per hour. At the time, Rick Hall had produced a couple of national hits, "Steal Away" by Jimmy Hughes and "Anna" by Arthur Alexander.

After arranging the session with Rick Hall, I convinced our band to record "Laugh It Off," originally a "B" side to the Tams' No. 1 hit, "What Kind of Fool." I liked "Laugh It Off" for its style, its rhythm. I felt it had potential for us. Our "B" side was Paul McCartney's "You're Gonna Lose That Girl."

After practicing for the recordings, we made the beautiful drive to Muscle Shoals, Alabama, from the panhandle of Florida. On our way we listened to WLS radio in Chicago; Dick Biondi was the DJ, as I recall. Later, we tuned in to one of my favorite DJs of all time, John R. of WLAC radio, Nashville, Tennessee. Listening to the radio, we envisioned ourselves having our record play on these powerful 50,000-watt stations that boomed all over the country. Like a basketball team, we were fired up. The next day we were going to record.

As we entered Fame Recording studios, Rick Hall met us. He, in fact, was the only one there. The studio was quaint and comfortable. We did the session quickly. As a matter of fact, I recall the entire session costing only $88.

At that time there was no record company for us. We had to distribute our own records. We sent the master tape to Cincinnati, Ohio, to have our records pressed. We used our own label at the time and called it Volume Records.

Now that we had made the record, we had to figure out how to get it on radio stations. We didn't have a promoter. We didn't have a record contract. I took it to the local radio station and they played it. I was driving along in a '63 Ford Fairlane and hearing our record played. It was the greatest thing in the world. I loved it all.

In Montgomery, Alabama, there was a huge radio station called WBAM, the Big Bam. It was a 50,000-watt station in the daytime. From Montgomery all the way down to Panama City, that's what everybody listened to. The Brennan family owned it; they had the market on the whole state, period. The Big Bam was a request station.

It hit me one day: "This song has to be on WBAM." I got in my '63 Fairlane. My brother, Randy, drove with me. There weren't any four-lane roads from Chipley. It was two hours and 15 minutes from my house to WBAM.

I can still remember the drive—Dothan, Ozark, Troy, and Montgomery. I didn't know where the station was, but as we were entering Montgomery, I saw this big tower. I figured that must be it. I got out of the car and went in. I'm sure the people at WBAM wondered who this brash kid was.

In the studio, there was a glass window where the show was being played, and I could see the disc jockey, Bill Moody. I said to the receptionist, "I need to see Bill Moody. I sure need him to play my record."

I even knocked on the window. I wasn't going away. He finally came out. He was very nice, even though he had no idea who I was or what made me think I had a record he would want to play. He took the time to listen, and I'll never forget that moment because he was willing to give our band a chance. Our friendship lasts to this day.

I said, "Mr. Moody, I'm Cliff Ellis of the Villagers. I have a record with me and all I want you to do is play it. If it doesn't get a response, then break it, but promise me you will play it." He said, "Let's go back and listen to it before I put it on the air."

He didn't act all that impressed, but he liked it enough to play it. He said, "That's not bad." He put it on the air, and I will never forget what happened. I was outside that glassed-in area. I was feeling like I was on top of the world. This son of a gun was on WBAM. I knew everybody between Montgomery, Alabama, and Chipley, Florida, was listening.

Before the record was half over, Bill Moody called me in. He said, "I don't let people come in here, but do you see all these phone lines?" Every one of the buttons was lit up. People were going crazy over the song. He said, "Son, you've got a hit."

WBAM rated its records by requests. The record in two weeks was No. 2. The next thing we knew, Rick Hall was calling to sign us to a contract with Fame Records. Not long after this, Roy Orbison was coming to Dothan, Alabama. We were asked to open up for Roy.

When Big Bam played our records, things got started for us. It was more than any of us ever imagined. We went from playing high school dances to playing with Roy Orbison, Charlie Rich, and people like that immediately. Instead of $50 per night, we could receive up to $600. We played colleges and fraternities all over the South. We ended up signing a contract with Atco, a major record label. We were hot, and I mean hot. It might not ever have happened if Bill Moody hadn't taken the time that day to be nice to someone he'd never met or heard of.

Rick Hall, who produced our records and signed us to a contract, would eventually go on to national fame, producing such great artists as Aretha Franklin, Etta James, Donnie and Marie Osmond, Wilson Pickett, and countless others.

When we went to Muscle Shoals for our second recording session for "Thank You, Baby" and "A Shot of Rhythm and Blues," we arrived while someone else was finishing recording. We walked in and saw a beautiful and robust African American woman sitting on a bar stool with a tiny poodle under her arm. When I heard her sing, I knew it was the inimitable Etta James, whose "At Last" is on my list of all-time favorites. I was so excited and happy to be there while she was recording that the producer asked if I wanted to participate. When you listen to the recording of "Tell Daddy" by Etta James, know that I'm the one playing the tambourine.

While I was going to college and entertaining as a musician, a major event in history was taking place, the Vietnam

War. I guess Vietnam had an impact on the lives of just about everyone in my generation. It was a horrible time, really horrible. Just about everybody had a friend or family member or someone close to him who was killed or wounded. A lot of protests were going on. It was a tough time for our country.

When I was at Florida State, my friend Robert Trammell would come over to my apartment that I shared with my cousin Ronnie Hatton; every day we would watch the news about the Vietnam War. I guess we all figured there was a good chance we'd end up over there some time or another.

We were in school, which gave us a deferment at the time. I was one of those who never went into the military because of being in college and eventually becoming a teacher. Eventually there was a draft lottery, but my number never came up. Had I been chosen, I would have served our country.

The '60s was a time of a lot of rebellion. The young people then didn't understand the war. Friends were getting killed or hurt, and they didn't understand why. I lost friends in the Vietnam War. I have a friend today, Dink Mills, with whom I enjoy fishing. Dink amazes me, as he never complains. His legs were blown off when he stepped on a land mine while in 'Nam. Today, he guides on Lake Eufala for bass fishermen and is an excellent speckled trout and red fisherman in the saltwater bays of Bay County in Florida. People sometimes never know his legs have been amputated. He loads his own boat, gets in and out of the boat on his own power, and he wears my little tail out fishing with him. The famed fisherman Tom Mann of Lake Eufala considers Dink one of the best fishermen alive. He and others like him who served in the war do not get the respect they deserve. I admire Dink.

Our band made a pact never to lose sight of our education. Every one of us, with the exception of one, earned his degree.

We never had long hair, even though that seemed to be a major part of the culture at the time. We were a fun group, what I call a beach music group. We didn't get too far out left or right. It was just good music. We all agreed that when we got our degrees it would be over, and it pretty much was. It was something we enjoyed doing, but we never lost sight of our goals in life.

It paid for our education. It gave me a great opportunity to travel and meet people. When it comes to public speaking today, I give so much of that credit to being behind that microphone. When a person is 18 and has 3,000 people out there and has to make sure they are in tune with what he is doing, he can learn a lot.

It taught me a lot about life. I traveled. I learned to communicate. I learned to make reservations for hotel rooms. I met countless numbers of people, and I did it with a great group of guys who had their heads on right. It was a fun experience, one of the very best times of my life.

Although music was occupying most of my time outside of studies, sports was never too far removed. I stayed involved in sports through the people I was at school with.

Milton Johnson, head basketball coach while I attended Chipola Junior College, shared his knowledge of the game with me, even though I didn't play basketball for him. I had his playbook, had his handouts, and watched his practices. Hugh Durham was head basketball coach while I was in school at FSU. He gave me his playbook, shared his philosophy, and allowed me to watch practices. To this day, I consider Milton Johnson and Hugh Durham mentors and great friends.

At Chipola and Florida State I enjoyed watching practice. I enjoyed the players playing. I wanted to be on the court, but my God-given ability wouldn't allow it. Anyway, I was now very content as a musician.

Some people felt in those days that if you weren't a college player, you wouldn't become a great coach. I found it to be just the opposite. As a matter of fact, many great coaches were average players or did not play a high level of college ball. Bobby Knight, for example, was a sub on the Ohio State team. Richard Williams, who recently took Mississippi State to the Final Four, never played college ball.

As for myself, I always felt that I never reached that satisfaction level as a player, and it gave me an even more burning desire to become an excellent coach. I have found that sometimes when one goal is not reached, it helps make you strive for another goal. I did not reach my goal as a player, but I was sure going to try to reach it as a coach. You could say I was hungry.

CHAPTER SEVEN

The Music Plays On

Nineteen sixty-seven and 1968 were very good years for the Villagers. We had signed a contract with Atlantic-Atco and were playing beautiful music. We were at the top of our game. By 1968 we would have three major regional hits. "Laugh It Off" in 1966 had become a No. 2 hit in the South; "Where Have You Been" in 1967 had become a No. 4 hit in the South; and in 1968, "Thank You Baby" also jumped to the No. 4 spot. We now had played countless places and had performed with some of the great artists of all time. It was something really special for a group of college students.

I graduated from Florida State in June 1968. I was offered a teaching job in Niceville, Florida, which would begin in mid-August. Others in the band were also receiving their degrees at this time. We decided that in August we were going to perform for the last time. We wanted to end right where we started, in Marianna, Florida. The place would be the National Guard Armory.

The armory was packed. It seemed like thousands were there, although the place could only hold a little over 1,000 people. It was show time, the grand finale. It seemed like everyone who had followed the Villagers was there. We were at our best. Twelve midnight struck, and we usually ended then. The people wanted more. We did an encore for about an hour. It was electric. At 1 a.m. I sang "Laugh It Off" with the Villagers for the last time. I put the microphone down, hugged band members, hugged friends, went to our tour bus, and cried. On Monday morning I reported to Ruckel Junior High School with a whistle around my neck.

I think so highly of all those guys who were part of the band. They've all been successful. Alan Myers is an attorney in Gainesville, Georgia. Walter Dover is in Tallahassee, Florida. His family has been involved in politics, and he's a very successful businessman. George Boyer is in business. Andy Murray was a banker. He left that job to be an engineer of a train because he could make a lot more money. Billy Bryan still is in the music business. He's a gospel music singer and has his own recording studio. He's the one guy who has stayed with the music. All are good people. I hear from them occasionally.

As for my music career, I basically had put performing behind me until I took the head coaching position at Clemson in 1984. Before then, I occasionally had been enticed to get on stage when a great band was in the area, but overall I had to let it go.

I went to Clemson in 1984 and received a call from a fan of Clemson basketball, Marion Carter: "I know you are our new basketball coach, but I know you are more than a basketball coach." To that I replied, "What are you talking about?" He said, "I've got your records." He said, "I own Ripete records." I said, "Are you the company that has the Ocean Drive album—that Ripete records?" It was, and I was impressed.

In the next few months, I went by the company in Elliott, South Carolina, and I saw that Marion had a big business. He had a huge market, and he had all of my recordings to boot. He said, "I want to get all of the rights to your stuff." We spent the day discussing music from its roots to my recordings. One day soon thereafter, he called and said, "Let's do a couple of projects." I agreed, but with reservations. After all, it had been a long time since I had recorded.

We went back in the studio. Marion was a Clemson guy who thought it would be a good thing to let people see me in a different light. It turned out he was right. The national TV networks have really gotten involved, and at various times have played these recordings coast to coast. I actually have gotten more national exposure as a musician since beginning coaching than I had gotten previously.

In '91 I did a song called "Love Land," which was played on the beach music circuit. Some people might not know there is a beach music chart. Along the Atlantic Coast, beach music is a huge industry. The group Alabama actually started in Myrtle Beach, South Carolina, and played a variety of beach music in addition to their own style. They are one of the top country music groups of all time, but their start was in beach music. I was hesitant to go back in the studio, but I did it, and I'm glad I did.

We put out a CD with all the songs I'd recorded and some new stuff. It included a tribute to Jim Valvano, whose battle with cancer was one of the most courageous things I've ever seen. I always wanted to sing "Amazing Grace." It's on that CD, and it was cut in one live session in honor of Jimmy. We could have gotten a better cut, but I think it sounds the way Jimmy would want it to. It was spontaneous. When I did it, I felt good.

It was through Marion Carter that I was able to have that chance to enjoy performing again. I was afraid people would take it wrong, but I was wrong. When the recordings were made available, the people loved it. The national media have loved it. I do not consider myself a great singer, but I can perform, and you do not have to be a great singer to sing rock 'n' roll. You have to have feeling and soul. Do this and do it without fear, and you'll succeed.

Once my music career was refurbished, people—especially in ACC territory—wanted me to perform. I have always been very reluctant to do this because I am not 18 years old anymore, but sometimes someone manages to get me to do it. I will say that once I do get up there and break the ice, I feel 18 again.

One incident of getting called on stage occurred in Greensboro, North Carolina, at the ACC Tournament. Our team and fans were staying at the Holiday Inn. Dick Vitale, famed college basketball analyst, was also there. We had gotten beaten in the tournament, and the next day, NCAA bids were coming out. Some alumni and friends asked Carolyn and me to join them to hear some beach music to simply relax and get away for a few hours. Dick noticed I was there, got up on stage, and along with the band, enticed me on stage. We rocked the joint. Dick was a hoot; he even tried to sing with me. I think we both need to keep our day jobs.

Every year, we had the ACC spring meetings, and all the ACC coaches enjoyed going out. If there was music, they would try to get me to perform. I never would do it until one night at a club called 2001 in Myrtle Beach, Bobby Cremins led a charge to have me perform. All the ACC coaches were there except Dean Smith. Bobby Cremins, Mike Krzyzewski, Gary Williams, Jim Valvano, Pat Kennedy, Dave Odom, and Terry Holland were there. The place was packed, and Cremins was on a mission.

I had already said I wouldn't do it, but the other coaches got involved with this mission. I said, "I won't do it unless all of you get up here with me." I got up and there they were—Cremins, Krzyzewski, all of them. We all performed together, with me as the leader, and we brought the house down. It was a moment to remember. I think people like to see you being human. We were all showing a different side of ourselves.

People today still seem to be fascinated with my involvement with music. I guess when you think about it, every person likes some form of music, and a lot of people simply like good old rock 'n' roll.

During the 1999 championship season at Auburn, I got a call from ABC to join John Saunders as a studio analyst. It was the weekend after we beat Vanderbilt to win the SEC championship, and we were not playing.

I flew to New York. John and I rehearsed the show. I felt well prepared. He was going to discuss various events of the day, and I was to respond. Then, all of a sudden, in one of the segments, I heard one of my songs being played on the air. I sat there stunned. I could hear them playing my song, and I had no clue this was going to happen to me. I looked at John Saunders and said, "You dog, what in the world are you doing?" He just sat there laughing. It threw me a complete curveball.

This was the second time I had done a national show with John. The other time was in 1990 while John was at ESPN. I enjoy being a coach's studio analyst. I think the music business and the coaching business have enabled me to be relaxed and informed when doing studio work. John has been fun to work with and has been a good friend over the years.

There have been moments in my 31 years of coaching when my music has been rekindled by either going back in a studio or occasionally getting on stage with an act. Yet, really and truly, I feel that part of the music business has never left me. This music business is a business where I learned to promote, and I have been promoting at every stop of my coaching career.

For example, at South Alabama there was no school band when I was hired. The administration was contemplating taking South Alabama from Division I to Division II. I knew I had to promote. I knew our games had to have atmosphere. I went out and heard a band led by Joe Lewis, a talented local musician. This band also had famed drummer Jabo Stark, who was the drummer for Bobby "Blue" Bland, as well as other R & B acts. Together we went over a song that would be up-tempo. No Blue Danube Waltz here. This band could flat-out play and were worth the price of admission alone. This promotional move proved priceless, as it ignited our crowds.

At Auburn, the promotion of our Cliff Dwellers in the student section and the refurbishing of our coliseum have helped create fan interest never before seen at Auburn.

From the music business, I learned a long time ago that when you put on a show and they don't like the atmosphere, they are not coming back. This goes for any performer. In basketball, I have tried to use these ideas I learned a long time ago from the music business. People love to be entertained. Basketball is a great entertainment sport, on and off the court.

I am very appreciative of what music has allowed me to do, and what it continues to allow me to express.

By the way, for you music lovers, here is a list of my Top 10 all-time favorite songs. This list was tough to pick, as I have so many favorites.

10. "Amazing Grace" by Judy Collins
9. "Silhouettes" by The Rays
8. "Night and Day" by Frank Sinatra
7. "Goodnight My Love" by Jessie Belvin
6. "Since I Don't Have You" by The Skyliners
5. "At Last" by Etta James
4. "Gypsy Woman" by The Impressions
3. "He Will Break Your Heart" by Jerry Butler
2. "Stand By Me" by Ben E. King
1. "Stubborn Kind of Fellow" by Marvin Gaye

My favorite all-time artists include Frank Sinatra, Tony Bennett, Marvin Gaye, Curtis Mayfield, The Impressions, Jackie Wilson, Clyde McPhatter, James Brown, Bobby "Blue" Bland, Willie Tee, Martha Reeves, The Vandellas, The Temptations, Etta James, George Jones, Merle Haggard, The Florida Boys Quartet, Jerry Butler, B.B. King, Brook Benton, and Roy Orbison. It may seem strange that the Beatles and Elvis Presley did not make it into this group, even though they wrote and performed many songs that I enjoy. The above simply had a way about them that turned my crank.

CHAPTER EIGHT

A Career Begins

My first coaching job was with the Okaloosa County school system in the panhandle of Florida. I took a position as physical education instructor and seventh- and eighth-grade basketball and golf coach at Ruckel Junior High School in Niceville. But my first task as a coach was to assist with the Ruckel Junior High Rams football team. I started out at the lowest level possible as a coach (junior high), but it was here that I started becoming comfortable with coaching basketball and had a truly great experience.

Junior high school coaching was the only coaching position I could find upon graduating from Florida State. I had not played college basketball and had not played football in high school. In the '60s, high school coaching positions were primarily going to people who had these backgrounds. As I moved on in my career, I don't think it made much difference that I had not played college basketball, but it was sure tougher to start out high in the ranks of coaching basketball without it.

I was paid $6,000 to teach and $100 to coach basketball, football, and golf in that first year. I guess you could say I coached because I loved it. Another important step in my life took place in December of my first year as a coach. I asked Carolyn to marry me. I wasn't making much money, but I was confident and excited. I was young and I had a lot to learn, but I was happy to be there. I was coaching, and that's what mattered the most to me.

I didn't know much about coaching football, but my first actual coaching assignment was to take the seventh-grade football team. Back in those days, it was three yards and a cloud of dust. That's how everybody seemed to play. And just like I like to play up-tempo basketball, I wanted to play up-tempo football.

I decided if everybody else was going to run, run, run, I was going to throw our team wide open on offense. We would throw it left, right, wherever. Everybody else was running, and we were throwing. And we were scoring and we were winning. The players had fun, and I did also.

Football was fun, but my major aspiration was to coach basketball. In my first coaching assignment, we did not even have a gym. We practiced outside. We played our games at the high school, but we practiced on an asphalt court. I never remember it being too cold or too rainy.

Trying to get your kids to learn to take a charge on an asphalt court is a challenge. A kid has got to be tough to take a charge on that kind of court. The 1968-69 season at Ruckel was an interesting year, a learning experience.

I lost my first game as a basketball coach to Richborg Junior High out of Crestview, Florida. At that time, since I had to coach football, I had only about a week to get ready and then went right into the first game.

I remember being a nervous wreck. What I recall most about that game is we got behind in a hurry. I used all my time-outs early. When it got down to the end of the game, I didn't have any left. I made many mistakes in that game, and I literally cost us the game.

First of all, I was nervous, and that probably carried over to my players. I can't tell you the score, but I learned quickly the importance of using time-outs in basketball. We ended up having a good year, 13-5.

One of my more interesting experiences as a coach was having to learn to drive those old yellow school buses. In those days, a young coach drove the bus, mopped the gym floors (once he had a gym), painted the lines on the football field, cut the grass, and performed any other menial task that was necessary. I can tell you I was really nervous about having to pass the test to get the chauffeur's license. After all, I wasn't going to move up in the public school ranks as easily without that chauffeur's license to drive that old yellow bus.

I did pass that test and started driving the bus to games. I think I was so nervous about driving the bus that it actually helped me settle down before games. I was so thankful I had driven the team safely that nerves for games were secondary.

As a young coach, I think I was too scared to fail. During regular school classes, my mind was constantly on getting ready for practice or a game at the end of the day. I was learning to enter what I call the "tunnel." The tunnel is my mind totally focused in on the task at hand—and that task was basketball— and I was going to succeed, not fail at it.

Across the street from Ruckel Junior High stands Niceville High School, home of the Niceville Eagles. The principal at Niceville High happened to be Colly V. Williams, the same guy who had whipped my rear end while I was a student and he was the principal in Chipley, Florida. The junior varsity football and basketball position came open, and he, along with athletic director and football coach Bobby Walton, offered me the job. I would remain in that position for two years.

Colly V. Williams was a good man. He had given me direction as a student and he'd taught me discipline. Now he was giving me an opportunity to prove myself very early in my coaching career. I will always be grateful to him.

It was the 1969-70 season. My football team went undefeated, and we continued to play wide open. We were defeating the three-yards-and-a-cloud-of-dust teams. My basketball team had a good year, finishing 15-3. The following year's football team would again go undefeated with one tie, and the basketball team finished 19-1.

CHAPTER NINE

Graduate School—A Step Closer to College Coaching

I was absolutely fascinated every time I stepped onto the basketball court to teach. Because I didn't play in college, I think I was more driven to learn every aspect of the game than maybe some people who had played. I bought every book I could get. I would read, read, and read. I studied nightly into the wee hours of the mornings upon coming home from practice. I read literally hundreds of books and articles on basketball. This game called basketball was consuming me, and I wanted to be the best at it as a coach. That was my mind-set. I've always wanted to be the best I could possibly be at whatever I was doing.

Carolyn and I were married July 12, 1969, while I was coaching at Niceville, and we both attended graduate school. She wanted her graduate degree, and so did I. I felt that getting a graduate degree could provide a winning edge in getting better coaching jobs for the future. I had not even become a head basketball coach at the high school level, but I already knew that I wanted to coach beyond the high school level. The question was how to get there.

It seemed like the best way to get your foot in the door was to be a graduate assistant. There were graduate assistantships available, but I couldn't seem to get one because of my not playing in college. It seemed that when head coaches at colleges hired graduate assistants, they usually hired someone who had played for them. It made it hard on someone who had not played at the collegiate level.

On the football staff at Niceville High was a Pennsylvanian named Bobby Hlodan. He had obtained his graduate degree from Middle Tennessee State University and had played football for the Blue Raiders out of Murfreesboro, Tennessee. The head basketball coach at Marianna High School, Bill Peacock, and his brother Jack, were attending graduate school at MTSU at the time. We were friends from college at Chipola and FSU. All had described how beautiful the campus was, how friendly the teachers were, and how it was a wonderful place to be.

Carolyn and I applied to and were accepted into graduate school, and in the summer of 1970 we packed our Ford and headed off for a new adventure, graduate school.

During the 1969-70 season as junior varsity coach, the head varsity coach was Ron Shumate, who later would become very successful as a head basketball coach at the University of Tennessee–Chattanooga and Southeast Missouri State. I learned a lot from him, especially about practice planning and organization. He also confided in me, which I appreciated, and we have a friendship that is everlasting. I also learned a great deal from Grover Hicks while I had coached Ruckel the previous year, particularly fundamentals of the game and discipline.

In the spring of 1970, Ron accepted an assistant coaching position at UT–Chattanooga. Colly V. Williams recommended me for the position I so badly wanted, but I did not get it. I was extremely disappointed.

The superintendent called me and said, "You are too young. They will crucify you. You're not ready." I thought I was. As I look back on it now, he was right, but at the time it not only hurt, but it hurt the high school principal as well. He'd already come to my house and said he was recommending me for the job. Bobby Welch was named the head basketball coach. Bobby was a good coach, and we worked well together the following year.

Had I gotten the head coach's position, graduate school probably would have been put on hold. I have always felt that God provides direction. This perhaps was a path He was choosing.

I might add that upon being recommended for the head position, it was implied to me by the superintendent that with another year's experience I perhaps would be the choice for the next available position in the county.

Carolyn and I finished our first summer of graduate school. We met wonderful friends, had wonderful professors, and were confident now that a graduate degree would eventually happen. It would take three summers to finish graduate school. A graduate assistantship, by the way, would only take one year.

CHAPTER TEN

Head Coach/Author

After finishing with the 19-1 season in 1970-71, Carolyn and I would again go to MTSU for the summer. Something that would change my life was about to happen. While we were in Murfreesboro, the head basketball position came open at what was considered the No. 1 school in the county, Choctawhatchee High School. Choctawhatchee was a large high school and known as a powerful program throughout the state.

The superintendent called me personally. He told me I would not be named head basketball coach at Choctawhatchee High, yet still encouraged me to be patient. I was incensed and was determined now to leave the Okaloosa County system if a good head job opened up.

In the meantime, I continued to enjoy graduate school. I would enjoy fly-fishing on Woods Reservation in Tullahoma, Tennessee, golfing in the beautiful mid-state courses, and got my first hole-in-one ever at a public course in Murfreesboro. It was a 5-iron from 165 yards out on the first hole of play. Carolyn and I would go to Nashville on occasion and we attended the Grand Ole Opry. Ryman Auditorium was where the Opry was held, and it was hotter than any gym I'd been in. No air conditioning, but the show was great. Loretta Lynn was the headliner.

Late in the summer I received another important call while nestled in my lovely quarters at Florida Trailer Park just outside the Murfreesboro city limits. It was my friend Robert Trammell, who, at the time, was graduate assistant to Hugh Durham at Florida State. Leon Rogers, principal at Ocala Vanguard High School, had called about the vacancy that had occurred at his school in basketball. The head coaching position had come up, and Coach Durham recommended me for the job. Robert felt I would be getting a call soon and I should be ready. I began to envision the title of Head Coach.

Leon eventually called me at my trailer and asked me to be his coach. He opened a major door for me, and I am eternally grateful. He now resides in Dunnellon, Florida, and has always followed my career and comes to the Florida game each time we travel to Gainesville. Carolyn would accept a job teaching English. I accepted and told him we would be there immediately following the summer school term.

During that summer, I spent many afternoons practicing my golf game in an open area on the MTSU campus. One day, while hitting shag balls, I met a person who would change my life professionally. As I was hitting balls, a middle-aged man was practicing about 50 yards away. I could tell he was a newcomer at golf. After several minutes he walked my way, introduced himself, and asked if I would give him a few pointers, and if I would play golf with him the following day.

He said, "I'm Don Fuoss. I was the football coach here, I've been fired, I'm tenured, so I'm going to ride it out for a year and learn to play golf." He and I would play golf frequently. One day while we were on the golf course, he looked at me and said, "Young man, what do you want to do with your life in coaching?" I said, "I'm about to go to Ocala, Florida, and try to succeed with my first head coaching position in high school at the varsity level." He said, "What do you want to do with your life 10-15 years from now?" He made me think.

I told him I thought I wanted to coach basketball on the collegiate level. He wanted to know how I planned on going about doing it. I really wasn't sure.

He said, "Separate yourself." He said, "The people calling the shots don't know a lot about athletes in a lot of cases. Most of the presidents at universities and colleges never played. They just smoke their pipes and talk a lot. They are into intellect."

He asked me if I'd ever thought about writing. He said, "I have the best-selling football book in America today. It helped separate me. What do you know about the game of basketball? Give me your best subject. I'm a close personal friend of Herman Masin of *Scholastic Coach* magazine." Don's book that was a best-seller was called *Encyclopedia for Football Drills.*

At that time, *Scholastic Coach* magazine was huge. He said, "You get me an article and I'll have it published." Now my thoughts turned to writing. I thought if I could cut records, play golf collegiately, I might as well write, too. Besides, I had a wife who could correct spelling and place commas where they needed to be.

I decided to write about the 1-3-1 press my teams were using. It was very successful for us, and I was comfortable writing on this subject. I wrote throughout the summer, usually late at night. Upon finishing the project, I placed the article in my golfing pal's hands.

This same summer I would get to know Jimmy Earle, head basketball coach at the time at MTSU. He was also an author. I was enrolled in his coaching class. I loved the way he taught this class. He was intense. He shared his knowledge of the game with the class, which was primarily made up of coaches. He made sure all the coaches in the class shared their philosophies with other members of the clan. It was a tremendous learning experience for everyone. Jimmy had written several books, and he shared with me ideas about writing as it pertained to coaching, ideas like giving your presses a name like mad dog, bull dog, etc. He showed me the proper way to diagram and illustrate plays when writing.

Following this summer term, Carolyn and I made our way to Ocala, Florida. We moved into an upscale mobile home, although not a double-wide.

One morning in the fall of '77, the librarian at Ocala Vanguard High School came to me and said, "Have you seen your article in *Scholastic Coach* magazine?" I couldn't believe it. There was my picture and the article. I was now an author. I had no idea the article would get as much attention as it ultimately did.

In January, there was enough interest in it that Parker Publishing called and asked if I would like to expand that article into a book. It would be called *Zone Press Variations for Winning Basketball,* but I could not begin the writing right away. I had a team to coach, the Ocala Vanguard Knights. I would start writing following the season.

Ocala Vanguard had experienced racial problems at the school the year before. Students were boycotting, and police were being summoned. The basketball team had won eight games. I took the job knowing I needed to help relieve tension at the school. I needed to help relieve any tension that might carry over into practice. I was looking for a winning edge.

When I started practice, I wanted tensions broken. I wanted practice to be fun. When the players entered the gym for practice and warm-ups, I would play James Brown music for about 20 minutes of practice. It was up-tempo. Songs such as "I Feel Good" and "Papa's Gotta Brand New Bag" stirred not only the coach's emotion but the players', too. My music career was having an impact positively with my basketball team. Next thing I knew, the kids were having a good time. We went 20-5 for the season and played without a senior on the team. All the starters were coming back. Little did I know, following this season, I wouldn't.

In the summer of 1972, during the last week of school at Middle Tennessee State, I was sitting in Jimmy Earle's office, thanking him for helping expand my knowledge of the game and also for his encouragement of my potential, when the phone rang. I was 26 years old and getting ready to go back to Ocala Vanguard. On the other end of the phone line was the president of Cumberland College, a junior college in Lebanon, Tennessee. His name was Dr. Earnest Stockton. He told Jimmy Earle that school started the next week and his basketball coach had resigned suddenly.

Dr. Stockton told him he needed a basketball coach, and he needed to find the best one he could in a hurry. He trusted Jimmy Earle to make him a good recommendation.

Jimmy Earle looked at me and told him, "Dr. Stockton, I may have your man right here. I'll send him over." God seemed to be steering me toward another path.

Carolyn and I drove over to visit and saw this quaint little school tucked away in the middle of the state. It was a beautiful campus displaying tradition like an Ivy League school. We both liked it, but the president wasn't so sure about me. I didn't know if I was going to get the job or not after I talked to him for the first time.

The president looked at me and said, "You sure are mighty young." I said, "Yes, sir, but if you give me a chance, I won't ever let you down." I could tell he was unsure. I then handed him the magazine article I had written. His attitude suddenly changed. He saw an academic side in addition to the coaching side, and I think that impressed him.

That separated me from the rest, just as Don Fuoss had talked about. The magazine article separated me and gave me that opportunity. There's no question in my mind about that.

Dr. Stockton wanted to listen to Jimmy Earle, but he needed a reason, as he was concerned about my youthfulness. Don Fuoss and Jimmy Earle paved the way. They gave me good advice, and I listened. I parlayed writing into a job. Writing got me in the door for my first college job at a time when I was still young and relatively inexperienced. It gave me the winning edge.

At age 26, I was hired as head basketball coach of the Cumberland College Bulldogs. I was also named athletic director, golf coach, and would teach physical education courses.

Chapter Eleven

The Cumberland Years

I almost got the opportunity to coach Larry Bird in my third year at Cumberland.

I came really close, I think, to getting to coach one of the truly great players in the history of the game of basketball, a player I have watched and admired over the years.

It was early September or thereabouts. I was heading into my third season at Cumberland. We had a point guard on the team named Danny King. He was from, of all places, French Lick, Indiana. Danny came running to see me at my office one day. He was so excited, he could barely get the words out. I mean, he was really excited. He said, "Coach! Coach! One of my best friends just left Indiana's basketball team and we need to get him to transfer down here. He is really a great player." I had no idea who he was talking about. I just looked at him and said, "Well, who is it?" He said, "It's Larry Bird."

Of course, at that time, Larry Bird wasn't nationally known. I knew he had been at Indiana. I knew he was a good player. I never would have thought about him coming to Cumberland.

Danny said, "I'm going home this weekend and I'm going to go find him. He's left Indiana for good. He wasn't happy there."

Danny went home that weekend and came back with the information. He said, "Coach, Larry needs to be with our team, but he has already enrolled at Northwood Institute and has been in classes for one day or so." Northwood Institute was a junior college that did not have a basketball program.

I was excited. I was thinking Danny King could really bring Larry Bird to Cumberland. Since Northwood Institute didn't play basketball, I thought he might be able to transfer.

I called the National Junior College Athletic Association and asked about the transfer rule from a school that did not have a team to a school that had a team. Since he had enrolled there, they said he wasn't eligible to play at Cumberland. It was a terrible rule. Danny went home one day too late.

If it had been one day earlier, we might have had Larry Bird. I've often wondered what would have happened and what direction my life would have taken if Larry Bird had played for us.

The next year, Bird went to Indiana State, and Danny King went with him. Danny King was point guard on that team, and Larry Bird became the player everybody heard about. Indiana State ended up losing to Michigan State in the NCAA championship game when Bird was a senior.

I really believe Danny King would have gotten him to come to Cumberland. They were best friends. Oh, well. It was one of those things that could have happened. I'll never know what it would have meant. Larry Bird went on and led a school that had never been there and probably never will be again to within one game of a national championship. I went on with my coaching career, and Larry Bird went to the NBA and became a national icon.

In 1972, I began my first campaign at Cumberland. I was 26 years old and really excited. I don't think *scared* is the word I would use. I just knew this was my opportunity, and I didn't want to fail.

It was a big step from high school to the college level, and I was taking the job very late, from a recruiting standpoint. We needed players. We had some, but we needed more. Cumberland had finished 8-18 the previous year. I had a lot of work to do, and it was not going to be easy.

The president, Dr. Stockton, was a man I dearly loved. He gave me this wonderful opportunity, and I did not want to let him or myself down. I found out quickly, however, that there were problems I had not been completely prepared for when I took the job.

The '60s brought about integration, and in the early '70s, schools were still getting accustomed to integration. Dr. Stockton was a warm, caring individual, but felt the community was still adjusting and not ready for a totally integrated team. Their feeling was that more than three African-Americans might not be accepted by the community.

There were eight scholarships to give for a 12-man squad, and scholarships could be awarded to athletes either partially or in full. Federal financial aid was available to anyone—red, yellow, black, or white. By law, nobody could be refused this if they qualified.

Upon taking the Cumberland job, I had little time to recruit before school started. I took the job in mid-August, and school would officially start in two weeks. I called friends Ron Shumate, UT–Chattanooga; Jimmy Earle, MTSU; and Lake Kelley, Austin Peay, for leads on players who might be available for junior college play. I took the school station wagon, and off I went through the states of Tennessee, Georgia, and North Carolina, following the leads. I saw student-athletes I liked and convinced them to apply for financial aid to come help me build a program at Cumberland College. Our team would have more than the so-called quota. It would prove to be a winning edge.

Charles Fishback was on this first team. He was the leader and was as good a guard as I have ever had. He was as quick as a hiccup, could shoot the lights out, was an adept ball handler, and was always ready to play. He was also a student of the game.

This first year at Cumberland, our record was 20-5. More important, the community and school bought into this team. They supported us and learned to respect wonderful human beings like Charles Fishback, James Britt, Willie Smith, John Garnett, and Walt Bellamy. The color barrier in athletics at Cumberland College was now broken.

In that first year, Cumberland fans saw a team on the floor that pressed with tremendous intensity. I like the theory of pressing the opponent when they get off the bus. This team could do that. Besides, the press was clearly in our favor. We played in a cracker box. The gym was dilapidated, built in the '30s. When teams tried to bring the ball inbounds versus our press, we could almost push the passer to the wall.

There was no rule at this time when you could start practice. Young, energetic, and nervous, I started our work the day after Labor Day. We had a tough conditioning program. I would run them and run them. We would usually practice no less than three hours. This team was hungry and had a great attitude about winning. We would win, as our record indicated, but would peter out towards the end of the season. We started to lose the legs and crispness we had had earlier in the year. From this season I learned not to overkill too early. Legs are more important at the end of the year than at the beginning.

This was a special team and one that is still very special to this day. I wasn't much older than the players, yet they bought into what I was trying to teach and they gave me respect.

One evening in the fall of 1972 on the Cumberland campus, Carolyn announced we would be having a child. I remember stepping outside and noticing the beautiful stars in the sky. Lightning bugs were all aglow. It was a sight to behold and a memorable day. I was going to be a father. I thanked God.

On the day Carolyn went into labor and her water broke, I had gotten up at 4 a.m. to go fishing with my assistant coach and now my longtime friend, Boone Swain. It was a lovely day to fish. We caught several, cleaned them, and decided we should grill them when we got home. Carolyn and Sally Swain, Boone's wife, met us as we came in to announce we were going to grill. They had the bigger announcement. Since it wasn't quite time for the hospital yet, according to Carolyn and Sally, we grilled and ate with our good friends. By this time I was full, sleepy, and dead tired.

Around 11 p.m. it became time to take our ride to St. Thomas Hospital in Nashville, Tennessee. Carolyn was beginning to have severe back pain that would progressively get worse. When we arrived at the hospital, Carolyn was put in the labor room. I massaged her back for hours to help alleviate the pain. I continually massaged until it was time for the doctor, which meant it was time for Chryssa Deanne Ellis, our first child. When Dr. James Johnston came in, I went to the waiting room and was so tired I fell asleep. The next thing I knew, Dr. Johnston was tapping me on the shoulder, saying, "Coach, you are the father of a baby girl."

Now you talk about a great feeling. Seeing that little baby girl was like seeing a miracle. I don't think anybody can ever prepare you for the feeling of seeing and holding your baby for the first time.

I've had a lot of great and exciting moments in basketball. I've been a part of a lot of big games, emotional games, but the greatest days of my life were the days my children were born.

Our children have meant so much and brought so much joy to Carolyn and me. I'll never forget the three special days each of our children was born. What a feeling!

The second year at Cumberland was a memorable season, a record-setting season at Cumberland. We had a tremendous basketball team that ended up with a 34-2 record. It was also in the summer prior to this season that I established a relationship with someone who would become a close friend. Willie Hamilton became a part of our team, and the following year, his younger brother Barry arrived. This started a long-term relationship with a coach who I think was ahead of his time as a recruiter in the '70s at Austin Peay, when I met him.

Their brother, Leonard Hamilton, is now, of course, setting school records as head basketball coach at the University of Miami.

The second year really was a pivotal year for my confidence. I'd been a junior high coach, a junior varsity coach, a high school coach, and the head coach one year at Cumberland. I'd never before had that team that just burned it; this one did.

That team won 27 games in a row. They averaged 105 points a game, which led the nation, and this was before the shot clock and without a 3-point shot. It was amazing. It was as ferocious a defensive team as I've ever been associated with, including the 1999 team at Auburn. They would not be denied. This Cumberland team would finish fourth in the nation and win the state championship of Tennessee.

In Tennessee there were two junior college divisions, the winners of which played for the state championship at the end of the year. We were undefeated in conference play going into this game, one of the more memorable contests of my career. We had played Martin Junior College, the winner of the other division, twice already in the year and had beaten them soundly both times. But defeating a team three times in one season is a difficult assignment, and this game proved that adage true.

At a neutral site, Motlow Junior College, we were behind by 13 points with a minute and a half to go in the game. There was no three-point shot in 1974, and there was no shot clock. Scoring 13 points in 90 seconds seemed impossible. The people in the stands were gathering up their coats and kids and preparing to celebrate or mourn, depending on whom they were supporting. But the players on my team were not finished.

Charlie Fishback and company stole the ball six times and scored, adding a free throw to tie the game with less than ten seconds to go. At that point, James Britt, Fishback's partner in the guard tandem, took right in front of our bench what was clearly a charge (in our unbiased eyes), but the referees saw it as a blocking foul on him instead. My assistant coach was so enraged that he jumped off the bench to let the referee know how wrong he was and was charged with a technical foul. Things did look bleak then: Martin had one-and-one foul shots and two technical foul shots and then the ball out of bounds. Martin missed all foul shots and two shots at the basket at the end of regulation, sending the game into overtime. The game was ours in overtime. I still tell my teams that few leads are too big to overcome—or to lose.

That team was so much like the 1999 team at Auburn. The leadership was there, the attitude was right, and there was talent. When Daymeon Fishback was born, I told Charles Fishback, his dad, that if his son played basketball, he would have a place to play if I was still a head coach. I was thrilled to be able to offer Daymeon a scholarship and get him to come to Auburn. It wasn't like I was doing him any big favors. He was Mr. Basketball in Kentucky and could have gone a lot of places. There is perhaps little coincidence that two of the most successful teams I've coached have had players named Fishback.

We didn't exactly travel first class in those years at Cumberland College. We traveled in station wagons. We'd get there the day of the game and play it and go home. There were no fancy hotels and no fancy eating. It was Hardee's, McDonald's, or Burger King. Some nights, we might splurge and have Kentucky Fried Chicken.

We'd load up three in the front seat, three in the back. It never fazed those players. We were a tight-knit group. Every player in the program graduated. It was family. Carolyn was their primary tutor. She would teach in the day, make lesson plans at night, and tutor our players. I remember many nights going to bed while she tutored players in the living room.

I was blessed to be associated with this team. They were fine young men. They could play. They would all become successful in their own right.

It was in 1973 that I made what I considered a real recommitment to God. I was raised in the First Presbyterian Church in Chipley, Florida. I was made to go to Sunday school and church. I was nurtured and also taught there. While in college, I backslid, one might say. In my early coaching career, I was too busy x-ing and o-ing, and if there was time left, I wanted to fish or golf.

Carolyn, a devoted Christian, would encourage me while at home, but a person must make that decision on his own. In 1973, I made a decision that was emotional and gave me great comfort and joy. I had tasted success in many areas, and success certainly had been a driving desire all of my life. What I was discovering was that professional, social, even marital success is good but not ultimately meaningful. What I was realizing was that ultimate meaning is glimpsed only as my professional, social, family relationships are empowered by my relationship with God.

The 1974-75 team at Cumberland finished 25-5 and 12th nationally in the final regular-season poll. It was a team with a strong front line, but we were not exceptionally quick, and our press game was not as effective as in past years. Nonetheless, it was an excellent team.

It was at Cumberland that I learned the value of the psychology of coaching.

During my second year, our team was on a roll. We traveled to play Gulf Coast, which was ranked No. 1 in the country, and beat them by 50 points; this was my first major victory as a college coach. The next night we played Chipola and Milton Johnson. We won by 19. It was gratifying and satisfying to beat the team of the school where I had attended yet had not been able to play and to defeat one of the finer coaches in the game.

It was the first time I knew the feeling of being ranked, and I did not want to have this feeling go. It was ecstasy. Our team was confident.

At that time, there were freshman teams at universities, and we had a game scheduled against the Middle Tennessee State freshman team. Their coach was a colorful character by the name of Stanley "Ramrod" Simpson.

Middle Tennessee had a brand-new coliseum. It was a 7 o'clock game, and the strangest event I've ever been part of, as far as a basketball game goes. "Ramrod," as well as all the coaches and their wives at Middle Tennessee, were friends of Carolyn and mine. Besides, this was another game against one of my alma maters. I was so excited I drove to Nashville to buy a brand-new green suit with matching green shoes. This was the '70s and the era of gawdy dressing, but at the time, I thought I was "stylin'." I wanted these green shoes to be shiny enough that they could reflect off the lights of their fabulous coliseum, where, ironically, Elvis Presley had just performed. I was proud, somewhat cocky, and confident.

We took the floor for warm-ups for the 7:00 tip-off, but the Middle Tennessee team wasn't warming up on the other end. As Cumberland warmed up, the pregame warm-up music that was played was my Villagers song. My players heard the music and started laughing among themselves. Their concentration was broken. I was somewhat taken aback myself. I never envisioned my song being used for pregame warm-ups.

As the clock was running down before the game, Ramrod came walking over to me with this very concerned look on his face and said, "Cliff, we've got problems. I don't know where my team is. If they do not show up soon, we'll have to forfeit. I thought to myself, "Gee, what kind of kids does he have who won't show up for a game?" I also was going to be disappointed if I could not wear my new green suit and green shoes.

During pregame warm-ups, as a rule of thumb, teams go back to their locker room approximately eight minutes before tip-off for last-minute instructions. I told my team that if the other team did not show up for the game by tip-off, it would be a forfeit. We took the floor with three minutes to go before tip-off, and still there was no team on the other end. With exactly one minute to go, the doors from an auxiliary gym near the coliseum burst open, and the Blue Raiders from Middle Tennessee took the floor as fired up as any team I had seen in my career. The fans were going wild and apparently knew of this psychological ploy. I now had to get my team's concentration back. A moment before, we had been thinking forfeit, and suddenly we were about to play, and our warm-ups had been lackadaisical due to all this.

The two teams took the floor for the tip. MTSU called a time-out before the game ever started. My team came to the huddle laughing and giggling again. We were not even close to being ready to play.

After the time-out, both teams went back out for the jump ball. We were going north and they were going south. We got the tip and scored on our end. MTSU scored on their next possession, knotting the game at 2. As we came down the floor on offense, they kept a player under their basket. We had five on offense versus four on defense in our half of the court. Our players and I were befuddled. We missed the shot on our next possession, and they passed for an easy basket. We could not get back in time. This scenario happened again, and we were behind 6-2. The next thing I knew, we were behind 10-2. I was upset. The players' concentration was broken. We were in a far different situation than we'd anticipated.

I now called time out and tried to reorganize my troops for this 5-4 offense with a snowbird on the other end. I could tell by the looks on my players' faces that we were in trouble.

After the time-out, though, we eventually would get ahead, forcing them to play the normal five-on-offense, five-on-defense game and we won.

We were much better than they were. We beat them by 50 points at our place later in the year, but this game went down to the wire; we won by only two or three points. It was a war game, all created by the psychological advantages they had.

Ramrod did a masterful job that night. He knew the situation. He knew he was outmanned, but he also knew he was playing a young coach. We managed to win the game, but he sure won the psychological battle and taught a young coach some lessons.

The best team doesn't always win in basketball. Sometimes the team that wins is the team that finds an edge, finds a little something extra. I've never tried anything quite like that, but we've won quite a few games over the years when we weren't as talented as our opponent. That game against Middle Tennessee State was one of those lessons that I needed to learn.

When I started coaching I thought that I needed to be very animated on the sideline. I think that is one reason I ran out of time-outs in my very first game. I had to do and say something immediately and loudly. I had a similar relationship with referees from the sideline. I argued every call—with animation and obvious doubt about the referees' ability to see and think. At Cumberland College I began to mature in my attitude toward the game and those who called the game, largely because of Ralph Stout.

We were playing Motlow State Junior College for the division championship after having beaten them at our place pretty soundly. It was a real battle, and I was contributing my own heat to the battle with yells to my team and to the referees from my bench. Ralph, who was calling the game, ran by my sideline, and of course, I took the opportunity to vigorously beg for help on blocking or charging or carrying the ball or jump-ball calls. Ralph turned toward me, puckered his lips, and threw me a kiss. I chuckled and calmed down.

In a few minutes, though, I was convinced that the referees needed my help again and yelled at Ralph again as he passed within earshot. This time Ralph wrapped his tongue around his whistle and pretended to swallow it; then he stuck out his tongue with the whistle lying on it. He did all this while running with the players and watching every move they made. It was a great trick that broke me up. Then he said, "This game will be controlled. I will make sure of that."

On more than one occasion, Ralph Stout proved he was stronger and smarter than most coaches, and certainly he knew the rulebook better than most coaches did. In that Motlow game, he made the gutsiest call I have ever seen made. At that time the rules of the game allowed no tap-ins as shots. In other words, a tap-in had to be in the cylinder to be counted at the end of a game. Other shots could be launched before the buzzer and counted after the buzzer, but not tap-ins.

At the end of our game at Motlow, they hit a tap-in to win the game. Their crowd and players were in a frenzy. I headed to their bench to shake the coach's hand, resigned to losing our second game of the season. From out of the corner of my eye, though, I saw Ralph Stout skipping across the court, waving his arms, indicating that the shot did not count. Everybody, including me, thought the game was over and that we had lost. It took unusual courage for Ralph to make the call and change the outcome of the game in a very hostile environment. He explained that the ball was tapped in and was not in the cylinder by the time the clock ran out. I decided then that referees make great contributions to the game because they know the rules better than coaches and players and because they enforce those rules. It helped that this call went in my favor.

The headline in the paper the next day amazingly agreed with my new assessment of referees. Under the headline was a picture of the basket, clock visible behind it, showing :00, and the ball hovering above the cylinder. Ralph Stout had made the right call. His skill gave me a deep and lasting respect for referees.

At Cumberland I finalized the book *Zone Press Variations for Winning Basketball* for Parker Publishing Company. I had now gone from magazine publication to a hardback book. This would prove to be a winning edge once again.

In August, after my third season at Cumberland, the director of development for Cumberland College came to me and said, "Cliff, the job is open at South Alabama." He had been the former basketball coach at Birmingham-Southern. His name was Bill Birch.

Fred Whiddon had been vice president at Birmingham-Southern, while Howard Phillips served as president. Ironically, Fred Whiddon was named president at South Alabama, and Howard Phillips went to South Alabama as Fred Whiddon's vice president. Bill Birch knew them both very well.

Bill Birch called them and said, "Look, guys, I've got the guy for the job." They said to send them some information. He sent my new book down. I flew to South Alabama for an interview.

South Alabama was considering dropping from Division I basketball to Division II. Nobody was attending their games, and nobody seemed to care about USA basketball in Mobile at the time.

In my interview with Dr. Whiddon, he immediately referenced my youth: "You are a little wet behind the ears, aren't you?" My answer was, "Yes, sir, but if you'll give me the chance, I'll never let you down." I was 29 years old at the time, and there was only one other Division I coach at the time as young as I was—Mike Krzyzewski, head coach at Army.

Dr. Whiddon was from Newville, Alabama, approximately 50 miles northeast of Chipley, Florida. I remember his next comment as if it were yesterday. "I come from sawmill country, and I know you are out of this same territory. I'll bet when you were young you had your nose rubbed into the pavement many times." I knew what he meant. I nodded, thinking of the times that I had had to fight to protect my recess money. Dr. Whiddon knew I could handle the tough situations I was about to be put into. He stepped out on a limb and hired this young person to be his head basketball coach. I wasn't about to let him down. With much emotion, I resigned at Cumberland to take the South Alabama job.

Carolyn returned to our apartment on the night that I had flown to Mobile for the interview, after teaching her night class at Cumberland. When she opened the door, all she saw were sad faces: Boone and Sally Swain both had their heads bowed; Harry Frank, whom I had hired as baseball coach and who was married to Carolyn's sister, was holding Mary Beth's hand as she wept. Carolyn's heart dropped, wondering what plane crash I had been in. Then she heard my voice from the bedroom, already on the phone, planning for the job at the University of South Alabama.

It was painful to leave Cumberland College. We were leaving good friends and family. Mary Beth was pregnant with their son, Brett, and she wanted Carolyn to be with her. I had developed relationships with players that would be everlasting. Cumberland had given me a chance, and I am forever grateful. I had to say goodbye to a place I loved and people I loved, yet I anxiously anticipated this next move.

CHAPTER TWELVE

The South Alabama Years

I was taking over a program that did not draw fans.
The administration made it clear that the school was going to
give Division II basketball a hard look. We were playing 13
miles away from campus in an auditorium that seated 10,500
people, and attendance hadn't been very good. An auxiliary
facility for basketball called Expo Hall could seat 4,000, and
we would play some of our games in that 4,000-seat arena.

There were only five players on scholarship when I took
the job in late August. They included point guards Alonzo
"Zeke" Lambert and Ricky Baker; wing guards Albert Gardner
and Jimmy Tate; and post player Rick Sinclair. It was about as
tough a situation depth-wise as I had ever been involved in.
Thomas Ledford and Johnny Farmer, who played for me at
Cumberland, were predictors out of high school, making them
eligible to play immediately, although I had to get Dr. Stockton to agree with this. The players were anxious and ready, and
Dr. Stockton was the type of person who wanted the

Cumberland students to advance. He knew it was in their best interests, and without reservation, he agreed to allow them to play at South Alabama.

George White, who had played at Columbia State Junior College, was also available. At the last minute I added three scholarship players to the roster, giving us a total of eight scholarships that first year. Dave Grube, a local Mobilian and student at South Alabama, would walk on and join the team, as did Kevin Courtney, a baseball player for the legendary Eddie Stanky, head baseball coach at South Alabama. Dave Grube, by the way, finished his degree at South Alabama, began a coaching career, and now is currently general manager of the CBA's Grand Rapids, Michigan, franchise.

My first game as a Division I coach was versus Centenary College. I thought I was about to have a nervous breakdown. They were No. 18 in the nation as we opened the season. None other than Robert Parish, who went on to be a star with the Boston Celtics, was their leader. This was not the Centenary that we know today. This was not a good basketball team— this was a great basketball team. We played at Expo Hall, which was sold out, packed to the rafters. Centenary won by about 14, but we didn't embarrass ourselves.

Our next game was against the University of South Dakota and we barely won. I'd won my first game as a Division I coach. It was close; I was relieved.

Now we had a major road trip ahead of us. We were going to Florida to play Jacksonville University, home of the great Artis Gilmore, who is from my hometown. He used to love to eat dates, a tangy fruit, from underneath our palm tree on 202 North Blvd. Jacksonville was in its heyday at that time, just recently coming off a Final Four appearance. We knew we were going to a tough place, and from there we were going to leave and go play Centenary. Then we would leave to face Nevada–Las Vegas to play one of the greatest Vegas teams ever. We were playing all these great teams, and the administration was considering going to Division II.

We bused to Jacksonville. The place was packed because it was their opening game. I mean it was absolutely packed. Don Beasley was the new coach at Jacksonville. Electricity was in the air in the Jacksonville Coliseum; we could not hear ourselves talk, as Jacksonville took the floor. Here I was in my first big Division I road game. Nobody thought we could win except our team. Media and fans had written us off—an impossible win, they would say. Besides, South Alabama had never won at Jacksonville.

As the roar of the crowd seemingly excited JU's players, my team got caught up in the emotion of the crowd. In the locker room all I said to the players was, "Spoil the party. Think of the celebration that we are going to have when we win this game. Go out and spoil the party."

We got the opening tip and scored, then stole the ball quickly for another score and led 4-0. The crowd toned down but was still loud. The teams went back and forth until our team made a sudden surge and, behind the play of guard Albert Gardner, we took an eight-point lead prior to the end of the first half. I made the decision to spread the floor on offense, to play a four-corner offense. I had quick and steady guards in Zeke Lambert and Gardner and George White. Jacksonville extended their defense and allowed our offense to get by them for more scores. We still led at halftime, and in the locker room our team was excited and confident. I told them the game was a 40-minute game. There were 20 minutes left before the "party would be spoiled." We needed to stay with the four-corner offense and focus on what we had been doing to get the lead.

We played a great second half, executing well and hitting foul shots down the stretch, and we upset Jacksonville by about 10! There was a shock wave in Mobile. South Alabama had beaten Jacksonville! No one had given us a chance. At the Thunderbird Motel, my phone rang until about 3 o'clock in the morning. Nobody could believe it! Nobody could believe we had won that game.

The next day, we took a plane from Jacksonville to Shreveport. It hadn't been but a little over a week since we had played Centenary and lost. Centenary was still ranked in the top 25. We were confident going in, though, and Johnny Farmer would hit a shot at the buzzer. We pulled off another major upset. We'd gone to Jacksonville and won. We'd gone to Centenary and upset this nationally ranked team that had beaten us in our first game.

Now we were going to UNLV, and they were in the top 10. The sports world was wondering what was going on with the South Alabama basketball team.

We flew to Vegas to meet Jerry Tarkanian and company. We spread the floor out with our four-corner offense and had them on the ropes. It was a one-point game with three minutes left in the first half. We didn't win or even come close in the end, but we had made another statement. This team would fight tooth and nail and was determined to win despite the odds.

At that time in NCAA basketball there was no shot clock. This team without depth had a hard time going hard for 40 minutes all out. We'd play awhile, then spread the floor out. We spread it against Nevada–Las Vegas, but by halftime, I had one player in the hospital who had taken a pretty good shot to the head and another guy in foul trouble. I got pretty upset at the officiating in the game, and Tarkanian and I got into a fairly loud discussion about the rough play. South Alabama ended up getting drilled.

The next weekend we played in a tournament at Arkansas State, getting a split. We had played five straight road games but were coming home 4-3 with two national wins on the road under our belt. Next up was our tournament—the Senior Bowl Tournament with Ole Miss, Rice, and Pan-American. We opened up the tournament playing Rice. We were so fired up and confident that we destroyed Rice by 60 points.

Ole Miss played Pan-American in the other round. I discovered the humor of Abe Lemons, head coach at Pan-American, at the pretourney press party. He is one of the funniest men I've been around. I remember a question asked by a local reporter: "What do you think about playing Ole Miss tomorrow night?" His response: "Who's she?"

Abe was famous for one of his weekly TV shows when he was head coach of Texas. Texas had lost a couple of tough games in a row, and the show began with funeral music. As the show opened up, the cameras focused on an open casket. Suddenly, Abe raised up out of the casket. In his funeral tux, he intoned, "We ain't dead yet." Abe knew, and taught me that humor can defuse many painful situations.

I was shocked to find that when we took the floor against Rice, there were only 1,500 fans in attendance. We had been on the road and accomplished some things no other USA team had. Ole Miss beat Pan-American to set up a matchup versus an SEC team. Surely this would bring in a crowd. Disappointingly, only 2,500 people were in attendance to see South Alabama play Ole Miss. On that night we pulled off our third major upset of the season.

As a coach on the floor, I had done my job preparing my team. It sent a strong message to me, however, that if this program was going to make it, I would have to incorporate the things I used to do as a singer—entertain the crowd and put on a show.

It put an exclamation point on what I had always believed about promoting and entertaining. You had better have the atmosphere in all situations. You had better have the popcorn right, you'd better hug babies, shake hands. The band has to be right. You have to put on a show. We did not have a school pep band at USA. I knew then that I was going to hire one.

We finished this season, miraculously, with an 18-9 record. It was a gutsy performance by a gutsy group of young men. I was totally satisfied with our on-court performance, but I had work to do in the off-season to get this community fired up.

It was during this time that I met one of the best friends I ever had in my life. His name was John Albert Counts. He was a South Alabama graduate who became my closest friend at that point in my life. He was a big fan. He felt the way I did about promoting. He didn't know anything about basketball, but he knew that city.

We would share ideas in the off-season. Who in the community can help? What band can we get? What companies did he know? He was the guy who continued to steer me in the right direction, showed me where to go and whom to talk to.

We set up a season-ticket drive to get the community involved. A plan to succeed was in the making.

We spent the entire off-season planning. John and I eventually found our band, the Lewis Brothers. We gave them a list of up-tempo songs we wanted them to learn. The season-ticket drive incorporated businesspeople to lead a charge to find season-ticket holders. Businesses donated prizes to people selling the most season tickets. We sold over 1,000 tickets initially. It was a start.

It was also in this year that South Alabama joined a conference, the Sun Belt Conference. Other members included UNC–Charlotte, Jacksonville, South Florida, Georgia State, and New Orleans. Along with South Alabama, these were the charter members. Vic Bubas, the famed Duke coach, became commissioner.

South Alabama had been an independent; by joining a league, we could now develop rivalries. Our league would not get an automatic bid for two years, but everyone had his sights set on the day this would come.

In our second season, attendance picked up, a band was in place, and our team finished 18-10. The highlight of this season was playing in the finals of the Vulcan Classic. It pitted Army vs. South Alabama. The two youngest Division I coaches at the time would face each other for the first time, not knowing their teams would face each other many times in the future. Army was coached by Mike Krzyzewski. South Alabama won in a thriller. South was led by Don Hogan, who would later become an assistant for me at South Alabama and Clemson. Don currently is head basketball coach at the University of West Florida. He was a hard-nosed player and today is an excellent tactician and coach of young people.

Vic Bubas, as commissioner, was leading our conference in the right direction. He gave our conference instant credibility. He immediately put a TV package together for the conference, which helped provide all of us with exposure. He could promote, and he knew how to get things done.

Joining the Sun Belt Conference gave us an opportunity to go to recruits and say, "We've got a conference. We are going to get to go to the NCAA Tournament."

Back in those days, there weren't a lot of recruiting camps. Nowadays, there are so many camps that most of the top players are seen before they ever enter their senior year of high school. There were "sleepers" back then. If a coach beat the bushes, he could find players out there who could play. If a coach had a staff who would burn the roads up, they would find something.

I was fortunate to have excellent coaches with me at South Alabama. Larry Phillips, who was a former Auburn assistant, did a phenomenal recruiting job for me at South Alabama. Robert Trammell, my best friend from college, had been with Cobb Jarvis until Jarvis was fired at Ole Miss and Robert came back to USA as an assistant coach. George Scholtz, who has coached in the NBA and at Jacksonville, was on my staff for a year. Drayton Miller and Larry Cone eventually became significant members of my staff and sparked our recruiting efforts. My last year at South Alabama, Eugene Harris and Dan Hogan joined my staff. Eugene has been with me ever since. Also, Bill Muse, current head coach at Connors State College in Oklahoma, spent time on our staff in our last year.

The third year, I started freshmen who had basically been recruited by Larry Phillips and Robert Trammell. My starting lineup consisted of four freshmen. John May was my center from Gulfport, Mississippi. He was 6-10. He was a shot blocker and an outstanding defender. At power forward was Rory White from Tuskegee, Alabama. The small forward was Ed Rains from Ocala, Florida. The guard was Scott Williams from Warner Robbins, Georgia. These four guys were recruited to come in and play immediately.

I said, "We are going to build this program with a solid foundation, and we are going to play these freshmen." The point guard was Lonnie Leggett, who had been a junior college transfer and was a senior. This team, composed predominantly of freshmen, would pull off an upset against a top 10 team on the road. That team won 18 games and went to the finals of the Sun Belt Conference Tournament.

Florida State was No. 10 in the country. As we took the floor, the Seminole pep band rocked, and the crowd was in a frenzy. We were huge underdogs. FSU was my alma mater; my mother and father, brothers and sisters, and many friends were there. I invited my mentor and coach, Phillip Rountree, to come and talk to the team.

The game was nip-and-tuck throughout, with FSU keeping a small lead throughout the game. We made a surge in the second half. Down by two with a minute to play, we stole the ball to tie the score. FSU inbounded the ball and played for the last shot. FSU missed the shot with about five seconds to play. South Alabama got the rebound and threw the outlet pass to point guard Lonnie Leggett, who caught the ball and fired a prayer from half-court. It went in! Florida State was beaten. All the drums were dead silent. I had beaten my alma mater while they were 10th in the country—what a special feeling.

Little did I know that this would be the beginning of a national program for South Alabama. We opened up in the Sun Belt Conference tournament against South Florida, the first televised game I'd ever been a part of. This was big. Media and fans in Mobile called it the biggest event in South Alabama history, because television cameras were bringing it back to Mobile. We beat South Florida.

The next night, in Charlotte, we were playing Lee Rose and the 49ers. They had beaten us the Monday night before by 30 points. We got the lead, spread it out, played a cat-and-mouse game with the press, and found a way to win. It was a huge upset. UNC–Charlotte was coming off a Final Four appearance the year before, and this loss would knock them out of the NCAA Tournament.

We played in the finals against New Orleans. Butch van Breda Kolff, who had taken Princeton to the Final Four and had coached in the NBA, was their head coach. After being beaten twice soundly by UNO, I devised a plan to try to give us a chance to win and perhaps get in USA's first postseason tournament, as well as win the conference championship. We spread the floor out. New Orleans banged in a buzzer shot from the corner to win 22-20.

Dean Smith was spreading the floor out a lot at North Carolina. The score of one Duke-Carolina game had been 7-7 at halftime. Nevertheless, the league was furious that I had spread the floor. Dick Bowers, who was the athletic director at South Florida, came to me after the game and said, "You set our league back light-years." I thought that what he said and how he said it was uncalled for. A coach plays to win. It was within the rules. I played to win. I didn't play as if it was a circus. I would never do that. If a rule is bad, change it, but people should not blame a coach for taking advantage of what the rules are.

Vic Bubas didn't come out and say it, but he didn't appear to be happy. He knew that if North Carolina or Duke held the ball, it was a little different situation. He saw that this wouldn't work for our league. There wouldn't be any fan interest. He was right. We were an upstart league, and we were not going to draw fans with a dull, spread-the-floor game.

Our game provided the impetus for Vic Bubas to get the rule passed that brought in the 45-second shot clock. It was South Alabama that caused it. The 45-second clock came in as an experimental rule the very next year. It was known for a while as the Bubas-Ellis shot clock in the league.

The shot clock is one of the greatest things to happen to the game, in my opinion. Some people had questions about it at the time, but I don't think anybody would want to do away with it now.

I didn't spread it out and hold the ball at home, but I would do it on the road. I had four freshmen; I gave them a chance to win. A postseason tournament was on the line, and I was going to give them a chance.

In that third year, we opened the eyes of Mobile with a team of mostly freshmen. We had a dynamite band, we were in a conference, and fan support was growing. The Mobile-area fans liked these freshmen. It turned out that in 1981 we had more draft picks when these freshmen had become seniors than any other program in America. Neither Kentucky, Duke, North Carolina, UCLA, nor any other high-powered program would have more draft picks in 1981 than South Alabama.

The people in Mobile and across America were beginning to witness a group of dedicated 17- and 18-year-olds who would turn the word *sleepers* into *giants* on the hardwood.

While building the program at South Alabama, Carolyn and I continued to build our family. On July 8, 1978, Robert Clayton Ellis was born. We call him Clay. He was born four days before our anniversary. We spent our anniversary adoring Clay, and we celebrated somewhat. I was able to talk the doctor and nurses into allowing me to bring a pizza into Carolyn's hospital room, as well as a small bottle of champagne for a toast. It was an enjoyable ninth anniversary.

Clay is a bright kid, thinks for himself, and is very independent. He basically is a quiet person, yet always thinking, and can express himself very well when called upon to do so. Through the years, some of my more satisfying times off the court have been taking Clay fishing, hunting, and golfing. These are special moments between father and son. I have regretted at times, however, due to coaching responsibilities, as well as a growing boy's own aspirations for independence and wanting to be with friends, that we have not been able to do more together.

As a kid, Clay was exposed to the game and had great hand-eye coordination, but the game was never a passion for him. This was fine with me, as long as he adhered to his work in the classroom. Early in his life I could see the pressure of being a coach's son. He was six years old and competing with kids in his own group, ranging up to nine years of age. He got into the championship of a contest and lost. The kid who won was nine years old and jumping up and down shouting, "I beat coach's son, I beat coach's son!"

He played junior high and high school basketball and tennis, but tore his ACL in his junior year in high school. Through this adversity, he showed me his mental toughness. He's been a good student and has made us proud. He never let the pressure of being a coach's son get to him. He never had to score a point to make me proud.

Meanwhile, the season-ticket drives continued. John Counts, my close friend and now soul mate, was named to the Board of Trustees in 1978. He was in a powerful position. There were some movers and shakers in the beginning to help make that program go—John Counts, Mayer Mitchell, and Bill Lubel were intent on helping us get on the national map. Mayer was on the Board of Trustees along with John. They wanted college basketball. They wanted it to be successful. Dr. Whiddon, who gave me the opportunity, loved it, too, but he was consumed with a lot of other things in his office as president. Without the help of these people, it would have been much more difficult. It might not have ever gotten done.

There were other people: John Pittman, Earl Andrews, T. M. Smithwick, Eddie Roberts, Larry Harless, and other boosters who were instrumental in the ticket drives and who helped energize the community. We were starting to move.

In 1978-79, the freshmen became sophomores, and we recruited talented Herb Andrew, a junior college player in Los Angeles, California. This is what I call the birth of the California connection. It was at that time I realized that the way the game was moving, we couldn't recruit in the State of Alabama and get the prime athletes.

We had to find a recruiting base where there were a lot of kids and go find the one who might have been missed. There wasn't a better place than Los Angeles. There were as many people in Los Angeles as there were in Alabama and Georgia put together. Florida had about 10 million and Los Angeles had seven to nine million. We started targeting those two areas. We felt that we could fill our needs targeting these areas.

The breakthrough season for South Alabama was 1978-79. ESPN was new in the television market, a sports channel network, and it needed games. Vic Bubas masterfully set up a TV package, giving ESPN any game it wanted. We were televised nationally several times that year. Major conferences such as the SEC, ACC, and Big Ten had their own networks at that time and did not realize the potential of this sports network. This marriage between ESPN and the Sun Belt Conference provided the spark both needed. We were televised in millions of homes that year, plus we were good. Abe Lemons, at the NCAA convention following the season, joked, "Cliff, you are on TV more than *Sanford and Son*."

This team went undefeated in the conference with a 10-0 record. The only other team to go undefeated in its conference that year was Indiana State, led by none other than Larry Bird. Indiana State lost in the finals of the NCAA Tournament to Michigan State in the first of many famed matchups between Larry Bird and Magic Johnson.

We won the regular-season championship, then lost in the conference tournament, but we still received South Alabama's first NCAA bid in history. The City of Mobile was in a frenzy, and so were our players.

They might not have been quite as excited when they found out who our opponent was. It was Louisville, and it would be nationally televised on CBS. Darryl Griffith was their leader. We played them in Dallas at SMU. I did my first live network interview with Jim Thacker of the famous Thacker-Packer television team. I thought they were the best TV hosting team at the time in college basketball.

We stayed right in the game. It was close, but Louisville led all the way. With about three minutes left to play, we were down one point and had the ball. We had a backdoor play for a wide-open layup—I mean it was there. We missed the pass on the backdoor play or we would have gone ahead.

It was now a one-point game and we had to foul. Louisville was visibly shaken. Darryl Griffith went to the line; it was a one-and-one, I'll never forget it. He banked the first one in—I mean he almost broke the glass. We lost a heartbreaker, or we would have played Arkansas in the Sweet 16. At that time there were only 32 teams in the NCAA.

We flew back to Mobile following the game to an unbelievable sight. The airport was packed. The city had gone mad. There was a platform built at the airport especially for a ceremony to greet the team. It seemed the entire city was there. Everyone sensed the program had turned. These four guys were just sophomores, and we had them for two more years.

The following year, a rematch would be set up on television between Louisville and South Alabama to open the season. The exposure would be great, and with a good showing, we could make a mark early with our team nationally.

We lost in a very close game, but we would lose something vital to our team for this year. Rory White, our star forward, tore his ACL and was out for the year. Rory had the best touch of any big man I've ever coached. He would eventually play for the Phoenix Suns and now coaches professionally in Idaho.

However, behind the leadership of Ed Rains and the chemistry this team already had, it would be a team that would not be denied. This team won the Sun Belt Conference championship and again went to the NCAAs. We played Alcorn State, which had beaten us earlier in the year. Alcorn won again.

It was disappointing to lose in the tournament to a team most people expected us to beat, but the program had proven it was on the move. It was obvious both on the court and off the court.

Getting to the NCAA Tournament for the second straight year validated us in a lot of ways. This program had been considering going to Division II, and now it had been to two straight NCAA Tournaments. A lot of people across the nation were sitting up and taking notice of this group of young men from the University of South Alabama.

Once we got to that NCAA Tournament, South Alabama basketball was established. This would be a year of sellouts. In 1975 we could not get people to come. This year there were games where people turned away at the turnstiles. It happened because a lot of people—players, supporters, coaches—worked hard to make it happen. I'm very proud of what we accomplished in those years at South Alabama.

The Sun Belt Conference continued to grow. Teams were being added and powerful coaches were being brought into the league.

UAB, the University of Alabama at Birmingham, came into the league as a full-time member in 1978. UAB pulled a coup, luring Gene Bartow from UCLA to build a program. I believe his package around then was about $85,000. (It might be noted that I came to South Alabama with a starting salary of $14,000.) Butch van Breda Kolff, a Final Four participant and NBA coach, was coach at New Orleans; Tates Locke, at Jacksonville, was coming off a stint as head coach of Buffalo in the NBA; Lee Rose, a Final Four participant with UNCC, had moved to South Florida; Paul Webb, one of the nation's winningest coaches, became head coach at Old Dominion; Clem Haskins became head coach at Western Kentucky. Those were high-profile coaches with fame at that time.

Upon our having success, other schools inquired if I would be interested in their schools. I could not leave the program at that time; it was a beauty to watch it, as well as this conference, grow. South Alabama was generous to my family. I got a nice raise and package to stay with the program. Competing against the other coaches and having success instilled great confidence in me.

In 1980-81, you could hardly get a ticket to a Jaguar game. Unfortunately, we opened the season with a devastating loss to Middle Tennessee State.

By this time, the group that started as freshmen were seniors. We had to regroup and go to Holy Cross for a tournament and play Don Haskins' Texas–El Paso team. We had missed plenty of free throws against Middle Tennessee to contribute to this upset loss.

After that game, I can remember at practice jumping in the end line and trying to rattle my players as they practiced foul shots. They were very tough kids; they weren't fragile. I think I got their attention. We didn't miss free throws that entire tournament at Holy Cross. We beat a good UTEP team and also beat Holy Cross to win the tournament.

The next week we flew to Ohio State to face a great Buckeye team led by Clark Kellogg. They were ranked seventh in the country. In Columbus, Ohio, we pulled off a major national upset. Even though we'd been to the NCAAs the previous two years, we'd never been a ranked team in the regular season. The next week we were ranked for the first time.

Following the Ohio State trip, which ended with our traveling to the University of Akron and winning, we came back home for the Senior Bowl Tournament. We would win this tournament, defeating Fordham and Navy for the title. We opened up the conference schedule with Georgia State, which was 0-13, on a Sunday afternoon. The doors had to be shut an hour before the game because it was sold out. That was an enormous feeling. This wasn't Ohio State—it wasn't anybody like that. The fans had come to see South Alabama, not the opponent. This was a milestone in the growing attitude of support for South Alabama basketball.

The team stayed ranked, going 15-1 before it was beaten by Virginia Commonwealth, and tied for the regular-season championship. We were beaten by UAB in the conference tournament, which was a huge blow.

Virginia Commonwealth won the tournament and received the automatic bid to the NCAA. We lost to UAB for the second time in three games that season. We were the higher-ranked team; we'd played with the pressure. UAB got an at-large bid; we were left out. I was devastated and shocked.

It was a sick feeling. We had been ranked all year. We had an outstanding basketball team that I felt could compete with most teams in the country.

I was upset with the system, not understanding how a team that had been ranked all year could be left out. And this was a group of seniors that had proved themselves not only this year, but in the previous three. I took my frustrations to Commissioner Bubas.

Now, I had to prepare my team for the NIT. The NIT is still a significant event, but was even more important then. At the time, only 32 teams received bids to the NCAA and 16 went to the NIT. Only 48 total teams received NCAA and NIT bids. It was special to be playing, even though we were disappointed at not being in the NCAA Tournament.

We opened the NIT by hosting UT–Arlington and won. The next round matched us with the Georgia Bulldogs, led by Dominique Wilkins, in Athens, Georgia. We defeated this fine Georgia team, with Ed Rains hitting both one-and-one foul shots with one second to go to win by one. We had forgotten about the NCAA Tournament by now, and it was on to Tulsa to face Nolan Richardson's excellent team for a berth in the finals of the NIT at Madison Square Garden in New York City.

We lost a hard-fought game to Tulsa in front of a packed house. I addressed those seniors for the last time. I broke down because I knew that I would miss that group of young men. They had meant so much to the program and to me. We hugged, and as we left to fly home, I recall how blessed I felt to have had this group of seniors.

With this senior class, national acclaim had come to South Alabama. NCAA bids, top 20 rankings, NIT play, and Sun Belt Conference championships were a legacy this group would leave behind. It was also in this era that the conference produced great teams, even though it was embedded in the deep south, where football was king. Basketball was marketed well, and people in Mobile, as well as those in the cities where other teams were located, were plugging into it. In those years, we would play UAB in Birmingham in front of 17,000 every year. UAB would play South Alabama in front of a sellout crowd of 10,500 every year. On the other had, the fierce rivalry of Auburn-Alabama would seldom ever sell out.

I learned during this era the mastery of Gene Bartow. He knew how to maneuver. When a coach had an at-large team, it was good to know people on the committee to sell his side. He simply sold his side. UAB owes that man a lot. He was a masterful coach, not only at putting together a great basketball program, but a football program as well. He's a very close friend who taught me a lot.

What I learned from people like him and the other guys in the league I would take with me to the ACC when I got the job at Clemson. Winning against those great competitors and coaches, I had no fear when I got to the ACC.

The backwoods and swamplands of the panhandle of Florida, where I grew up, is an environment where you can meet some very interesting people. One day Robert Trammell and I were riding from Blountstown to Bristol across the Apalachicola River, when we passed a guy named Bloke Johnson walking on the railing of the bridge, about a hundred feet above the river. We slowed down and asked what in the world he was doing and wondered if he was afraid of falling. He answered in his backwoods drawl, "I got confidence in myself." We laughed and drove on. But I have often thought of Bloke and agreed that confidence can help a person avoid falling. I gained confidence because I had achieved success against what I considered great coaches.

Gene Bartow was appointed athletic director, as well as head basketball coach, upon coming to UAB. In 1980, the South Alabama athletic director position came open. The president and the board wanted the same athletic administration structure as at UAB, and I was appointed athletic director. I was somewhat reluctant to accept, but after reviewing the situation, eventually felt compelled to take it. I had experience in this position at Cumberland and felt somewhat comfortable. Eddie Stanky, former major league player and manager, was our baseball coach and had his program on top. I needed his support and got it; without it, my appointment would never have worked. I hired my friend and associate Robert Trammell to be associate athletic director. I delegated much authority to him in overseeing the nonrevenue sports. I would oversee basketball; Stanky, the baseball program; and Robert, the nonrevenue sports. It was a good mix.

In 1981 I also met someone who would help chart a different path in my life. His name is Bobby Lowder.

Bobby is an astute businessman who was the CEO of an upstart bank in Alabama, Colonial Bank. John Counts became president of this new bank in Mobile. A friend of ours, Jack Miller, an attorney in Mobile, was putting together board members in the community for this bank. I was asked to be a member of the board. I gladly accepted and thought it would be a great way to learn business. I added my support to the bank, learned about the banking business, and enjoyed this venture.

Bobby Lowder masterfully put a plan together with this board to make Colonial Bank work in the Mobile area. Through these meetings, we developed a deep respect for one another and a friendship that is lasting. We shared thoughts and ideas not only about banking but athletics as well. Bobby is the most avid Auburn fan I know. At that time he was a powerful alumnus and would gain an appointment on the Board of Trustees at Auburn. Little did we know that this relationship would eventually help lead to my appointment at Auburn.

I learned to love Auburn while at South Alabama and serving on the bank board. On fall Saturdays, John Counts and I and our wives would travel to see one or two football games and be the Lowders' guests. I saw on these trips why Auburn is such a special place.

In my opinion, Auburn has been able to rise to the top athletically in all sports due to the influence of this businessman and Board of Trustee member, Bobby Lowder. He knows how to manage business, and that is vital to any successful athletic program. Through the years, in building his reputation as a powerful trustee, he has taken a lot of criticism along with praise. He stands strong on what he believes, and if people agree, fine, and if not, he will stick to his beliefs regardless of the consequences. I wish more people knew the humane side of Bobby. For example, when my daughter was married, he picked up a friend of mine who was dying of cancer, and he and Charlotte, his wife, took my friend and his family to my daughter's wedding in Clemson, South Carolina. He is a kind, compassionate, and generous person who has his friends, as well as Auburn, in his heart.

We'd had a great run for five years prior to entering the 1981-82 season. It was a year in which we seemingly lost every close game. It was my first losing season. It was difficult because I had never been involved with a losing season as coach.

We had a great front line, but I learned for the first time that you can't win without excellent guard play, no matter what else you have. We'd be in every game, but when it got down to the last four minutes, we couldn't hold on. I've said for a long time that when you get down to the last four minutes, your big men don't win the game for you—guards do.

A team has to take care of the ball and hit foul shots. If a team is behind, the guards have to be able to pick up the pressure and get the ball. We lost one-pointers and two-pointers. We lost a horde of close games.

It was tough on me. I'd never been through anything like that, but I just took it as a learning experience and moved on.

My first losing campaign as a coach occurred in the 1981-82 season, but it was a highlight year for me personally, as Carolyn would become pregnant with our third child, Anna Catherine Ellis. She was born November 16, 1982.

Anna Catherine is a witty child and a very caring person. She makes a positive impact on those people she surrounds. In the summer of 1999, she and her mother went on a mission trip together in Honduras to help those in need. She works to earn her money and spent some of her own money to make this trip.

The 1982-83 season was a comeback year. We had a lot of young kids, and I was determined we would bounce back. We won 16 games playing primarily freshmen and sophomores. We were led by future NBA star Terry Catledge, only a sophomore. We were still winning mostly with players who weren't highly recruited, but we were also starting to recruit more high-profile players.

At that point in 1983, the NBA draft from South Alabama would include Ed Rains, Rory White, Scott Williams,

John May, Reggie Hannah, and Herb Andrews. My NBA train had started rolling down the tracks. This would help us get in the door with high-profile players.

Terry Catledge was now our leader and was somewhat of a high-profile player out of high school. To sign him, I had been involved with one of the most interesting recruiting events ever.

In Catledge's senior year of high school, there was no fall signing period. South Alabama was interested in two excellent prep post men: Catledge of Houston, Mississippi, and Bobby Lee Hurt of Huntsville, Alabama. At the end of our season I would leave on Monday morning to go see Catledge. On Tuesday evening I would leave Houston, Mississippi, for Huntsville and visit Bobby Lee and return home on Friday. I did this every week until both signed.

It was a long process. Back in those days, recruiting rules were different. I talked the South Alabama president into going and meeting with Bobby Lee Hurt. The president flew to Huntsville, Alabama, and visited with him. I thought we were in good shape.

Bobby Lee was playing a recruiting game with me, and with coaches from Hawaii, Maryland, as well as others. I thought he was actually going to Alabama, where he eventually signed, all along. I kept recruiting Bobby Lee, because he was telling me he wanted to come to South Alabama. But he was telling other coaches he wanted to go to their schools as well.

I got a call one night and Bobby Lee said, "Coach, I want to come to South Alabama. I'm having my press conference in Huntsville."

I rolled into Huntsville thinking I was going to get him, and that I was really about to pull something off. I was excited. This was going to be a real coup. South Alabama was going to get Bobby Lee Hurt.

I pulled up to Butler High School, where Hurt played, and noticed Lefty Driesell was there. Then I saw coaches from Hawaii, Larry Little and Riley Wallace. They had been in California on their way back to Hawaii and got the same call I got. They hadn't shaved in two days. I turned to Larry Little and said, "I think we've been snookered."

The good news regarding this recruiting adventure was that Terry Catledge would sign with South Alabama, and it would turn out that he, not Bobby Lee Hurt, would go to the NBA.

Catledge led us into the 1983-84 season. I had no idea it would be my last at South Alabama. On this team were Dexter Shouse, a point guard who would eventually play in the NBA; Michael Gerron, a two guard who would play abroad; Dale Osborne, small forward, who would later coach at USA. Inside positions were manned by Catledge and Joe Waitman, who also played abroad. Kelly Blaine, a seven-foot center, and Willie Jackson helped make us stalwarts inside, along with Catledge and Waitman. Anthony Barge and Calodeus Cannion gave us reserve strength in the backcourt. This was a dynamite team with tremendous potential and no seniors. I knew that by the following season, it could be my most talented ever at South.

We came out of the box in a hurry. We won a couple of games early on to start the season. The Colonial Classic was set up to build goodwill between Colonial Bank and the community. With Bobby Lowder ties, Auburn agreed to play, setting up only the second matchup between Auburn and South Alabama, should both teams win in the opening round.

In the opening round versus Florida A&M, we could not play dead in a cowboy show. We won, but barely. Auburn blew out Youngstown State. This set up an Auburn-South Alabama matchup in Mobile.

I called for an unusual practice at noon, requiring our team to tape up and put on practice gear. We practiced intensively for 45 minutes, taking charges; they were catching the wrath of my disappointment at the previous night's play.

I had a knockdown, drag-out, ferocious practice on game day. Coaches do not normally do this, preferring to keep their team rested. At the end of practice I told them, "I don't know what is going to happen in this game or who is going to win, but one thing is for sure—we will be the scrappiest, toughest team on the court."

By this time the team was not thinking of playing Auburn. They were thinking they never wanted to go through this routine again. There was a huge crowd at Municipal Auditorium to witness this event. Auburn brought a fine team, led by Charles Barkley and Chuck Person. Charles Barkley and Terry Catledge would be matched against each other. We were on fire and in an unbelievable mind-set, hitting virtually every shot and playing like wild animals. We won 95-73. Charles Barkley fouled out and did not score. Auburn would go on to have a great season, and it was no embarrassment to them to lose to South Alabama. These were two very good teams.

We built a 10-1 record and were off to the Orange Bowl Classic and won the championship, making us 12-1. We were primed for conference play. We finished second in the conference, 22-8 overall, went to the NIT, and defeated the Florida Gators, yet lost the next round to Virginia Tech.

It had been a very good year. We had no seniors on the team, and I was excited about the prospects of the next season with this team. However, the Virginia Tech game would be my last as South Alabama basketball coach.

A few days after the 1983-84 season, the phone rang. Dwight Rainey, who was the assistant athletic director at Clemson, called. He wanted to know if I was interested in the Clemson job. I said I wasn't interested, and I went on a recruiting trip.

We had this great team coming back, and we'd been recruiting Vernon Maxwell out of Gainesville, Florida. Florida had not really recruited him hard. I went into his home ready to sign him.

He looked at me and said, "Coach, I love your school. You guys have done a phenomenal job recruiting me, but I've always wanted to go to the University of Florida."

I was really dejected as I went to the Gainesville airport, leaving Vernon's house. I decided on the way to the airport that I would call Clemson and see if they were still interested. I felt I didn't have anything to lose and thought the interview would be something I needed to try.

I called Dwight and said, "I'm going to Atlanta from Gainesville, Florida. I'll be in Atlanta tonight. If you still want to talk, I'll be available." He immediately said Clemson wanted to talk and that they would have a plane in Atlanta to pick me up the next morning. I'd never been in a small plane in my life.

When I was a young kid, even being on a high bridge really made me nervous.

Dwight Rainey picked me up and arranged a meeting with Bill McClellan, the athletic director, and Bobby Robinson, the assistant athletic director. Bill, Bobby, and I met in Bill's office. After about an hour of talking, Bill McClellan said, "Let's cut the crap. What's it going to take for you to be the head basketball coach at Clemson?" I said, "This is what I make. You'll have to make that offer." They huddled for 20-30 minutes and came back with what they would do. I said, "Put that in writing. I'll go back and get my wife and we'll give you a decision in 24 hours."

I went back to Mobile to think about and discuss the situation with Carolyn and bring her back with me to Clemson for her to see it. I called Vic Bubas and I called Hugh Durham. They both said I shouldn't take it. I couldn't find anybody to say I should take it except my wife and Bobby Lowder. I came back to Mobile to meet with Dr. Whiddon. I was crying; I was very emotional. I was having a hard time letting go of South Alabama.

Carolyn and I went to Clemson, for they had put everything we'd talked about in writing. We were at the Ramada Inn. I said, "Look, hon, I've bounced you all around, and you've always been supportive. I have to have your input." She looked at me and said, "I think you ought to take it." That sealed it.

If Vernon Maxwell had said he was coming to South Alabama, I might not have made that change. I had a tremendous team coming back, and they were all young.

It was a difficult decision because those were nine great years for my family and me. South Alabama was like my baby.

By the end of our journey, South Alabama had come from being an infant in college basketball to a grown-up. Three conference championships, five postseason trips, top 20 rankings, and several players making it professionally gave me a lot to be thankful for upon departing this great school.

There is no doubt that I grew the most as a coach while at South Alabama. I had competed against icons, legends in the coaching business.

We had promoted well, going from small crowds to sell-outs, and we did it with a small alumni base, as South Alabama's first graduating class was in 1968. The city, made up of alumni from other schools like Auburn and Alabama, joined the South Alabama contingent to help us build a strong support.

I had made my decision. It was an emotional one. We had so many really close friends and so many fond memories in Mobile. Now, time had come to move on.

Chapter Thirteen

The Clemson Years

A lot of people told me I would be making a mistake if I took the Clemson job. It would be too much of a football school. Besides, they had achieved very little success in basketball. I had gone from two colleges where there were no football programs to one that had recently won a national championship in football, but it just felt like the right thing to do.

I thought the success of the football program could work to the benefit of the basketball program. The first thing that I did, because Clemson had won a national championship in 1981, was meet Danny Ford, the head football coach. Danny became a very good friend.

We went through a lot together. His family and my family became very close. We attended the same church. Our wives were close. Danny Ford didn't need Cliff Ellis. He had won a national championship. I knew that to survive, it was important that I be able to sell the program to people. One of those people, to me, was Danny Ford. He had been successful. People admired him. I was surprised to find out Danny had gone to Alabama on a basketball scholarship, eventually giving it up to play football for Bear Bryant. He liked basketball.

I took the job in April, and my family stayed until school was out, so I would go to Mobile to see my wife and kids on occasion. On my way home one trip, I got about 15-20 pounds of crawfish from friends Mr. and Mrs. Bosage and took them over to Danny's house. He'd never had a crawfish, but upon eating one, absolutely loved them. It forged a bond that would prove instrumental in my success at Clemson.

Danny directed me to people I needed to know, the ins and outs of Clemson. I would go and watch his team and this event known as college football at Clemson. I'd always liked college football, but I'd mostly watched it on television. I'll never forget the first football game I attended at Clemson.

People try to compare Clemson and Auburn, some calling Clemson Auburn with a lake, but Auburn is much bigger than Clemson. Clemson is a very small town. When I saw that first game, how 80,000 people were coming into that stadium, it set something off in my mind. I was seeing an event, an event like the ones I had tried to create at Cumberland and South Alabama—on a larger scale.

State troopers were directing traffic with great effort and mechanics. Their uniforms looked good. Their movements were crisp. They got traffic in and out; it was well organized and done with much class. To heck with the football game; the event surrounding the game fascinated me. I smelled barbecue outside the stadium every time I would take a step. This went back to what I've always believed—make an athletic contest a happening. The whole scene was impressive, everything about it.

I'd come to know the man who had it going on. I would meet some wonderful people along the way, soul mates like Steve "Ace" Bowie and Ansel King. They would provide me with important knowledge concerning the roots of Clemson.

Ansel King worked in the horticulture department. Ace Bowie awarded the Paul Bowie MVP trophy, named for Ace's father, to a basketball player every year. His father was a tremendous basketball fan, and the love of the game had trickled down through the family. Ace was a former singer himself, so we had a common bond there.

Clemson is a very special place with a lot of very special people. Friends like Billy and Claudia Ware; Ann and Ed Harris; Russ and Judy Hebert; Jim and Nancy Hellams. They welcomed me with open arms. I made a lot of friends. We had a lot of good times at Clemson.

Upon my taking over the Clemson program in 1984, spring signing period was already in gear. Grayson Marshall had committed to Clemson but was considering other options with the coaching change. I flew to Washington, D.C., met with the family, and he followed through on his commitment. He would eventually become the ACC's all-time assist leader. Clemson had played .500 or below three years prior to my taking the job. It looked like a long year ahead.

I met with our team and let them know we were going to take a blue-collar approach. I didn't know how many games we would win, but we would play harder than anybody we played. I also let them know that I knew North Carolina and Duke were in our league, and I was not going to be intimidated by them. I had faced the likes of Bartow, van Breda Kolff, Rose, Hoskins, Locke, and all the fine coaches in the Sun Belt and I was prepared. I stated to them that my goal was to win Clemson's first ACC championship.

It was hard for them to buy into this immediately, but once they started diving for loose balls in practice drills, enduring strenuous rebounding drills, and rising for practice at 5 a.m., the dedicated players bought into it. Several players left the team, but those who stayed became tougher than nails. It might be noted that at that time, the NCAA did not limit teams to practicing 20 hours a week, as is the rule now. In 1984 we had two practices a day the first two weeks.

The first game was against Tennessee Tech. We lost. Everybody was thinking it was going to be a long year. Dwight Rainey, the assistant athletic director, had also been a basketball coach. He is still a close friend today. He didn't think we had much of a chance. He said, "Man, I feel for you. It's just going to be a long year."

Ironically, five years earlier at South Alabama we had scheduled to play in the 1984 IPTAY Tournament. IPTAY, an acronym for Clemson's athletic booster organization, stands for I Pay Ten A Year. Now it should be I Pay Thousands A Year. Now I had to play in this tournament and potentially play my former team, the same team I thought was going to be the best one I'd ever had at South Alabama.

In that tournament were Campbell, South Alabama, and Houston, which had Akeem Olajuwon and company. I played Campbell, of course. We beat Campbell. South Alabama beat Houston. Their win was a significant game for me personally.

Many Mobilians made the drive to Clemson up the interstate. There was a lot of interest in the game. On the opening tip, South Alabama jumped out on us and would eventually take an 18-2 lead. I looked toward the ceiling and said,

"Lord, I can handle a defeat, but don't let them massacre me in front of the home crowd." Led by the steady play of Vincent Hamilton, we would come back and win decisively. It was a relief to me. Grayson Marshall in this tournament would entrench himself as the starting point guard and make the all-tournament team.

Our team now had a good win, and we were feeling good about ourselves. The only thing we were lacking was depth. We were down to a minimum of players. Marshall and Hamilton were our guards; Chris Michael and Anthony Jenkins played small forward; Horace Grant, a phenomenal player, along with his brother Harvey, a redshirt freshman, teamed with Glen McCants inside. This was young talent, combined with some veteran players, but our bench was not deep.

We fought and clawed our way to a 6-2 record, broke for Christmas, and then headed to Nashville, Tennessee, for the Music City Invitational. At the pretournament party, I got to sit and visit with Brenda Lee and Richard Sturber (of the Oak Ridge Boys) about the music days. I also found out that Richard's wife was Carolyn's English student at Shaw High School, Mobile, Alabama. This event was my all-time-favorite pretournament banquet.

We opened up with UMass and won. This was a huge win. We had Vanderbilt next, and somehow we found a way to pull it off. Son of a gun, we were now 8-2.

The conference race was next, and we would open on a Tuesday night at Georgia Tech, which was ranked eighth in the nation. It was the only televised game that night, and the whole world would be able to watch. I was excited; this was my first ACC game.

My players had confidence, but I could almost hear, "Here we go. We are in the ACC." This group hadn't had any success in the ACC.

When the bus pulled up, there was a long line of fans waiting. We went to the dressing room, and I could tell the players were a little bit nervous. Alexander Memorial Coliseum was sold out. I'll never forget my locker-room speech. Throughout all of the preparations, I was calm, cool, and collected. I was confident. I told them, "Fellows, we are going to Georgia Tech and we are going to win. We are going to surprise people. It's on national television. It's a great opportunity. Let's go get this win."

When we came back in the dressing room from our pre-game warm-ups with eight minutes left, fans were still lined up deep in the ticket line. I opened the windows in our dressing room where our boys could see the line. I said, "Guys, I want you to look at all the people coming to see *us* play tonight. Since they are coming to see *us* play, we are going to go out there and kick Georgia Tech's butt." And that's exactly what we did!

We threw every defense at them, and Georgia Tech was stunned. We sent a message. I knew through the ACC race we would have some struggles, but we'd let it be known that we were ready to compete.

We came back home and met North Carolina State. Jim Valvano had a great team, and they won a close one.

As we moved on into conference play, I would have my first matchup with the legendary Dean Smith. I respect and admire this man as much as anyone in this business. What he did at North Carolina as head coach is phenomenal. He had winners and championships on a consistent basis, year after year.

North Carolina rolled into town for the Clemson game. Another sellout crowd—Clemson fans would rather beat Dean Smith and North Carolina than anyone.

The game would be one that kept fans out of their seats on almost every possession. It was a good, old-fashioned see-saw battle. In the last minute of the game, with the score tied, North Carolina had the ball; but with the shot-clock rule, we would get the ball back. North Carolina missed the shot on its possession. Glen McCants rebounded the ball to Marshall, who passed to Chris Michael for a shot up the floor. It was an 18-foot jumper. The ball was in the air, the crowd held its breath as it gently touched the net, hitting nothing but bottom. Clemson won! Clemson fans stormed the floor. Cliff Ellis was now endeared to the Clemson faithful.

In that same year, Lefty Driesell brought Maryland to town looking for his 500th career victory, a milestone in coaching. The game would be televised. The print media and ACC media were at this game to see Lefty celebrate his 500th win. Lefty would have to wait; Clemson won.

This gutty team would go on to a 16-12 record and an NIT appearance. They succeeded with the blue-collar approach and laid a sound foundation for our first year. Vincent Hamilton, who now coaches and is involved in the CBA, was a great leader as well as player. Unfortunately, this was his senior year. His leadership reminds me of the leadership Bryant Smith provided for our 1999 Auburn team.

There was a lot of turmoil during my first year at Clemson. The president and athletic director who hired me were forced to resign from their positions. I was stunned, wondering what direction would be taken by Clemson. I had gone to Clemson with this administration, and within eight months they were gone.

There was controversy and sadness that surrounded the departure of the AD and the president. I hated seeing it, but it had obviously started long before I had gotten there. There wasn't anything I could do about it. I felt my basketball team had given Clemson a lift during this time.

Walter Cox was the vice president and was immediately named to take over as interim president. B. J. Skelton took over as interim AD. He was the faculty rep and admissions director.

Eventually Bobby Robinson took over as permanent athletic director. Danny Ford and I were called by Walter Cox and asked our opinions about who should be the athletic director. We both recommended Bobby. There didn't need to be an outsider at that point. There were too many unhappy people for that. Dean Cox heeded our advice.

The second year began; there were changes being made all around us; we had a young team. Grayson Marshall was developing as an excellent point guard; he was also becoming a very good leader.

Horace Grant was developing into a great player. As everyone knows, he eventually went to the NBA and had a stellar career. Horace has a twin brother named Harvey, and a situation would arise involving the two of them that would become a real big test for me.

This is my
first portrait.
I was three
months old.

Courtesy of the Ellis
Family Collection

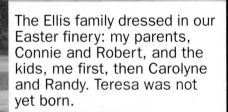

The Ellis family dressed in our
Easter finery: my parents,
Connie and Robert, and the
kids, me first, then Carolyne
and Randy. Teresa was not
yet born.

Courtesy of the Ellis
Family Collection

I graduated from
Chipley High
School in June
1963. This is my
senior portrait.

Courtesy of the Ellis
Family Collection

CLIFF ELLIS: THE WINNING EDGE

Courtesy of the Ellis Family Collection

Our first band was called the Uniques. Pictured (left to right) are Billy Bryan, who still sings in the gospel music field; Paul Uhrig, songwriter and musician in Nashville today; Alan Myers, a lawyer; me, with a cast from a pickup football injury and without a musical instrument (I could play a mean tambourine, but mostly just sang); and Norman Jackson, lead guitarist.

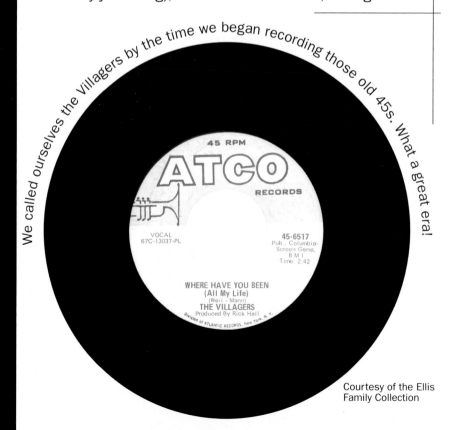

We called ourselves the Villagers by the time we began recording those old 45s. What a great era!

45 RPM
ATCO RECORDS

VOCAL
67C-13037-PL

45-6517
Pub., Columbia-
Screen Gems,
B M I
Time: 2:42

WHERE HAVE YOU BEEN
(All My Life)
(Weil - Mann)
THE VILLAGERS
Produced By Rick Hall
Division of ATLANTIC RECORDS, New York, N. Y.

Courtesy of the Ellis
Family Collection

Courtesy of Cumberland College

Dr. Ernest Stockton, president of Cumberland College, welcomed Boone Swain and me to campus and the new basketball coaches—despite our '70s hairstyles and polyester suits.

Courtesy of Cumberland College

Boone and I posed for a yearbook picture in front of the big red bulldog with Keith Dean, James McClellan, and Johnny Farmer. That suit I had on was red, white, and blue—the school colors—and was one of my favorites.

In the huddle with me at the University of South Alabama were (clockwise from left) Eugene Harris, who has coached with me for 18 years; Drayton Miller, who became a businessman in Mobile and still lives there; and Don Hogan, who is now head coach at the University of West Florida.

Courtesy of University of South Alabama Sports Information

Terry Catledge was among the first great "big men" I've had the privilege to coach. He played outstanding ball for South Alabama from 1981 to 1985 before joining the NBA.

Courtesy of University of South Alabama Sports Information

Rory White (44) and John May helped build a basketball program at South Alabama that drew thousands of fans to the coliseum instead of hundreds.

Courtesy of University of South Alabama Sports Information

Eddie Stanky brought his baseball prowess and his feisty personality to the University of South Alabama baseball program. I was fortunate to be able to work with this legend.

Courtesy of University of South Alabama Sports Information

Courtesy of University of South Alabama Sports Information

Ronnie Davis, Ed Rains, and Lonnie Leggett helped to decide on the philosophical graffiti we wanted in our locker room.

At South Alabama my sideline demeanor was pretty intense.

Courtesy of University of South Alabama Sports Information

In my first press conference at Clemson University, I greeted the fans and wished Frank Howard, the Clemson football legend, a happy birthday. It was a pretty happy day for me, too.

Courtesy of Clemson University Sports Information

Here I am discussing strategy at Clemson during a time-out. Elden Campbell, now making millions in the NBA, always questioned and listened in the huddle.

Courtesy of Clemson University Sports Information

In 1987 Clemson was so happy to finish second in the ACC, its highest finish thus far, that the fans wanted to cut down the nets. Horace Grant was happy to participate.

Courtesy of
Clemson University
Sports Information

AND CLIFF SAID "LET THERE BE BASKETBALL"

Courtesy of Clemson University Sports Information

Clemson fans were very appreciative of the achievements of our basketball program. I, in turn, was very appreciative of our loyal basketball supporters.

Courtesy of Clemson University Sports Information

Clemson players Ricky Jones, Shawn Lastinger, Wayne Buckingham, and Kirkland Howling, along with coaches Tom Denboer, Rick Marshall, and Len Gordy, celebrate an NCAA Tournament win. I think I must have already been planning the next game.

Courtesy of Clemson University Sports Information

At my last game at Clemson—against Maryland in 1994—Clemson folks presented me and my family with many gifts that are wonderful mementos of our great time there. I knelt down and kissed the floor. Clemson had given me the wonderful gift of coaching in the ACC and working with gifted people—coaches, staff, and players.

When I took the job at Auburn in April 1994, I knew that the job of building a winner would be a challenge. I also knew that I was grateful for the opportunity and that our relationship was a satisfying match.

Here I am overseeing an Auburn practice session. The most joy I get out of coaching is the day-to-day routine of practice. The gymnasium is my classroom—that place where I teach and establish relationships with my players and coaches.

I have learned through my 30-plus years of coaching to respect and appreciate the contribution of referees to the game of basketball. I'm sure that is what I am discussing here.

Courtesy of Auburn University Sports Information

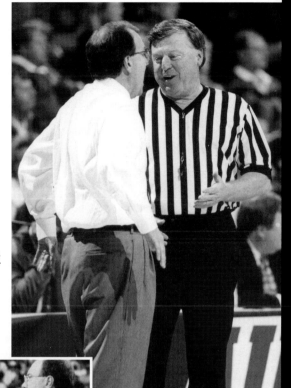

Here I lend some advice to Chris Porter, who came to Auburn from Chipola Junior College—the same school I attended. Chris brought a level of play and excitement to Auburn basketball that I will always appreciate—no matter what.

Courtesy of Auburn University Sports Information

As the head coach, I do most of the standing during the games. Seated behind me (left to right) are people who have been major contributors to our success at Auburn: Shannon Weaver, assistant head coach, and assistant coaches Mike LaPlante and Eugene Harris.

Courtesy of Auburn University Sports Information

My buddy "Raff," Bill Raftery, and I are discussing the ACC championship win over Duke in 1990. A former head coach at Seton Hall, Bill is one of the most respected and well-traveled commentators in the game of basketball.

Courtesy of Clemson University Sports Information

Courtesy of Clemson University Sports Information

Mike Krzyzewski and I were the two youngest head coaches in Division I basketball when my South Alabama team played his Army team in 1976. We went on to share many classic battles, especially when we were in the ACC together. He and his wife, Micki, have been great friends.

The legendary Dean Smith is with his assistant and now head coach at UNC, Bill Guthridge. Dean has one of the best minds for the game I have ever known.

Courtesy of Clemson University Sports Information

I miss Jimmy V. The game misses him.

Courtesy of Clemson University Sports Information

This was my first national TV studio work. John Saunders, Dick Vitale, and I are at the ESPN studio in Bristol, Connecticut, in 1990.

Billy Packer and I are discussing my first ACC win ever, an upset of No. 7 Georgia Tech in my first ACC game. Billy is one of my all-time favorites. He calls it like it is.

Cliff Ellis: THE WINNING EDGE

Courtesy of the Ellis Family Collection

Carolyne and I are extremely proud of our family: Chryssa and Tony Rutland, Clay, and Anna Catherine.

I had to ask Harvey to leave, which is one of the toughest decisions I have had to make. In my mind, however, it would eventually make Horace and Harvey better and help them grow up. Harvey would go to a junior college, then to Oklahoma to finish his collegiate career.

I'm as proud of Harvey as I am of Horace. They have a lovely mother, Barbara, who had to work hard to see that they had food on the table. With Horace and Harvey's success, she can eat about anything she desires. I am happy for this family.

The 1985-86 team, led by Marshall and Grant, got off to a strong start and won 11 in a row. The highlight of this season was beating Bradley in the Rainbow Classic in Hawaii. That was the year that Bradley went 30-1. Their lone loss was to Clemson.

We stumbled through the ACC. We lost close games and couldn't seem to get over the hump. We did get in the NIT and opened with a win over Middle Tennessee State, my graduate school alma mater.

The next round sent us to Georgia. Georgia is a huge rival of Clemson's. Clemson fans were ecstatic and made the 65-mile trip to Athens, Georgia. Led by Horace Grant, who was returning to his home state, with friends and family all around, we handled the Georgia Bulldogs.

The third game would be for a trip to the finals of the NIT. We had to travel to the University of Wyoming and we lost. Wyoming was the loudest, rowdiest place I had been to, including Duke. They are also at a high altitude, making oxygen intake more difficult, especially if you are not used to playing at that altitude.

The NIT had given us some confidence as we ended the season. We would finish 19-15 for the year, and this team would start getting primed for a breakthrough year at Clemson.

In 1986-87, our third year, we had a remarkable season for Clemson. It was a team that started out the season winning and just got more confident as the season went on. We won our first 17 games. The fans were going wacko over basketball.

We opened our nonconference slate by winning 11 straight games, capped off by winning the Hawaiian Pacific Christmas tournament.

Our team knew our biggest test lay ahead. We had played in Hawaii on a Saturday night and did not return to Clemson until Monday. On Wednesday we would play our first conference game versus NC State in Clemson.

With our 11-0 start, we got ranked for the first time of the year in the AP and UPI polls. I knew we were tired from the travel and was concerned about jet lag. Usually it takes about three days to recover in basketball from a trip to Hawaii. We had only Tuesday to prepare them mentally in our dressing room. I let our team know what our goals were: to win the ACC and go to the NCAA tournament. I told them I would not trade this group of people for anyone in our league and to go out and make their statement the next day.

I knew we had to get the lead early versus No. 18 NC State in order to win. I felt our legs would get very tired in the second half. Amazingly, we built a 20-point halftime lead. Our legs did get tired, NC State made a surge, but we won the game.

Following this game, we won two more conference games to build a record of 14-0. Back to conference play, we defeated Maryland at home and Georgia Tech on the road to go 16-0.

Clemson fans were hysterical. We were 16-0, and Duke was coming to town. Duke was on a tremendous run nationally. Duke was poised, confident in their own way. Some of the best games I've been a part of involved Duke, and this game was one of them.

The game went back and forth. Clemson fans were going mad, making it hard for the Blue Devils of Duke. Clemson basketball had not been a part of anything like what was taking place at Littlejohn Coliseum on this day. We were ranked No. 10 in the nation and were 17-0. Duke was in town and highly ranked. It couldn't get any better than this for our fans.

It was a war game in Clemson, South Carolina. Players would make big plays throughout the game for both teams; Tommy Amaker and Danny Fery, in particular, made big plays for Duke, as did Marshall and Grant for Clemson. Larry Middleton and Michael Brown would score big buckets, and Clemson would take the lead in the second half.

The game went down to the wire. At the end of regulation, we were up three, and the game was winding down. Tommy Amaker got a screen and put a shot up from behind the three-point arc with less than five seconds. You could tell the ball was going to be short.

The ball hit the front of the rim and went to the top of the backboard. The ball stopped. It seemed like it sat there for minutes. The entire crowd was watching that ball—it seemed to be an eternity. Amazingly, it came back down and went in the basket. The game went into overtime. Duke won it in overtime, 105-103.

We were right there, a chance to go 18-0 and move up in the rankings. What a ball game it had been. I think some of the best basketball games in the country were between Duke and Clemson at Clemson.

Next up was North Carolina at Clemson. The fans had put it on the line in the Duke game; they were still fired up but a little down from the loss. The players were, also. We could not recover, and the Tar Heels won. It was now two losses in a row.

Everybody was down. The fans were doubting us. It was like "Well, here we go again." We were 4-2 in the ACC and sitting at a critical point of the conference. We were to play Virginia next. Because of the losses to Duke and North Carolina, I felt that if we could not win this game, we would be on a major downward spiral. I had to come up with a plan to rally this team.

Danny Ford and I had an IPTAY speaking engagement in Columbia, South Carolina, prior to the Virginia game. We drove together, and on the way back we were talking about the upcoming game with the Wahoos. This is when I really turned to football to help. I said, "Danny, I need your help. We need a boost. We need a spark. Your team has had much success, and our players respect you. Would you mind coming to the locker room and saying whatever you feel compelled to say? Would you give the pregame talk?"

He wanted to know when we practiced. I wasn't sure why that mattered, but he started coming to practice that week just to make the players feel comfortable around him. He didn't want to shock them by appearing in the locker room by surprise. He'd sit in practice and watch and talk to the players as they went through practice routines. I didn't tell the players he was going to come into the locker room before our game. He kept saying, "We're going to whip Virginia. We're going to whip Virginia." He was already inspiring our team for the upcoming game.

It was game day, and Virginia was in town. Danny came by my office to give encouragement. He was getting me pumped for the game.

Our players dressed for the game in our locker room and were told to be ready for pregame talk, our usual ritual, 20 minutes prior to our taking the floor for warm-ups. The players were seated, and the door to the locker room swung open. Danny Ford was ready to address this basketball team. He would challenge each one of them individually.

He'd call out each player and whom they were to defend. "Somebody is going to win that battle," he said. "Is it going to be you or is it going to be him?" He challenged every one of them in this manner. They listened to every word he said. When Danny finished his remarks, the team almost tore the door down going onto the floor for warm-ups, they were so fired up.

We won the game. We were now 5-2 in the league and had put Duke and North Carolina behind us. From there we would win six in a row. Our confidence was again soaring.

At Maryland we won a buzzer-beater on Michael Brown's last-second shot. At NC State we found a way to win. We were starting to win major games on the road. We went to Georgia Tech and won. Now we had to go back to Virginia.

It was one of the most fascinating comebacks I've ever seen. We were down by nine with just a little time left. Michael

Brown hit a big three-point shot falling out of bounds. Horace Grant hit the only three-point shot he'd taken and sent it into overtime. We somehow found a way to miraculously win another road game. We eventually went 5-2 on the road in the ACC—quite a statement for this group of young men.

Our last home game of the year was against Wake Forest, and from this game we would finish the season on the road versus Duke.

If we could beat Wake Forest, we would clinch second place in the regular-season ACC race. Clemson had never finished as high as second. We did win, and the win was so huge for Clemson that the fans and players cut down the nets in the coliseum. It was like we had won the championship. It was a moment to remember and a great way to end a home career for our seniors.

We now traveled to Duke with a 10-3 record, second place clinched and no way to catch North Carolina, which was 13-0 in conference play. The game had no meaning at all for the record books but would have significant meaning for the rest of our season. In that game, Grayson Marshall would suffer a stress fracture in his foot, putting him out of the ACC Tournament.

Wake Forest beat us in the ACC Tournament. Most people called it an upset, but I did not think it was because we were playing our first game without our starting point guard. A team's chemistry is altered when something like that happens.

The following Sunday, NCAA bids were announced. We drew Southwest Missouri State, led by Coach Charlie Spoonhour, in Atlanta, Georgia. Grayson Marshall was not making very good progress with the stress fracture. He tried to play but couldn't. We lost a heartbreaker.

The loss in the NCAA was disappointing, but it still had been a significant year for Clemson. We finished 25-6. Horace Grant, Michael Tate, Larry Middleton, Michael Brown, and Anthony Jenkins were a special group of people who had played their last game at Clemson but left with the satisfaction of knowing they had achieved in the ACC what no other team in the history of the school had been able to do, and that was a runner-up finish in the regular season. Their NCAA bid was also only the second bid in the school's history.

While I entered my third year, a new president came to Clemson. His name was Max Lennon. There was a movement nationally for presidents to become more involved in athletic matters. There were some big issues arising. One issue was the athletic dormitory. A strong opinion in some circles was to do away with athletic dorms. This opinion eventually prevailed.

Danny Ford and I were asked to meet with Dr. Lennon. We discussed the dorm issue. Dr. Lennon wanted to do away with athletic dorms, and Danny and I were opposed. We felt if student-athletes were spread over campus, coaches could not keep certain discipline measures with their teams. We had curfews to assure we knew where they were and what time they would be in bed. Eliminating dorms would make this impossible. We also felt that team camaraderie is built with student-athletes staying together as a team.

This meeting would be the first sign of philosophical differences between Coach Ford and me and our new administration.

We were asked specifically not to talk to any members of the Board of Trustees about the dorm issue. Danny Ford had been on top of the heap, had won a national championship, and had done great things for Clemson. He was incensed. I could see the steam coming out of Danny's ears.

Now, when Danny has an opinion, he has an opinion. Eventually, in 1990, Danny was asked to resign. It was a sad day for Clemson. It was a tough time for me, because this guy had been willing to stand up and help me at a time when he didn't need me at all. Thousands of Clemson fans would march on the president's doorsteps upon hearing of his resignation.

This third season at Clemson, 1987-88, was a rebuilding year, but it was the beginning of the best tandem I have ever coached, Elden Campbell and Dale Davis. Elden was a sophomore and had played behind Horace as a freshman. Dale Davis would enter the program as a freshman from Toccoa, Georgia. Campbell and Davis were both 6'11". This was my first set of twin towers. We were going to center our rebuilding efforts for the future on these two men.

We would finish this regular season 14-14. At the end of this particular season, No. 9 Duke would travel to Clemson for a regular-season finale. In a major upset, led by Davis and Campbell, Clemson won 79-74. It propelled this young group into the NIT. It, however, was the final season for point guard Grayson Marshall, one of the finest to ever wear a Clemson uniform.

The off-season would involve intense training for this post tandem of Campbell and Davis as well as the rest of our players. Marion Cash would be signed to take over the helm at point guard. He came from Pratt Community College, Kansas. Another Californian, Kirkland Howling, joined the team as a wing player, as did Derrick Forest of Malone, Florida. These recruits would pay huge dividends in the games ahead.

Also on this squad were power forward Jerry Pryor, center Rod Mitchell, guard Tim Kincaid, and guard David Young.

This 1988-89 team finished the nonconference slate with a record of 7-2 and felt relatively comfortable with our play. The strength program in the off-season seemed to be paying dividends, as Campbell's and Davis' strength and weight had increased. We were out-bounding opponents rather avidly.

Enter NC State, our first conference game. NC State would win. I became concerned about our confidence level. We were playing Maryland next, and I had to come up with some kind of locker-room talk that would get something going. I challenged our basketball team. I really had confidence this team could go somewhere. I gave an emotional, positive locker-room speech that centered on Campbell and Davis becoming a force in our league inside. We beat Maryland and went on to win three games in a row in our conference. Suddenly, our confidence was growing.

We then dropped consecutive games to ranked opponents—Georgia Tech and Duke. We now had to face No. 8 North Carolina following those two losses.

I felt that, at this point in the season, our team was feeling stress. They seemed tired and were not having fun. I decided to use a play I had used at South Alabama successfully. For practice on this day we set up volleyball nets on the basketball court, chose sides (with coaches playing), and played volleyball. We all had fun, it was stress free, and when it was over, I said tomorrow we will prepare for North Carolina.

North Carolina came to Clemson and lost a hard-fought battle between both teams. This was a win Clemson badly needed.

During this season, I had a situation where I had to get some players' attention. I had a policy about missing study hall. I've always been strict on my policies for academics. If a coach doesn't enforce them, he might as well not have them.

Prior to our game at Duke, Campbell, Davis, and some others missed study hall. I had given them a warning previously that if they missed again, it would cost them. I found out shortly before the Duke game that they had missed study hall.

I don't know what they were thinking. Maybe they thought that because we were playing Duke I wouldn't do anything. They were wrong. I took six players to Duke in uniform. I even dressed out a manager. I had the disciplined players travel and sit on the bench in coats and ties. The game was televised, and everyone watched Duke absolutely annihilate us. I even ended up playing the manager. The Play of the Day on CNN was our manager scoring a basket.

North Carolina was the next opponent. My team policy had been set. Our players stormed out of our locker room, and there was no way they were going to be denied winning this game. Clemson beat the Tar Heels.

Now we were headed for the last week of the season. Duke and Georgia Tech would come to town with an NCAA bid on the line.

Duke was the first encounter of the week. I rehashed the first Duke game with our team, letting them know that Duke had not seen our real team, nor had the nation. The thrashing we took at Cameron Indoor was going to turn around tonight. No managers would have to play in this game against Duke. Clemson succeeded in downing Duke.

Georgia Tech came to Littlejohn for a weekend regular-season finale and a classic. We won in overtime, and this win, coupled with the Duke win, propelled us to an NCAA bid. This would be Clemson's third bid ever, but its second in three years, and with a team that had very few seniors.

We traveled to Boise, Idaho, for an NCAA matchup with St. Mary's, ranked No. 19 in the nation. We were not ranked. Behind Campbell and Davis and a three-point barrage led by David Young, the Tigers would get a come-from-behind victory. Next up, No. 1 Arizona, coached by Lute Olson.

Arizona won, but through this tournament, as well as through the season, people saw the potential rise with these Twin Towers.

I had high expectations for the 1989-90 season. At our first meeting, I restated the goals of our program: Win the ACC and get to the NCAA Tournament.

We opened the season with the San Juan Shootout in Puerto Rico. We lost in the finals to Alabama, coached by Wimp Sanderson.

Gene Corrigan and Dave Garitt set up a national marketing event for television, calling it the ACC-Big East Challenge. Corrigan was commissioner of the ACC and Garitt was commissioner of the Big East. This event took place following the San Juan Shootout, and our opponent was Providence, coached by Rick Barnes. We lost to Providence in this section of the challenge.

After going through nonconference play with a 7-2 record, we opened the conference with a loss to NC State. We were 7-

3 and it was gut-check time. I put our team through intense, harsh practice drills. I thought we were playing too soft.

We won four straight, defeating Maryland, Virginia, Georgia Tech, and Wake Forest. This was a great comeback from the opening loss. Two of the games were on the road at Virginia and Wake Forest.

I have always felt that championship teams must learn to win on the road. This team won not only at Virginia and Wake Forest, but at Maryland and Georgia Tech as well.

Down the stretch, we came into the last week of the season at 8-3 in conference play with home games remaining versus North Carolina and Duke. If we could win these two games, we could become ACC regular-season champions. Throughout our preparation, I reaffirmed our goals. I also made sure practice was positive and fun. The national media, as well as the local media, had traveled to Clemson for this week of basketball. I needed to make sure our players didn't get too distracted.

Back in 1986-87, North Carolina and Duke beat us in that dream season. Now we had the same scenario at Clemson, and the race was such that if we could win these two ball games, we were going to win Clemson's first ACC regular-season championship, or at least tie for it.

The game with North Carolina was on a Saturday. On Thursday morning, students, to help ensure that they got a ticket, pitched tents outside the coliseum. It was late February, and the weather was cold and blustery.

I knew the students could help give us the home-court advantage, and I wanted to do something for them. It got so cold that we opened the coliseum throughout the night so they could stay warm. The students did not seem to mind the cold.

They were excited, and you could smell the nice aroma of the barbecue grills in the early evening.

I went to a local pizza place in town and said, "I need some help. I want to show these people I appreciate them. For every pizza I buy, will you give me one?" They said they would. I took my car and loaded it up with pizzas. I had pizzas in the trunk, in the front seat, and on the floorboard. I let those students know how much I appreciated them. When I passed out the pizzas, I asked them to yell hard when the Tar Heels came to town. I kept those pizzas coming Thursday and Friday.

North Carolina came to town and we won 69-61, led by Dale Davis' 20-plus rebounds. If we could beat Duke on Wednesday night, we'd have a share of the ACC regular-season championship. It would be nationally televised on ESPN; every network was in town for this championship game. I kept the pizzas rolling. Those tents never went down from the UNC game. Momentum was growing—students would cheer the team from the tents when we entered the coliseum for practice.

When Duke came to town, electricity was in the air. The premier event for college basketball in the history of the school was about to take place. Every Clemson fan would be able to see it by attending the game or watching on national television.

The game was another of those classic Duke-Clemson matchups. Marion Cash propelled Clemson to a great start, only to get his third foul in the first half. Sean Lastinger, a seldom-used freshman guard, replaced him. He and the other members of the team held Duke at bay until Cash could re-enter the game. Both teams made great plays. Campbell and Davis, with backup support from Sean Tyson and Ricky Jones, established themselves inside. Cash, Forrest, Howling, and Young hit major baskets and kept Duke in check on defense.

Down the stretch, it was a close game, with Clemson taking a late lead, forcing Duke to foul. I can remember shouting to our players when they toed the line for the foul shot, "You are the champions, you are the champions." We hit free throws to win.

It was a madhouse. Students stormed the floor. We cut the nets down. Clemson had won the first ACC championship in its history. It was a warm feeling. My closest friends were there—my friend John Counts had come from Mobile, family was there. All my buddies from Clemson, guys I had fished and hunted with, were there. It's hard to describe the feeling. It was euphoria—it was the moment of a lifetime. History had been made. It was a wonderful, exhilarating feeling.

I was ecstatic, but I wanted to look composed and stay composed. I knew how Duke felt. I went to console my friend Mike Krzyzewski. He had a lot of class in that situation, congratulating my team and me. He had admired our effort and determination to win.

The championship meant a lot to Clemson, particularly the 1990 year. When Danny Ford had resigned, Clemson needed something positive to happen during the upheaval. I personally felt he had been wronged. In the midst of all the turmoil, this basketball team won the ACC. It gave Clemson a rallying point. That ACC regular-season championship for Clemson, I think, will stand for long time. It is tough to win the championship there.

Those players bought into our goals and system and were relentless in the task. Clemson will forever cherish this group of young men. It is a team that will be talked about for life.

We headed for the ACC Tournament trying to come down from the excitement of winning the ACC regular-season championship. We lost to Virginia in the semifinals. I was disappointed in the loss, yet happy for Terry Holland, who was retiring as basketball coach at Virginia at the end of the season. Terry had built Virginia into a consistent winner. He and his wife, Ann, had become good friends of Carolyn and mine throughout our times at Clemson.

We received an NCAA bid for the third time in four years in 1990. Our opponent in the opening round was Brigham Young University, and we played in Hartford, Connecticut. The BYU game was a low-scoring, dull game, and we would manage a 49-47 win. Our next opponent was La Salle, led by Lionel Simmons.

La Salle entered the game as the No. 5 team in the country; we were No. 13. I cannot explain why we got off to a sluggish start. We fell behind, playing with little emotion. We were down by 23 at the half.

At halftime, I wouldn't go in the locker room. They knew how I felt, and there really wasn't anything for me to say that hadn't been said in a time-out. They were waiting to hear the wrath of God from me, but I didn't go in. I wanted them to sort matters out.

I could hear what was going on. Dale Davis usually never says much, but he was speaking quite frankly with his teammates. He and Derrick Forrest were taking over the locker room at half-time, challenging their teammates to scrap and claw and find a way to win. I kept looking at my watch. When I finally did open the door to the locker room, I didn't say much. I told them they were better than what they had shown, but that they needed to decide if this was the way an ACC championship team was going to go down. It was for them to decide.

La Salle hit a couple of more baskets and we were down by 28 points early in the second half. It seemed like we had no chance. We came back, however, and won 79-75. It was, at the time, the biggest comeback in NCAA Tournament history, and it was against the No. 5 team in the country. It was an amazing victory. We performed like true champions in the second half. Davis and Forrest led the charge.

We played UConn in the Sweet 16. Now we were on our way to the Meadowlands. We were behind at halftime. In the second half, we started to chip away at the lead. I encouraged my troops during each time-out, trying to keep them positive and believing in themselves and their teammates. This group had never been in a Sweet 16. I wanted them to believe they could do it. We never led during the first 39 minutes of play.

With less than a minute to go, down by two, we were running a play to feed David Young, our three-point shooter. I can remember David being in the left corner right in front of our bench. I kept yelling at him, "Take it! Take it! Take It!" The ball came out of his hand, and it was like time stood still. The ball went in, and we took the lead by one with 30 seconds to play. He had made the 3-point shot.

Connecticut missed a shot on the following possession and Sean Tyson rebounded. UConn fouled Sean with 1.6 seconds left to play, and we were in the bonus. It looked like we were going to win. I took everybody off the line. I knew if we could just hit the bonus, it was over. Even if we missed, it was going to take a miracle for UConn to win.

Sean missed the front end, and UConn got the ball and called time out with 1.3 seconds left in the game. They had to go the length of the floor. Scott Burrell, who also played minor league baseball, would inbound the ball for UConn. I put Elden Campbell, who is 7 feet tall, on the ball. Scotty Burrell threw an absolute strike to Tates George in the corner. He caught the ball with his feet off the ground, came down, turned and shot. The ball went in. That all happened in 1.3 seconds. I don't know how all that happened in 1.3 seconds, but it counted. It was a great pass and a great play. UConn won the game, and our season was over.

As happens in so many Sweet 16 games, fortune was on the side of Connecticut. We were crushed. My immediate thought was, "My gosh, get to these players." I didn't think about anything but getting to those players. This was such a heartbreaking loss. I knew they were crushed. It was one of those unfortunate moments. We were unlucky, but there were more plays to the game than that one play.

I knew my talk was going to be painful. I told them, "We are going to handle this loss with class." I told them I wanted them to understand what a monumental season they'd had, what it meant, what they had done for Clemson. I also knew I was addressing valuable seniors who would never play again for Clemson in uniform.

I've always had a ritual of telling each senior following his last game how much I appreciate what he has done, that I would be there for him until the day he died. I meet with each senior one-on-one immediately following the season finale, whenever and wherever it happens. After meeting with

Campbell, Forrest, Howling, and Cash for the last time, I met with the entire team. I said we were going to give Connecticut credit and we were going to handle the loss with class. I told them there were going to be tougher losses than losing a basketball game, that life isn't always going to be fair. You have to get through it. That's the message I sent.

This culminated a great season in a league with great coaches. I was named Coach of the Year for the second time. This was a tremendous honor for me.

We didn't have a good year on the playing floor in the 1990-91 season. It was a tough year on and off the court.

We'd lost several players from the previous year's championship team. We won 11 games. We played the season without a true point guard. That goes back to that adage, proved once again, that without a real point guard, a team is going to struggle. We played with combination guards, and they were freshmen. We lost a lot of close games.

A very significant issue would come up in the fall surrounding a player by the name of Wayne Buckingham. Our faculty rep was also our admissions director at the time. He had also been an interim AD. The admissions office cleared Wayne Buckingham to play and accepted his core courses. I personally overheard a phone conversation between the admissions director and an official from the NCAA office. Even though this NCAA official said Wayne was cleared, the NCAA later took issue with whether or not certain courses should have been counted as core.

As the situation progressed, this administrator resigned under pressure, an unfair development, because he had had the proper assurance from the NCAA. With Ford resigning and Skelton, the admissions officer, resigning, I was beginning to become concerned with all the changes that seemed to be taking place.

Wayne Buckingham had come to Clemson in good faith. There was a move administratively to oust him. I stood up for him. I made a stand right then and there. I let our administration know that there was a process for resolving this question, and he deserved a chance. In standing up for Wayne, I would be pitted against the university for the first time. The process eventually worked. This kid was exonerated, but it took two years. Casualties occurred.

This situation would never have happened if there had been a clearinghouse in place, as there is today. It was because of this kind of situation that there is a clearinghouse. In previous years, high schools sent the colleges the transcripts, and the admissions office decided what was acceptable. There was no clearinghouse, so the university and the NCAA were pitted against each other whenever there was a disagreement.

Initially, Clemson University had strongly defended Wayne Buckingham's case. So what happened? The NCAA came in and checked on virtually every player who had ever been recruited by Clemson.

In the painstaking and nitpicking investigation, a coach misstated information, and he lost his job. That's how sensitive everything was. An administrator had lost his job and a coach had lost his job. I was devastated; this coach was also a close friend.

I was frustrated that I was eventually forced to defend Wayne myself, without much support from the administration. Clemson had made a commitment to him. He had lived up to his end of the bargain. I had to get down in the trenches with him. A player becomes like a son to a coach.

It wasn't a fight I was looking for. I did what I would want a coach to do for my own son. I knew this was beginning to cost me. I knew that the philosophical differences might force me into another coaching direction. In 1990, after the ACC championship, I thought Clemson would be a great place to end my career. Our family absolutely loved Clemson.

For 23 years of coaching, everything seemed to go the way I scripted it. Now I was seeing something I'd never seen before. I was in something I'd never been in before, but I loved this place and I loved the people. I loved the fans. Clemson fans and Clemson faculty, as a whole, remained supportive. But these philosophical differences between the administration and me were eating at both of us. It was a joy to see Wayne finally exonerated, but things were never really the same for me at Clemson after that.

As we moved on toward the 1991-92 season, we knew we had to find a point guard who could come in and play. We combed the junior college ranks. Chris Whitney was at Lincoln Trail Junior College in Illinois. I took the school plane from Clemson to Lincoln Trail. Chris is from Hopkinsville, Kentucky. I'd already had a great point guard in Charles Fishback from nearby Bowling Green, Kentucky. I knew what those kids were made of.

When I saw him, I knew Chris Whitney was the real deal. He joined the team, and we had recruited another great young inside pair in Sharone Wright and Devin Gray. Both of them were freshmen.

We finished the year 14-14, but with those two freshmen inside, we beat Georgia Tech, which was ranked 24th, and Florida State, which was ranked 16th at the time. Duke came in at the end of the season ranked No. 1 in the country. This young team led by almost 20 points. Duke ended up winning by one, but we made a statement. That was the start of a young team that was going to get better and better. A coach wants to win every game, but sometimes, even games you don't win can mean a lot. That was one of those games.

As the 1992-93 season approached, I was enjoying working with my young post players, Wright and Gray. They were sophomores now. The Grant era had passed; the Campbell-Davis era had passed, and it was time to take these two young men to another level of playing.

This was a young team, yet Chris Whitney was a senior. We traveled to Georgia Tech and won. We beat ranked teams in Florida State, Wake Forest and Georgia Tech. We missed the NCAA, but we got into the NIT. Our first opponent was Auburn. On this particular day that we played Auburn, I found out my grandmother Carlton, 102 years of age, passed away. It was a very sad day for me. I dedicated that day to her.

When I met with my team before playing Auburn, I couldn't help but reflect on life a little bit that day—how much my grandmother had meant, how basketball really was, in the end, insignificant. What she did for me was significant. Her memory still means a lot.

I never hold back my emotions from my teams. They knew I was hurting. I just said, "I want to dedicate this game to a person who has helped you without your knowing it. I want you to go out and give everything you've got to this game. It would mean something to me personally."

This Auburn team found itself behind early, and it really was not a contest. Clemson won that game, but next, we had to go to Alabama and play UAB, where we lost a buzzer beater. We missed a tip-in at the buzzer and lost by one point. We were finished for the year, and UAB moved on.

I had sensed before the 1993-94 campaign that it was time for me to start looking for a new challenge. We went to Hawaii for the Rainbow Classic in December. I had dinner one night with the entire family. I said, "I think it's time for me to make a change. I plan to resign when we get back home."

Carolyn and I had been talking about it, but I wanted to get the kids' response. The kids all concurred; they had seen what I was going through. We played No. 19 Oklahoma State the next night. We beat them in a great win. We came back to Clemson and faced Duke in a national game. Even after the joy of that win over Oklahoma State, I still felt the same. I knew it was time for me to leave.

I didn't want the resignation to be a distraction, what with the Duke game on Wednesday night. On Thursday morning, I was going to resign—only my family knew.

I'd made the decision while the team was on a high after having defeated OSU. It was in my own mind the right thing to do at this time. I'd had a love affair with these people for 10 years. I was going to show my appreciation for those 10 years and the people whom I loved. On Thursday, I first met with my team and let them know. I asked them for their support. I wanted them to understand that we were going to go through this season, play hard, have fun, and meet the challenges that lay ahead. I would not leave until the final hour of the final game.

I went to my athletic director and told him I was resigning. He asked me not to do it. I said, "It's time. It's simply time." I agreed to give it one more day. I went back home and slept on it. I walked in his office Friday morning and told him to be prepared for a press conference. I told him I wanted to do it that afternoon. He asked me again to stay, but I knew it was time. I had an emotional press conference, just as I'd had an emotional press conference when I left South Alabama.

As we went through the ACC race in that last season at Clemson, I was impressed with the effort of our team. It would have been easy for them to ease up in their effort. Our players played their rear ends off. My last game of the regular season was against Maryland. It was an emotional day. Clemson had a ceremony before the game for my entire family and me, acknowledging my teams' accomplishments. Our family was presented with a table that was built from the 1990 ACC championship floor. My daughters were in tears.

We played the game and won 73-67. I had a warm feeling and a sad feeling. I had so many great memories from games in that building. I have not been able to go back. That last team finished with 19 wins.

Every road game in the ACC was special. Every stop included a ceremony prior to the game honoring me for my contributions to the league. I was humbled at each place. I appreciate those people. Those ceremonies brought me to my knees. I carry with me today strong friendships and relationships that started while in this league.

The league at this time was close knit. We competed when we were on the court, but off the court, we spent time with one another. There were so many memorable times while in the ACC, like the night at the ACC spring meeting when the coaches got on stage together. We would play golf or tennis together. After winning the ACC championship, I did clinics for the Air Force and asked Dave Odom to go with me. Mike Krzyzewski, while coaching the Goodwill Games, asked me to go with him to help select the team for the USA. It was a league of coaches that bonded together as friends.

As coaches and friends, our most devastating moment came with the news of Jim Valvano's cancer. It put life in perspective for us coaches. Winning games would have less significance for the moment. Each coach rallied around him, his wife, Pam, and their family. I immediately called Jim and Pam upon hearing this news. Jim was distraught over the situation, and I would reach for words of encouragement. I continued to call him weekly, trying to find ways to help his spirit.

Jim lost his battle to cancer in 1992, but his legacy remains with us. The Jimmy V Foundation, which raises money for cancer research, is helping to pave the way to find a cure for cancer. The ACC coaches, past and present, were all there at Jim's funeral. There was not a dry eye among us.

This camaraderie among coaches is going to last for a lifetime with those coaches who were there. When we made our run at Auburn this year, as an example, I got a letter from Bobby Cremins, and phone calls from the other guys. Those guys were happy for me; every one of them made a point to call or write. That says something. Friendships are valuable.

As we walk through life, I think the essence of what we are on earth for is to care about other people. I think that's what the Bible teaches us. If I had to offer one word the Bible stresses, the word would be *love*. Love means friendships, love means caring. I will value those friendships. At the end, that's what it's all about. Do we make a difference in people's lives? Do we touch people's lives?

We had that camaraderie in the Sun Belt as well. In the SEC, it hasn't happened so easily because there has been so much change that no one has gotten the chance to really know anyone else. I make it a point to try to care for the other coaches in our league. For example, John Brady mentioned that when he went through a tough time at LSU in 1999, there was only one SEC coach who called, and that was me. I called Richard Williams upon his stepping down at Mississippi State, and I still stay in touch with him. I called Dale Brown through his tough time at LSU. Friendships are too valuable—I cherish them.

There are a lot of great memories from those years at Clemson. Not all of them are about games we won. Just playing at Duke is an experience. There's no question it is the toughest place I've ever taken a team. Cameron Indoor is small and quaint. I'll never forget the first time I ever went into Duke. I was excited going into this historic place. I had an orange suede jacket given to me by the IPTAY people, and I decided to wear my new jacket.

When I took the floor, the two sides of the gym started yelling back and forth. ORANGE! JACKET! Needless to say, I didn't wear that orange jacket anymore when I went to Duke.

One of the strangest incidents of my coaching career happened at Duke. After the 1986-87 team lost our last regular-season game at Duke, I crossed the court to shake the hand of Coach K. Suddenly, I heard the words, "You're no good!" Then someone spit in my face. I didn't know what to think. We didn't win, so I thought this was an irate relative of one of our players I didn't play in the game.

The team physician was next to me, grabbed me, and escorted me off the court as security moved in. After meeting with my team following the game, I opened the door, and one of the great athletic directors of all time, Tom Butters of Duke, was waiting. He said, "Cliff, are you all right?" I said, "I am okay, but I cannot understand what happened. I don't know who that was. I don't know who I offended." Butters was somewhat shaken and explained that the guy who spit on me was the father of a Duke player.

I could have embarrassed Duke, because it was seen publicly. I told them not to worry about it. It never reached the press. Now that it's been 10 years, I tell the story because of the uniqueness surrounding it. I think that's one of the reasons for the ceremonies at the end of my ACC career. People don't shower you with praise at the end if you are a jerk.

The following year at Duke I walked out and immediately got hit by a tennis ball. Before game time, Duke fans toss tennis balls across the court. It's all in fun, but Duke is the only place that can get away with it. It's cute if it's at Duke. I sincerely believe that if other schools tried this, it would be stopped. It's acceptable at Duke because it's unique and part of their mystique. TV networks embellish this action. Duke's game atmosphere is one of the special things about college basketball.

One thing I've always encouraged while our teams travel is to see significant sights that relate to our country's history. When I take teams to Hawaii, I take our teams to see Pearl Harbor. While in Europe, I took our team to Anne Frank's home. I recall taking a team to Duke and showing them the monument where the Rose Bowl was played in 1942. The Rose

Bowl was moved from California in 1942 due to the concern of bombing from World War II. Duke would be a safer place to play, it was felt.

We had two games at Clemson that stand out as they relate to a historic event.

One event occurred while traveling to Duke. We were in a bus going to play Duke, and we heard the space shuttle *Challenger* had blown up, taking the lives of every astronaut. There was a schoolteacher on that flight also. We were stunned listening to these events over the radio as we traveled. The next evening we played the quietest game at Cameron Indoor I would ever encounter.

Another game was almost canceled. We were about to tip the ball up in 1990 in a home game against Western Carolina when we got the news that the Gulf War had started. We decided to play, but our thoughts were with our soldiers in the Middle East.

Al Muskewitz, a writer for the *Anderson Independent-Mall*, asked me to pick my top 10 wins at Clemson before that last game. I agreed to do it, but it turned out it wasn't easy to pick just 10.

Here's what I came up with:

1. Clemson 97, Duke 93, on February 28, 1990. That's the game we won to clinch the only ACC regular-season basketball championship Clemson has ever won.
2. Clemson 69, North Carolina 61, on February 24, 1990. That was the game that set the stage for us to play Duke for the championship four days later.
3. Clemson 79, La Salle 75, on March 17, 1990. We were more than 20 points behind in the second half and came

back to win in the second round of the NCAA Tournament.

4. Clemson 90, Georgia Tech 81, on January 8, 1985. It was my first ACC game, and Georgia Tech was ranked No. 8.

5. Clemson 52, North Carolina 50, on January 30, 1985. It was our first game against North Carolina and Dean Smith. What a thrill!

6. Clemson 81, Georgia Tech 79, on March 4, 1989. We won it in overtime, and that was the key to our getting into the NCAA Tournament.

7. Clemson 83, St. Mary's 70, on March 16, 1989. It was our first NCAA Tournament game at Clemson. St. Mary's was good, but we played a good game and won it.

8. Clemson 77, North Carolina 69, on February 17, 1994. It was my last season at Clemson. We were a decent team, but North Carolina was ranked No. 2 in the country. It was the highest-ranked team we had beaten.

9. Clemson 87, Florida State 75, on March 12, 1993. Florida State was ranked, and we beat them in the ACC Tournament.

10. It was a tie between beating Duke 79-74 on March 1, 1989, and beating Bradley 81-76 on December 28, 1985. The win over Duke got us a step closer to the NCAA Tournament. Bradley did not lose another game after we beat them.

With all of these wonderful memories and accomplishments at Clemson, it was even more difficult to leave behind the great fans. I left due to philosophical differences with the administration, and I left on my own terms. The day I re-signed, I got in my car and played Frank Sinatra's "My Way" perhaps a dozen times. It had significant meaning to me.

To this day I love the Clemson faithful.

CHAPTER FOURTEEN

The Auburn Years Begin

Two schools had shown an interest in me following the 1993-94 season: Auburn and Western Kentucky. Both were good places, and I liked both schools.

I got the call from Auburn shortly after Tommy Joe Eagles resigned. The first official conversation I had was with David Housel, the athletic director, who called me. We agreed to talk when my season was over. They were in the process of talking to people. I had no idea where I stood with them or whether it was a situation I wanted to be involved in.

At some point, it was reported that Auburn had hired Mike Brey, who was an assistant at Duke. I think he said he would take the job and then changed his mind a couple of days later. That was before the Final Four in Charlotte, North Carolina, 1994.

I met with David at the Final Four. On that day, I had a choice to go to Auburn or to Western Kentucky. Western Kentucky was attractive because they had a full team coming back and had basketball tradition over many years. Auburn was in a better conference, it was near home, and the program needed rebuilding. It was my cup of tea.

I said, "Let's go for the grand slam." That was my immediate thought. The Grand Slam for me would be winning the championship at each school: Cumberland, South Alabama, Clemson, and now, Auburn.

I was told when I took the job that it could be the worst team Auburn had ever had. They'd won 11 games the year before, and Wesley Person, Aaron Swinson, and Aubrey Wiley had departed as seniors. Wesley Person was one of Auburn's best scorers ever and is in the NBA now. Aaron Swinson was an all-conference player. Aubrey Wiley was the leading rebounder. Even with them, the team won just 11 games, and just three in the SEC. It didn't look bright for the upcoming year.

I walked into Beard-Eaves Coliseum the first time and it looked antiquated. The seats were old-fashioned, and the paint was drab. There was no character in the coliseum. The west end-line seats were so far removed from the floor, it appeared binoculars might be needed on certain plays. I said to myself, "I've got a lot of work to do with this structure."

I immediately started looking for ways to improve the situation, and I wanted students and fans to get involved and comfortable once they got to the game. David Housel, Jay Jacobs, Chuck Gallina, Terry Windle, Tim Jackson, and I sat around and tossed ideas back and forth.

One of the first things we wanted to do was get the students involved, get them closer to the floor. The first thing we did was to install portable bleachers at the west end of the court near the floor so that students could be close to the game. This filled the open-space area in the west end.

It was there that the Cliff Dwellers were born.

The Cliff Dwellers, named by Susan Housel, David's wife, are students who, at the time, sat in those portable bleachers at the end line and harassed opponents and referees. They were given T-shirts, and they were proud of those shirts. Some still sit at that end, but most have moved to a more prominent position, behind press row. They have meant a lot to our program because they add spirit. They have become the sixth man on the floor, because they will not let a mistake by the other team or a questionable call by a referee go unpunished.

I go many places in the country now and see Cliff Dweller T-shirts; I've had people tell me they've traveled to Europe and seen those T-shirts. I've been walking on the beaches of Florida and seen those T-shirts.

When we played Ole Miss and Arkansas back-to-back that first year at home, and those students got to see themselves on TV raising Cain and contributing to some great wins, the Cliff Dwellers became a vital, established part of the program.

We didn't want to just take care of the students. We needed to take care of the people who offered financial support, our scholarship donors. We installed comfortable seats in the sideline bleachers, improving the seating for these special supporters, at the same time enhancing the look of the coliseum.

At the time, we needed everything: new dressing rooms, new sound system, a lighting system, a new floor, and painting. Name it, and we about needed it.

I wanted everything right. Being a former entertainer, I knew how important these issues were. The public address announcer would be vital; cheerleaders, dance team, and the pep band would be vital also.

I wanted the food at the concession stands to be the best. If people were going to come to a weeknight 7 o'clock game, they needed to eat in the coliseum. If good food was available, it would make it easier for someone from Montgomery to come.

I wanted the people directing traffic and guarding entrances outside to have uniforms. They are the ones who make the first impression on the fans coming to the games. They needed to look important and impressive. I wanted loudspeakers outside so people could hear the action inside even before they entered. During that initial summer and fall, plans to build this program were being made, leaving no stone unturned. I wanted everything in place as soon as possible.

Chuck Gallina, our basketball sports information director, came up with one of the better quotes after we'd put in all this time and effort creating plans for improving facilities and promotion. Somebody said, "What do you think, Chuck?" He said, "Just win, baby. Just win." I still kid him about that to this day.

Winning is the greatest marketing tool I've got. But you have to crawl before you can walk. We had to do all those things to be ready for the day when we did win. Auburn has had some really good teams, but they didn't have the fans captured even then.

A coach has to be a lot of things. He has to be a teacher, a disciplinarian, a substitute parent. And sometimes he has to be a politician.

At any university, the Board of Trustees is a key. The Board of Trustees is part of a political process. Its members are appointed politically. As I coach, I need to understand the political process.

Politics, to me, is the process of trying to get people to agree with you. Through the years, I have become a better politician. I've learned that nobody has necessarily the same perspective I do. I have to be empathetic with the people I am dealing with. I have to be persuasive.

Lowell Barron is the ultimate politician and has influenced my understanding of politics. Lowell Barron and his wife, Susan, have taught me as much as anyone about the value of knowing when to stick to your guns about a position and when to compromise for the good of the overall program. Lowell is a state senator from north Alabama, president pro tem of the Alabama Senate, and a member of the Auburn Board of Trustees. I have relied on his advice and his friendship to guide me through some prickly situations, and I can always count on his support, win or lose. Coming from the Sandhills area of Alabama, Lowell grew up in a rough time and place. He knows about working hard to overcome obstacles; he knows about not letting low expectations determine his outcome; he knows that sometimes creative use of your wits can overcome disadvantages. He and Susan and their family have become people whom our family love and enjoy.

The coliseum needed a new look. This place had not had any refurbishing to speak of in 25 years. The board, chaired by Jimmy Samford, put $5 million into the budget to restructure the coliseum. That was the first win. It took awhile to get it done, but that was a huge win. Our athletic department bought into it, our president has been supportive, and our board has stamped it.

We have new offices and a new scoreboard now. The seating has been changed, and we don't have to have that curtain anymore. The dressing rooms have been redone; the floor has been redone.

As we sit in these nice offices today and we look back and see where we were, it's really amazing. The facilities have made a major difference, and that is very important in building a basketball program.

I remember my first Auburn team meeting very well. David Housel was there and introduced me to the team. The first thing I tried to do was say something to lift the players up and give them some hope.

I could see a lack of confidence in their faces, kids wondering what was going on. I also saw some concern. They hadn't won, they'd lost their coach, and they weren't sure what to expect.

I said, "We are going to work hard. You are going to surprise people. I've never seen you play, but I do know this: You've been here. We will find a way to be successful. We are not even going to think about wins. I'm going to determine whether we are winning by how hard we are going to play. Winning will not be determined by the score at the end of the game, but winning will be determined by whether we put our best effort on the court."

I told them they were going to be a foundation. I took off my ACC championship ring and let each one of them hold it. I told them that I wear it for a reason. It's something I'm proud of. I told them, "You are going to be the foundation for a group of young men who will wear an SEC championship ring one day."

I left the room feeling pretty good about the interaction that had taken place.

We were off to a late start recruiting in that initial year. That year I didn't take the job until a week before the spring signing day. We needed players. We basically just looked at junior colleges. Junior colleges need an academic clearing-house like the one we have now for high schools. If we had had that, then we wouldn't have gotten into the situation we found ourselves in.

In the summer, two names popped up. Moochie Norris and Chris Davis were available. They were both very good play-ers. I went to David Dials, the compliance director, and David Housel. I told them these were borderline academic situations, but the players were available. I don't remember the exact words, but I told them I wasn't moving on it unless they felt it was the right thing for us to do.

Both men gave me the go-ahead, and these two young men joined our program. Moochie Norris was a crowd-pleaser. He was a great point guard. People liked him.

As a team, we took that blue-collar approach. Pat Burke was at center; Wes Flanigan, Lance Weems, and Moochie Norris were at guards; Chris Davis, Jim Costner, and Franklin Will-iams, who was a redshirt freshman, played inside.

Even though our team lacked depth in this initial year, we were determined to employ our run-and-press game and unleash it for the Auburn fans to see. We wanted to entertain them. However, we played an exhibition game and lost. We had to score at the end to get 40 points; it was rough. It looked like it was going to be a long year for Auburn.

Lynn University was our first regular-season game. I used an Abe Lemons line and asked, "Who is she?" I'd never heard of them, and they were from my home state. It was a close game that we almost lost.

Our next game would be at UAB. We were expected to lose. It was an ugly game, but our press took over, and we found a way to win. That was a very significant win in that first year and instilled some confidence in our team.

We went through our nonconference slate at 7-2, losing to Ball State and Kansas State. Our first conference game was at Kentucky against Rick Pitino and company. It would be a disaster. I was worried about our confidence going into our dressing room after the game, and I knew we had Ole Miss at home the upcoming weekend. I was disappointed that we had lost, but more disappointed in our effort. It was inexcusable. I reiterated to the team that winning would be judged on our effort—not on the scoreboard. "We are 0-1 in effort, and for that I am disappointed. We play at home this weekend for our first home conference game. It's televised, and all of you must decide how much effort you are willing to give. The next time I address you, I expect us to be 1-1."

Ole Miss came to town. Our effort was great, and we won handily. The Cliff Dwellers were on television for the first time and making their impact known immediately. The band was upbeat, and the opening show at home was a success.

Arkansas was our next home game. Arkansas came in No. 4 in the country. ABC was in town. Nobody gave us any chance to win.

It was an emotional game. My good friend John Counts was coming to the end of his battle with cancer. Bobby Lowder sent his plane to pick John up. We both knew he wouldn't be here long. We knew there was something special about this day. John loved Auburn, and he loved the fact that I was its coach. His son Jac was attending Auburn at the time.

For some reason, I just felt we were going to win. I tried to convey that to the players. "We are going to win. We are going to win." I had videotapes of our team doing things well, like Pat Burke making a dunk or Franklin Williams making a three-point shot. I showed them those clips before they took the floor.

We took the court. Lance Weems put on a show. He stuck every shot. We couldn't miss. We played the No. 4 team in the country and scored 104 points. We won handily. That sent a major signal to our ball club and to people around the league. We weren't going to win the league, but we were going to have to be dealt with. Fans were going nuts. It was the first time scalpers had been seen at Auburn in some time.

Florida was the next ranked team to come to town. Florida was coming off a Final Four appearance and had an excellent team. Fans could not wait for this encounter. Auburn loves its rivalry with Florida. A packed house watched the Auburn Tigers upset the Florida Gators.

Another ranked team was upcoming: Mississippi State. Auburn swept the Bulldogs of Starkville, Mississippi, upsetting them in both encounters.

What a game it was at Mississippi State. Moochie Norris put on a show. It was the Moochie Norris and Daryl Wilson show. Moochie and Wilson would make play after play. Moochie made the baskets for us to win, and it was our first road win against a ranked team.

We eventually ended the season 16-12, better than anyone ever envisioned. This team had come so far since their opening exhibition loss. This team had pizzazz and flair. They played with emotion. Talent was there, even though the bench was short, and the fans loved this team and the way they played.

I knew we weren't going to the NCAA Tournament, but I believed that this team deserved to play in the postseason. I knew the people at the NIT, so I flew to meet with them in New York and took David with me. Auburn had never hosted a national tournament game. I felt that in the first year this would be a great reward. I asked them, "If we get in, please consider that we are a program that has won some big games but never has had a home NIT game."

We received a bid and hosted Marquette, where Al McGuire had won a national championship. This was a national program.

It was an event; the fans really got into it. It was a great game. We built a big lead, but couldn't hold it and lost. Marquette went on to the finals in New York. It was disappointing to lose, but it was a great event. It had gotten the people excited.

We had started the season with 1,000 people at our first game. By the end of the year, there were thousands. The coliseum was full for the NIT game—it was loud. It was a great atmosphere. We had won fans over, and it was really a significant win for the program.

That first year, my daughter graduated and was married in Clemson to my new son-in-law, Tony Rutland. He was a chemical engineering major at Clemson. They were married and moved to nearby LaGrange, Georgia. When I walked down the aisle to give my daughter away, I had a strange feeling. I realized how fast time goes by. It had seemed like yesterday that she and I were playing on the lawn of the campus of

Cumberland College. But I knew I had to let go.

Following our first year at Auburn, we would find a new little haven, Lake Martin. Dr. James Herring, a veterinarian and former South Alabama trustee, was living at Lake Martin and was encouraging me to look at a lake house. When I saw it, I saw a piece of paradise. I knew this would be a great place to retreat to from a short distance. We bought our lake home, and I retreat there before the season with my staff and utilize it during the season on our days off to break film down at times; our family loves to spend time there in the spring and summer when we can.

I felt really good after the first year. I had won some Coach of the Year awards. I thought we were headed in the right direction. We had overachieved as a team and had nearly everyone back for the upcoming year.

The fall of 1995 began our first full year of recruiting, and it would have a major impact on our future. Our first team had won 16 games and had beaten some ranked teams. They had laid a foundation for others to follow with their run-and-press game, and fans were turning out to watch them play. The blue-collar approach in that first year of play had been successful. It was time that we knocked at the door of some All-Americans.

Doc Robinson, a point guard from Selma High School, was heralded as the No. 1 recruit in the State of Alabama. In addition to the state schools, Duke and Florida State were recruiting him. Willie Maxey, his coach, loved our system. His mom and dad and aunts appreciated Eugene Harris, his character and his truthfulness. Doc Robinson chose Auburn to be his school in the fall. This was a major step for us. Alabama's Mr. Basketball had said, "I do" to Auburn. This sent a signal in recruiting that Auburn's stock in basketball was about to rise.

At the same time, a young man from Bowling Green, Kentucky, by the name of Daymeon Fishback was being recruited. His father, Charles, had played for me at Cumberland. His son would choose Auburn in the fall period. He was named Mr. Basketball in Kentucky. Mr. Basketballs from Alabama and Kentucky were coming to Auburn. Wow!

In this same period, a young man named Chris Porter from Abbeville, Alabama, signed with Auburn. Surprisingly, he was not heavily recruited. Mississippi State was the only other SEC school to recruit him. Chris would eventually go to Chipola Junior College following his senior year in high school before joining the Auburn Tigers.

Mamadou N'diaye, a seven-footer from Senegal, was the last signee to join this recruiting class. This recruiting class would be a top 15 recruiting class.

I went into the second campaign really excited. Fall recruiting had been successful, and I had my entire team back from the year before. I had the feeling this team could be good and could get us to the NCAA Tournament.

Our season would open in San Juan, Puerto Rico, for the San Juan Shootout on Thanksgiving weekend. Our team would depart on Monday.

David Housel informed me the weekend prior to our departure that Moochie Norris and Chris Davis might not be eligible. There were questions regarding whether all their credits were valid and acceptable from their junior college work.

This questioning by the NCAA is why there is a clearinghouse for high school students today and exactly why there needs to be a clearinghouse for junior college prospects. Clearinghouses decide whether a young man in high school qualifies, taking the decisions out of the hands of the NCAA and admissions offices at schools. Junior college prospects need to be cleared for eligibility through a clearinghouse instead of by the admissions offices or an NCAA representative.

At the time, Auburn was serving an NCAA penalty for problems relating to football. When questions arose from the NCAA about Moochie and Chris, Auburn took the stance of not taking a chance by playing these young men. Under the circumstances, it was the correct thing to do at the time, but it was very hurtful.

Moochie and Chris were seniors, and it could take a while before a ruling could be issued. Time was not their ally. They were both NBA prospects and could immediately play at the non-division level. Both would transfer. Moochie Norris would eventually make the NBA, playing with the Seattle SuperSonics. Chris had knee problems and would not make the NBA, but he and Moochie won Auburn people's hearts in the way they managed themselves. I am very proud of these two young men. They have reserved a special place in Auburn basketball.

It was a tough time. I had lost two players I loved. I felt support from David Housel, Dr. William Muse, our president, and our Board of Trustees. Removing Chris and Moochie was something the administration felt had to be done, and we had to get through it.

We traveled to Puerto Rico, having gone through preseason preparing with Moochie as our point guard and Chris as our power forward. We had two days to practice before our opening-round game with La Salle. We had been playing a three-man rotation at guard—Moochie, Lance Weems, and Wes Flanigan. It was now a two-man rotation—Lance and Wes.

Without much practice and with a new starting five, we would use our press as our main weapon and defeat La Salle by 10. Next up was James Madison University, led by Coach Lefty Driesell, my old buddy from the ACC. We found a way to win and would be in the finals of the San Juan Shootout playing the No. 13 team in the country, Louisville.

Louisville took the opening tip and never looked back, building a 20-plus-point lead at halftime. Our players looked as if they were ready for the game to be over, but I had seen my teams come back before. In the locker room I stated, "We're playing not to lose as opposed to playing to win. We also played the last several minutes with our heads down, showing lack of fight. We must show we are better than this. I don't know what the score at the end of the game will be, and right now I don't care, but what I am going to see when we come in this locker room at the end of the game is a group of young men who are going to play to win and play with their heads up, and you will show determination regardless of the score."

Lo and behold, in the second half our press created turnovers and havoc for Louisville. Lance Weems drilled three-point shots. Wes Flanigan, as our point guard, led the charge on the press. This team came from behind and upset the Louisville Cardinals. It took sheer will, guts, and determination to pull off that upset. It was a win I'll never forget and one I don't think Auburn fans will ever forget. It marks one of the great comebacks in Auburn basketball history.

We flew home and prepared for the upcoming Dr. Pepper Classic in Waco, Texas. Our team won its second tournament championship, defeating Baylor on its home court.

From Waco, Texas, the team was off to Mobile, Alabama, where I would face my old school, South Alabama, and it was my first trip back to the arena. I received a warm reception prior to the game, but once the ball was tipped, I knew who the South Alabama fans were pulling for. Auburn would win a thriller led by two uncharacteristic three-pointers from Adrian Chilliest.

We finished our nonconference schedule on fire at 12-1. It was an unbelievable start. This team was overachieving.

We opened up the conference race on the road at Tennessee, losing a close one to the Vols. The Razorbacks of Arkansas would be next in Auburn.

The Arkansas game was a sellout. Once again, scalpers could be seen on street corners. It was as if the script from the previous year had been written again. Lance Weems again launched a barrage of three-pointers and propelled Auburn to a 101-76 victory.

We followed this win with two more victories against ranked opponents at home, Georgia and LSU. We were 15-2 and, amazingly, this group was ranked.

Next step, Ole Miss. Ranked No. 21, Ole Miss pulled off the upset. The loss began a downward spiral for us. The season was taking its toll on our depleted team. We finished the season 19-13, losing to Tulane in the NIT.

I was proud of these overachievers. Not many people expected a winning season under the circumstances they were dealt.

The 1996-97 season started a new era for Auburn basketball. My first major recruiting class became freshmen, and as with my previous programs, I was determined to get these young men some playing time early. A foundation had been laid, but that freshman class would help determine whether we could win a championship.

Doc, Daymeon, and Mamadou entered the Auburn program. It was a strange mixture—these freshmen to go along with seniors Wes Flanigan and Pat Burke. Bryant Smith and Adrian Chilliest were still sophomores. It was a team composed mostly of underclassmen. Franklin Williams was a junior.

The greatest triumph of that season didn't come in winning a game. It came when Wes Flanigan was on the floor for our first home game.

Shortly after our second season, we got news that was almost impossible for any of us to believe. Wes had cancer. What had been thought to be calcium deposits in his arm turned out to be a malignant tumor.

He underwent surgery in Birmingham. They had to remove part of the bone and graft bone from his leg in its place. Basketball seemed very insignificant at the time. I waited it out at the hospital with his parents.

What Wes did was one of the most inspirational stories I've ever witnessed. He absolutely would not give in. It was the story of the year, as far as I was concerned.

Here was a young man who had bone cancer, had surgery, and was not able to play for several months. He battled it from day one. When he came out of recovery, the first thing he said to me was, "I will be back."

It showed his character. It showed his desire, his hunger, and his nature. He is just a winner. This was one of the most unbelievable comebacks I've seen in 30 years of coaching.

We went through the season and it was a .500 year. We won some significant games. We beat Mississippi State home and away again. We beat LSU. We beat Alabama, our intrastate rival. We ended up 16-15, but we played freshmen, and we didn't have a losing season. We had gotten through the first year of these freshmen with a winning season.

In the fall of that year, we signed the most heralded junior college player in America in Michael Spruell from Albany, Georgia. He'd won a junior college national championship. He wanted to come to Auburn, but before he got to Auburn, he was charged with rape. This was a real blow, because I had not seen any character flaws in him at all. While we were recruiting Michael, with his coach, with his family, with his background, I didn't see anything like that.

I didn't know what was going to happen at this point. I did know there was a process for him. I was going to be a human being before being a basketball coach. I asked him forthrightly, "Did you commit this crime? If you did, you don't need to be here." He said he didn't. I stayed with him through the process. He came to school, but he did not play. And then he was convicted.

The incident happened before Michael came to Auburn. He was convicted and sent to prison. Until he was sent to a facility in South Carolina, I would go and visit him.

When a situation like this happens, God knows it's awful. I felt for the victim and certainly don't condone the behavior, but Michael had no one outside his family. All I did was let him know that I cared about him as a human being and prayed for him. My wife went with me on one of the trips to visit him. I wrote him letters and encouraged him. I still write to him, though not as often.

Before that incident, I got a phone call about a young kid. I liked a player from Columbus, Jasper Sanks, who ended up playing football at Georgia. Richard Mahone was Jasper's coach. He said, "You like Jasper Sanks? You better get over here and look at another kid. He just did a number on us." This young kid was Scott Pohlman.

Scott Pohlman and his dad drove to Auburn after the season for an unofficial visit. He had had one scholarship offer to Pepperdine. I told them I didn't have any scholarships. His dad said, "If you feel like he can play, I'll send him as a walk-on."

As it turned out, due to the Michael Spruell situation, a scholarship opened up. Scotty Pohlman came and made an immediate impact as a freshman. We went 7-9 in the SEC. We were very close to a big year, but we lost our last five conference games.

We started out strong, solid. We were in great position. We were 7-4 in the conference. We were ready to go to the NCAA Tournament, but once again, just didn't have the depth to pull it off. We were young and we were good. We had a very good first five, but we didn't have that necessary depth. We just stumbled down the stretch.

We went to the NIT. We beat Southern Miss in the opening game at home. We went to Marquette and we had the doggone thing won. We had taken the heart out of Marquette. Clifton Robinson, a football player who played that year because we didn't have the depth, did a great job. We had a five-point lead in the final seconds, but we missed some free throws, and they hit a desperation three-pointer to send it to overtime. We didn't have any legs left, and they blew us out in overtime.

We had one of the most remarkable wins that year I've ever been a part of. Alabama had dominated Auburn in recent years.

In 1996-97, I could see it changing. It was now the 1997-98 season, and I remember the day Alabama came to town. It was a Sunday. My father-in-law was in town; sadly, he was dying of cancer. Somehow I knew this was going to be his last game. Our family went to Sunday school and church. There was a calm that day. The players were ready.

The most perfect game that I have ever been associated with happened that day. Everything went right for us, and everything went wrong for the other side. We beat Alabama 94-40. It was the largest margin of victory in the history of Auburn basketball, and it was against Alabama. That was a major win.

That win ranks right at the top with any I've had because of the significance attached to that game by those who support this school.

I did not coach against David Hobbs, the Alabama coach, again after that season. He was told before we played them in Tuscaloosa that he would not be retained. They beat us and finished out the season. I felt for him.

David has been a friend for a number of years. I think he will eventually return to coaching. It's a part of the business that some people think about. We coaches just take it one day at a time and do our jobs. I don't think any one of us dwells on whether we are going to get fired or not. Lack of job security is just a part of this business.

Some situations are tougher than others. Every situation is different. In my situation, I try to go out and do the very best I can in every circumstance. Very seldom do I see a coach walk out on his own completely satisfied. Al McGuire did it at Marquette. John Wooden did it. But it's a profession where very seldom does a person walk away on his own accord.

When the 1997-98 season was over, we had another good recruiting year, and the future was bright. As it turned out, we were on the brink of a championship season.

CHAPTER FIFTEEN

The Climb Begins

I knew it. I knew, if things went well, the 1999 team would be something special. I started talking about it before we ever tipped it up. I told our players after we lost a heartbreaker at Marquette in the second round of the NIT in 1998 that this team had a chance to be really good.

We had four starters back, and we'd had another good recruiting year. We had added Chris Porter, whom we'd signed two years earlier out of Abbeville when nobody knew much about him. He ended up having to go to junior college, but he told us he would come back and he did. I guess you could say the rest is history, since he was the SEC Player of the Year.

We also added David Hamilton, who was really coming on strong before he got hurt and missed most of the conference season. Jay Heard and Mack McGadney also came into the program to make huge contributions.

We'd had two good recruiting classes, and those players had gotten good experience, because I had been able to give them quality playing time for two to three years. We were adding talented freshmen to mature, experienced upperclassmen. We'd been shorthanded since our second year at AU. Now, finally, we had the same numbers everyone else had. I knew we had to have help from some freshmen, but I felt that this was the first time we really had a legitimate shot.

I felt good. I had a team that had two blue-collar seniors in Bryant Smith and Adrian Chilliest. Doc Robinson would be a junior at point guard, and he made some All-American teams. Scott Pohlman was a sophomore guard who could shoot it and just knew how to win. We had Mamadou N'diaye, a 7-footer who could block shots. We had solid players and solid citizens, like Daymeon Fishback, whose daddy played for me at Cumberland. I told his daddy when he was a baby he'd have a scholarship, wherever I was. He was Mr. Basketball in Kentucky, and he had come to Auburn two years earlier.

My goal was to do as well as we could, do as well as we could in the West. I never envisioned an SEC championship. I never envisioned Sweet 16. I never envisioned No. 2 in the country. I never envisioned any of those things. I told them we were going to work hard and have fun. That was still our motto.

I want to say something about Bryant Smith. He came here and believed in us when this staff was just getting started at Auburn. He's the best leader I've ever been around. I mean, he took that team over; I could see it in the summer. A coach never knows for sure what kind of chemistry a team is going to have, but he and Adrian Chilliest, our seniors, made sure everybody did what they were supposed to. They made sure team members made curfew.

Bryant recognized that a freshman player was going into a shell because of academic and social problems and alerted the coaches so that we could address that freshman's needs with counseling and tutoring. Sometimes players will have problems and be gone before coaches know that anything is wrong. It helps very much to have a mature player/coach on the floor and in the dorm who cares and who takes the initiative to guide the players where he wants them to go. You could see Bryant asserting himself out there from the very start. If we hadn't had that leadership, I don't believe we would have accomplished what we did. He set a standard others followed. Those freshmen watched him. When they get to be juniors and seniors, they'll know what to do.

We were picked second in the SEC West by the media, but we didn't start the season ranked nationally. If you are not ranked early, it's difficult to become ranked in November and December when all teams are in their nonconference schedules. They are going to play a couple of tough games, but not enough to put their rankings in jeopardy.

Our team started out with four straight home games; then we went to Hawaii. We were opening with Rutgers. I knew they were good, even though some other people might have not known it. They made a big run at getting into the NCAA Tournament and probably should have been there. When we beat Rutgers, I knew something was going on; it wasn't a close game. Then we had Hawaii. Hawaii ended up not having a good year, but I knew Indiana and Kansas had come in there and lost the year before. They had been nationally ranked and been in the NCAA Tournament. We won by 27 points on their home court. It was never a game. I came home from Hawaii feeling very good.

The next week we were going to Florida State, a good ACC team that we played in their house. They lost their center after that and struggled a bit, but they were good at the time we played them. They had just gone on the road and won their first ACC game over Virginia. I told the staff then, "If we pull this off, we are for real." I had not been sure how it would play out, but we should have been up 25 or 30 at the half. We won handily. I knew we were there then. We were 7-0.

Then we went to UAB. I knew this was the best UAB team we had seen. Nationally, this kind of game can hurt you. We know how good UAB is, but people in New York, California, or Washington don't know how good UAB is. I was nervous about this game. I believed it was a game that could hurt us if we lost. It was the toughest nonconference game we played. We were behind at halftime, and it was close down to the last minute. It was a war game, a battle we ended up winning going away in the end.

We still had another road game at Navy. They'd won the Patriot League, and Don Devoe is a good coach. We went to Navy and won. Chris Porter scored 39 points. They couldn't do anything with him. Now we had gone on the road and won five pretty significant games. We were undefeated, 11-0. People were starting to talk. Maybe this Auburn team was better than what they had thought.

After one more nonconference game we were 12-0, and it was time for conference play. We were ranked, but we were still not getting a whole lot of attention. People were talking about us, but their talk included lots of questioning about whether the team was "for real." I knew it was. I didn't know where we were going to finish or how many games we were going to win, but I knew we had a good basketball team. There was no question about that. Those freshmen were already playing better than anybody would have imagined, including me.

Tennessee came in for the first SEC game. They had won 20 games the season before and had everybody back. They were ranked No. 9 in the preseason polls. Even though we were playing at home, it seemed like a lot of people expected us to lose.

Tennessee ended up winning the East, so they were good. They came in, and we were ready. The score was 90-62. Good gracious alive! We were 13-0.

Our next SEC game was at home. Arkansas came in, and we won by 17. Actually, it was a 20-point game until our players started celebrating a little early. An Arkansas player hit a three-pointer with Doc Robinson already standing on the press table and celebrating with the students. That didn't matter. I was just happy with the game. Now we were 14-0.

Football had been through turmoil that season, and the team finished 3-8. Terry Bowden had resigned as head coach halfway through the season. People were upset that Auburn was taking a beating nationally. Auburn people were having a hard time.

It was a very similar situation to 1989-90, when Clemson was going through turmoil in football, and we won the ACC championship in basketball. It was almost an identical story. Football had all these problems, and now the basketball team was giving people something to feel good about, to be excited about.

The first conference road test was LSU. Auburn hadn't beaten LSU in Baton Rouge in 10 years. LSU had been struggling for most of the time I'd been at Auburn, but we had never played very well in Baton Rouge. People were starting to notice Auburn. We were climbing up in the rankings. *Sports Illustrated* wanted to do an article. They said, "If you win at LSU, we're going to write about you." *Sports Illustrated* was big time. That was significant.

We went down there and, as in a lot of other years, nothing went right. LSU was throwing in three-pointers from everywhere at the start of the game. We weren't playing well. We were down 19 at halftime. It looked like another disappointing trip to Baton Rouge for Auburn.

In the locker room, I took my time. I basically gave a talk I had used in years past at Clemson and South Alabama. I told them I didn't know the outcome of this game, but I knew this: "This next half we are going to play the kind of game we've played the last 14 games. We are going to play hard and play smart and see what happens." It was a great effort; Chris Porter put on a show. We were still down 19 with 10 minutes left, but our players played intense defense and were strong enough to shoot with strength and confidence. They found a way to come back and win. When we got back to the locker room, we hugged and high-fived as though we had won a championship that night. We had proved to ourselves that we could win a close game. We proved that to a lot of other people, too, and *Sports Illustrated* sent Tim Crothers to write an article titled "Long-sleeping Auburn a bright-eyed, bushy-tail 15-0."

My wife Carolyn's brother, John Alan Ratzlaff, an Auburn graduate, listened particularly intensively to the LSU game that night. He and I had talked the night before when he told me that his chemotherapy had failed to stop the spread of his stomach cancer. His cancer had been diagnosed in May of 1998, two weeks before their dad died on June 2. We talked of faith and of living fully and completely. And I told him that I wanted to dedicate the season to him—that I would keep him in my thoughts and prayers throughout the season.

John Alan listened to the game on the Auburn network with more and more disappointment; about halftime he told Debbie, his wife, "Cliff's dedicated this season to me, and now they're going to lose their first game!" He slunk to his bedroom, and Debbie thought he was going to try to sleep. With about three minutes left in the game, she heard cheers and yells coming from upstairs. When the game was over, John Alan came bounding down the steps with more energy than he had had in months. He cried, "We won! Auburn won this game!"

The perfect conclusion to this story would be that the miracle, which seemed to happen in the LSU game, would now work in John Alan's life. Often it does; working hard and never giving up are important decisions to make in the game of basketball and in the game of life.

Another good understanding of basketball is that it is a fun diversion from hard work and hardship. For two or three hours twice a week, John Alan could forget his pain and enjoy the thrill of vicariously playing well and winning. We had an off weekend on February 20, and I was with John Alan watching Kentucky lose to Tennessee, giving us the outright SEC championship.

Wherever he was, in however much pain he was in, John Alan wanted to listen to or watch Auburn—in the SEC tournament, through the NCAA tourney, to the Sweet Sixteen. We lost to Ohio State on March 18, and instead of traveling on to play another game, we went to Marianna, Florida, for John Alan's funeral. He died just a few hours after we lost our last game.

In many ways, 1998-99 was the worst year of our family's life. Carolyn's dad and her brother died of cancer. Our daughter Anna Catherine's best friend, Ashley Bridges, died of leukemia in January after a valiant three-year struggle.

Carolyn's best friend in the Auburn area is Cindy Cannon. She met the love of her life in the summer before the season. Cindy and Blade Kelley fell in love and were going to be married in June. They enjoyed the season with gusto. They rejoiced with us in victory and overcame defeats with humorous, level-headed perspective. Tragically and unfairly, Blade died of a heart attack in April, two months before the wedding date.

At the very same time that we were experiencing one of the best years of our life—enjoying with a wonderful group of young men the happy fruits of preparation and hard work—we were in intense pain because of tragedy. Perhaps basketball, this year and always, is best understood as a gift, not as the most important aspect of life, but as fun, respite, therapy.

Another mingling of the good and bad occurred in January in Tuscaloosa, Alabama. Chris Porter, top rebounder and scorer on the team, had been suspended for three games just before the Alabama game. Mack McGadney had been chosen to start in his place. About midnight on Friday night before the game, we got a call that Mack's grandmother had passed away.

Jessie Mae Feggian was more than just Mack's grandmother. She raised him and loved him and helped him to become the wonderful young man he is. Mack loved her and recognized how much he owed her. One of the reasons that he chose Auburn over Indiana was so that he could stay close to Mobile and his grandmother. The last time I saw Ms. Feggian, she was at an early nonconference game and she said to me,

"I'm so happy I saw where he is. This is the right place for him." She would never see him play again.

When I had to break the news to Mack that his grandmother was gone, I explained that I have always believed that family comes first and suggested that he prepare to go home and be with his family. Mack looked hurt. He insisted, "Coach, my grandmother would want me to play before I went home." In Chris Porter's spot he tallied 11 points, scoring baskets at significant times, grabbed seven important rebounds, and defended like a man possessed. Basketball that night for Mack McGadney was therapy, respite, and solace.

CHAPTER SIXTEEN

Reaching Peak #1—
The SEC Championship

Our players just kept doing what it took. They weren't just winning; except for the LSU game, they were blowing people out. We were climbing in the rankings, and the attention was growing all the time.

In the home game against Arkansas, when the starting lineup was named, Arkansas' players did a dance on our emblem. Not a sign of disrespect, this dance showed tremendous respect. They wouldn't have bothered four or five years ago. Now they knew they needed to get fired up; they knew they were facing a formidable foe.

Ole Miss had won 29 straight at home, and we went in there and won by double digits. When Florida came in, CBS was there, and we won big. We were 17-0.

As we were getting ready to go to Kentucky, and because we'd won 17 straight, everybody wanted us. We were on the "Sports Babe Show," ESPN, in all the state media.

Now it was becoming national. It was magical.

We went to Kentucky, another team we hadn't beaten in a long time. Our players were very confident, but we lost. Doc

Robinson and Adrian Chilliest couldn't do anything. They were sick as dogs with the flu. Chilliest didn't get on the floor; Doc tried to play but was too weak to perform up to par.

Nevertheless, we stayed in the game all the way. We got behind and came back, got behind and came back. We didn't win, but I was as proud of our team as at any time. We came back after this loss and won eight straight. Some people might have thought we would sag because we lost to Kentucky. I never worried about that with this team and the mind-set they had.

Most people had begun to realize that this Auburn team was something special. Beating Tennessee earlier was a major step in gaining national respect.

One of the most interesting parts of the season was the three-game run after the Kentucky game without Chris Porter. The suspension was painful, but rules are rules. We won the first game of the three at Alabama in the emotional contest with Mack McGadney substituting for Chris and playing despite his grief at losing his grandmother. Mack left to go to Mobile after that game, and the staff had to prepare for a Wednesday night game against Mississippi State without both Chris and Mack. Enter Adrian Chilliest. He was a senior who hadn't played much, but when his time came, he was there and ready. His response was typical of this team's. They pulled together, cared for each other, and willingly did whatever it took to get the job done.

The final game of Porter's three-game suspension was in Athens against a talented Georgia team. Auburn won 85-74, our 20th win of the season before the end of January. No Auburn team, nor anyone in the game's history, had ever done that.

We went to South Carolina. Chris returned and was like a mad man. We won in a blowout. LSU came into Beard-Eaves, and we got another win and yet another blowout. We were 22-1.

ESPN televised the next game, the rematch with Ole Miss in Beard-Eaves. For whatever reason, it was the only game we had all season on ESPN. I don't think that will happen again anytime soon. Curry Kirkpatrick did a feature for ESPN on our inside guys—Porter, Smith, and N'diaye. He called them "Flying Tigers." He called Chris "Sovereign of Dunk."

There was electricity in the air. It was the most phenomenal first half anybody would ever want to see. The score was 50-20 at halftime. We were on fire. We won 95-66, playing everybody. For the first time this season, the nation watched the Auburn Tigers. Auburn was for real and stood at 23-1.

We were now in position to win the SEC West Division for the first time ever. Alabama was the next opponent. If we could beat Alabama, we'd have the SEC West title. The place was on fire. Everything was just right. I was primed. The year before, we'd beaten Alabama 94-40 in one of the most amazing games I've ever seen. We beat them just about as badly this time.

At halftime we were ahead by a greater margin than we had been the year before. This time we won 102-61 and called off the dogs. The place was hysterical, and it happened against Alabama. Toomer's Corner was rolled. Toomer's Corner has been rolled for basketball games before, but that has usually been reserved for football. People were excited. It was big. We won Auburn's first division championship.

Now, if we could beat Vanderbilt in our last home game, we would win it all. The place was on fire again. Students were excited. Everybody was talking about it all over the country.

Even when we won the ACC championship at Clemson, it wasn't as much of a Cinderella story as this was, for whatever reason. Everybody had bought into this team. Every day was an interview with national media. If we could do this, we were going to give Auburn something it hadn't had in 39 years.

Two weeks prior to the Vanderbilt game, I got an interesting call.

It was from Bo Jackson. Bo is a real hero at Auburn, of course. I guess most people think that he's the best football player who ever played for us. Of course, he's one of the better-known athletes of recent times on a national basis. I had met Bo the summer before in Akron, Ohio, on the golf course at Firestone with Dr. Jimmy Andrews and Mailon Kent. That's when I got to know Bo a little bit. There were a lot of people around, so we didn't spend a lot of time with each other. We weren't even in the same foursome.

But then I got a call from Bo. "Cliff, do you know what's going on around you?" He said, "I go to Hollywood, I go to Phoenix, I travel all over the country. Every time I step off a plane, people want to know what's happening with Auburn basketball."

He continued, "I'll be honest with you. Auburn was playing some pretty good basketball when I was there, and I think I went to three games in four years." I interrupted to tell him that I wanted him to come and see a game. He said, "I do want to come and see this team for myself." Bo Jackson wanted to come to Beard-Eaves, and I was sure going to try to accommodate him.

After looking over the schedule, I explained, "Bo, if we win the next three or four games, we are going to play Vanderbilt for the SEC championship in the last home game." My prediction came true, and on Monday of the week we were to play for the crown, Bo called and made me promise that I wouldn't tell anybody that he was coming. That was very important to him. If his attendance had been public knowledge, he would have been mobbed, taking attention away from the game. I agreed to have somebody meet him at the loading dock at the coliseum so that very few people, not even the players, knew he was there.

Bo came into the dressing room to talk to the players before the game. Man, our players' eyes got real big. Not only were they in the SEC championship game, but there was Bo Jackson just to see them. When they were young kids they watched Bo. He was really good with those young men. He let them know how much he appreciated what they were doing, how much what they were doing meant to Auburn people all over the country. Then he left the dressing room and went into the coliseum. Our players were impressed. They were ready.

It was a magical moment.

There were so many emotions, so much pride in what the players had done, so much excitement. People were going crazy. Everyone was hugging and slapping each other. It was loud, really loud.

Auburn had done it. Auburn had won the Southeastern Conference championship. It's a night I don't think that anyone who was there will ever forget. I know I won't. We beat Vanderbilt 81-63. We really didn't play one of our better games, but it didn't matter when the horn blew and the streamers came down and everyone came out on the floor.

I'd have to say that that was the most significant night in Auburn basketball history in a long time, and perhaps ever.

A conference tournament championship is a three- to four-day affair; on the other hand, the regular-season championship is a long, grueling three-month affair. To go through that regular season in a league as tough as the SEC and to reach your goal is what you dream of as a competitor, whether you are a player or a coach.

The team was ranked as high as No. 2 in the country in the last two weeks of the season. Winning the championship was the crowning achievement. Remembering those few hundred early, diehard fans who came out when we played and almost lost to Lynn University in our first game at Auburn back in 1994—all that made the moment very special.

Those thoughts of the early days at Auburn went through my mind when I saw the players cutting the nets down, the students on the floor, everyone so excited. It was a great time of joy and achievement during a period when Auburn University had been having some problems in other athletic areas. I thought also of the '90 year at Clemson when we had beaten Duke on our home floor to win the ACC championship. That championship had also offset some controversial athletic times. Our experience at the University of South Alabama in 1979 had a similar feeling, when we went undefeated in the league, won the Sunbelt Conference, and got to the NCAA Tournament for the first time. All these moments were with me on the floor that night and will always be with me.

As it got late in the Vanderbilt game and became obvious we were going to win, I thought about the people who helped me get where I was. I thought about my family, my own mother and father. I thought about Carolyn, my wife, who has always been there for me. I thought about our children. I thought about all that these players had gone through to get to this point.

I knew that this joy was why we'd worked hard, why the players had worked hard.

We felt exhilaration. We felt satisfaction. I felt pride in what the players accomplished. A coach feels all those things when it all comes together and the team has a night like that. It was something—the coliseum was full; people were into it. The atmosphere was incredible.

There were two especially significant people in the stands. One was Bo. The second was a man who was supportive with telegrams, phone calls, and other gestures even before the game. It was Gov. Don Seigelman, who was in attendance with his children. In my time at Auburn, there had not been a governor before who graced us with his presence at a basketball game.

Our players really felt the support when they took the floor. Bo Jackson, one of the most heralded athletes ever, was there. The governor of the state was there. We knew it was a special night. It was a spectacle.

We didn't beat Vanderbilt as badly as we had beaten a lot of other teams, but that didn't really matter. We had it well in hand at the end. It was fun being on the bench with our kids as it began to sink in what they had done.

It took a long time to get to the locker room after the game. It was a wild scene on the floor. The players were enjoying it. Everyone wanted to slap them on the back. They got their SEC championship T-shirts. They cut down the nets, which is something they will remember for a lifetime.

One of the first guys in the locker room was Bo. He wanted to know where his shirt was. I gave him mine. Anyone who would fly from Chicago down here to be a part of our victory deserved that much. The governor also came through, and we were appreciative of that. I could see pride on the players' faces. I could see their feeling of accomplishment. I could see they were a proud, proud group. Everyone was hugging. There was happiness. There was joy. There were tears. Everything. It was very special.

Who would have ever believed it? It was like a Hollywood gala that night. The stars came out.

Moments like that are why I play the game. Everyone was so happy. Auburn hadn't had that championship feeling for 39 years in basketball. Most of the people there weren't around the last time it happened.

"We Are the Champions" was playing. People were hugging necks, slapping backs, and giving high fives. My mind went to the players, and tears flowed down my cheeks as I watched them. I sat back and tried to hide in the crowd. I just watched our players. I smiled and I cried. Gosh, what a night! It was just an ecstatic feeling.

It was a Wednesday night, but people kept coming by the house until 2 or 3 in the morning. The good thing is we didn't have to come back and play on Saturday. We could celebrate on Thursday and be able to savor the win, that wonderful feeling. It was a time when scheduling worked out well. After all that excitement, it would have been really hard to come back and get ready to play a game in just a couple of days.

It was almost like destiny. Vanderbilt was our last home game, and that's when we clinched Auburn's first championship in 39 years. Even if we hadn't won that night, I think that we would have still done it, but the championship would have been won on the road. It would have still been special, but it wouldn't have been the same as doing it in Beard-Eaves, with our players getting to celebrate with our fans. That's the way a coach, a player, or a fan wants it to be.

From a professional and competitive standpoint, it was truly one of the greatest days of my life. Auburn people are very loyal. When something like this is going on, Auburn people all over the country want to be part of it. What those players accomplished meant so much to so many different people.

CHAPTER SEVENTEEN

It Ain't Over Till It's Over

We did it. We were SEC champions, but the season wasn't over.

The next Wednesday, we went to Arkansas. I don't believe Duke or anybody else could have beaten them that night. What I saw at Arkansas again was a matter of respect. Nolan Richardson told me personally after the game and at the SEC meetings that that was the loudest he'd ever heard Bud Walton Arena from start to finish. You'd have had to have been there to understand. That's one of the loudest places you'd ever want to play, anyway, and it was a lot louder than usual that night.

The point that makes is how far the Auburn program has come. I can remember during my first year the noise when Arkansas came to Auburn in 1995 and they were at the top of the heap. Now Auburn was at the top of the heap, and Arkansas was giving us respect. Arkansas won and handed us our second loss of the season.

I don't think our players were shaken by the Arkansas loss. We still had a road game to go to at Mississippi State, and we went to Starkville and won a big game. I felt that showed a lot of character. Mississippi State was fighting to get in the NCAA Tournament and had lost only once at home. They were pumped up. They played really hard and really well, but we went in there on their Senior Day and pulled that win off. The regular season was over, and Auburn had finished the regular season 26-2. Over three months, over the long haul, Auburn had proved it was the best team in the SEC.

Now we were going into the SEC Tournament. Tennessee upset Kentucky and won the East. We got Alabama in the first game and Kentucky on our side of the bracket. I thought the pressure game was Alabama. We had beaten Alabama badly twice. Alabama was confident. They had just beaten Arkansas; they had beaten Kentucky. They were talking about, "It's another day. It's another day."

There was so much focus on the Alabama game; Kentucky wasn't the pressure game. Alabama thought they were going to win, but we won by 31. It was a big relief. We had swept Alabama three straight games by almost 90 points. No other Auburn team had ever made that statement and perhaps none ever will again.

The Kentucky game came up, and I thought that was the SEC Tournament championship game. Whoever won that game was going to win it all. They knew it and we knew it. We had put everything on the line, playing our archrival the day before. We knew we had become the hunted. That's the way it was going to be from now on. We lost, but so did a lot of other people around the nation.

Now the question was about No. 1 seed. Some people said we didn't deserve it. That's the way it was all year, but who else was going to get it? Who else was going to be the No. 1 seed? We were right there; we had proved it for three and a half months.

If it was based on the regular season, we flat-out deserved it. It doesn't make sense to base the decision on the conference tournament. The tournament makes a lot of money because people come. It's in March. It's an event that happens over a weekend. Television pays the conference money, and that's why we do it. But the best team is the team that can win for three and a half months. This team proved it was a No. 1 seed by being the No. 2 team in the country going into the last week of the season.

We came back to Auburn for the NCAA field announcement. Fans were in the coliseum to watch the seedings on the big screen. Cameras from local television and from ESPN and CBS were in the dressing room and on the floor to get our reactions. Being picked the No. 1 seed in the South was a wonderful testament to the season we had had. We had gone into the season hoping to just make the NCAA Tournament field. By playing one game at a time as well as we could play, we had turned those individual steps into a giant leap. It was an extremely satisfying moment.

CHAPTER EIGHTEEN

The Climb—A Peak Experience

We went into Indianapolis for the first round. Even though we were playing a No. 16 seed, I thought we had jitters early in the Winthrop game. Some of the Winthrop players had celebrated when they saw they were going to play Auburn. They said they thought they matched up well with us.

They did play hard, but they couldn't stay with us. We were simply a lot better than they were.

What a game the next game was! Our game with Oklahoma State was one of the best college basketball games I've ever been part of. The beauty of the NCAA Tournament is that the elite players are competing. Spectators are watching these players who have done well through the year and who are now going against each other, sparring, playing at the top of their games.

Oklahoma State guys made plays; our guys made plays. Scotty Pohlman had the game of his life, scoring 28 points. He really was the guy who broke Oklahoma State's back. Winning a game of this intensity and caliber and getting to the

Sweet Sixteen, I think, finally quieted any skepticism that we were seeded where we should have been. There is a reason that winning the first two rounds is called "sweet."

The Sweet 16 for us was held in SEC country. We went to the University of Tennessee campus and played Ohio State. Where Scotty Pohlman made shots the week before, Scoonie Penn, who had not shot well the first two games, made the plays for Ohio State. We put everybody on Scoonie Penn, including Bryant Smith, whom we had gone to war with against the best defensively for three years. Bryant, our stopper, was on him, and Scoonie still made shots.

It came down to making plays. We had a couple of open looks at the basket, and we didn't get them. They were the same looks we'd had the week before. I think the key play happened with a little more than a minute left. Chris Porter grabbed a rebound and had a wide-open layup ahead. We were one point down. Chris lost it off his knee. Instead of us scoring a layup and taking the lead, Ohio State got the ball and was fouled by Porter. Chris fouled out, they made the free throws, and we were in trouble. Ohio State won. Our great run was over.

What can you say? We were in the locker room. The players were crushed. We wanted to go as far as we could, obviously, but the further the team goes, the worse it hurts when they lose. We were so close, and we didn't get there. We were all hurt. That's the way it is.

In the end, when it's all over, only one team is happy. Duke had a great season, and I think they had the best team in the country, but they lost to Connecticut and they felt crushed. Connecticut went home happy after having won the national championship. Everyone else left with a sad feeling.

I wanted our players to feel the loss, but I didn't want them to dwell on it. I let it soak in a little while, but I would not let them leave that locker room without telling them, "You're not going to walk out of here with your heads down. You put on the best fight an Auburn team has ever put on from day one until the last day. You hold your heads high. You are still SEC champions, you are still a No. 1 seed, and you had a tremendous year. I love you for it, and Auburn people love you for it."

It was very disappointing for us all, but if you can't appreciate a regular season like we had, then why play during the year? Let's just fold up and play the conference tournament at the end of the year and whoever wins, plays. Then we can go straight into baseball.

The regular season is what the game has been centered on since it started. It's been built up around kids playing and going to tournaments. The regular season is what sets things up. We have the opportunity to show other teams we are good, and that's a buildup to postseason play.

All the teams that have played in the regular season showcase their talent. In the NCAA, there are 64 teams that have earned that route. If you didn't have a regular season, I don't think that you'd have March Madness.

What our guys did was amazing. They went 29-4. They won more games than any team in state history. They won the SEC championship. They were a No. 1 seed, and they deserved to be a No. 1 seed. They got to the Sweet 16. It really was a magical season.

The 1999 season all started with more than building a basketball team. There was so much to be done. A lot of people out there were saying we couldn't get it done at Auburn. I would never have taken the job if I hadn't thought it could be done.

Building this program and that season involved reconfiguring the coliseum to make it more fan-friendly and tougher on the opponents. It involved getting the nice offices we have now. To see the new scoreboard, to see the promotions, to see the arena packed, to see that celebration when we won the championship, to see it all play out was something that meant a lot.

A lot of people had a hand in it—our assistant coaches, the promotion people, a lot of people. But it was the players who went out there and got the job done.

Because of what our players accomplished, I got a lot of National Coach of the Year awards. Those awards are very special, especially the AP and CBS and John Wooden awards, but the players and people around me are a lot more deserving than I am. Those things are team honors. I'm just proud I was able to be a part of it.

Those players set a high standard for the teams to follow them. That's what I want. We have arrived. We're not going to win every game, but we can make each game exciting.

Our players can't get caught up in the expectations or the media hype. They can't think it's the end of the world if they happen to lose a game. They've got to play one game at a time, just as they did when they won that championship. I believe there are going to be a lot more exciting nights for Auburn basketball in the years ahead.

Our players have to play every game as the hunted now instead of the hunters. People are going to be after them. Auburn is going to be a team everybody wants to beat. That's good. That's the way coaches want it to be.

I think our future looks very bright. We have a lot of good players now, and we are going to get more. When a team wins a championship, recruits look at that program a little closer. They see us in a little different light. They see that the things we do can work at the highest level.

Championships are to be treasured. A team never knows when it will have an opportunity to win another one. There are a lot of great teams out there.

Whatever happens in the future, nobody can ever take that season and that championship away from our players. Nobody can take away the feeling of that night when they knew they had done it. None of us will ever forget it.

CHAPTER NINETEEN

The Roller-Coaster Ride

The first regular-season game of the 2000 season was our victory over UAB. The four seniors, Doc Robinson, Daymeon Fishback, Mamadou N'Diaye, and Chris Porter, were the double-figure scorers for the game, and N'Diaye and Mack McGadney had 14 and 13 rebounds, respectively, career bests for both of them. A sold-out Beard-Eaves Memorial Coliseum and the best effort of our opponent were both signs of the times of the season.

In late November, after a 100-44 win over the University of Arkansas-Pine Bluff, Auburn traveled to Anaheim, California, for the John R. Wooden Classic, one of the premier basketball events of the year. In a seesaw game that was a great early season matchup, Curtis Burchardt hit a three-pointer with 1:35 to play to break a 56-56 tie. We still trailed by only three with less than a minute to play, but Scott Pohlman and Chris missed back-to-back three-point attempts, and then we were forced to foul. Scott had a game-high 21 points, including a 10-0 run by himself to pull us from a 49-40 deficit.

The Wooden Classic was a great event. Our family got to visit with Coach Wooden's family at the banquet the night before the game. I loved having the chance in my banquet comments to say what Coach Wooden has meant to me professionally and what he has meant to the game of college basketball. Always the teacher, Coach Wooden came to the podium and emphasized again for us all that the glory of a game, of a season is ephemeral, that there is a more eternal glory of relationship with ultimate glory, with God. He quoted from a poem entitled "God's Hall of Fame" (author unknown).

> *I tell you, friends,*
> *I would not trade*
> *My name however small*
> *Inscribed up there*
> *Beyond the stars*
> *In that celestial hall*
> *For any famous name on earth*
> *Or glory that they share.*
> *I'd rather be an unknown here*
> *And have my name up there.*

Bill Walton was at the Wooden Classic as a TV commentator, and it was a joy to see how much he and others of the UCLA family love this coach.

The next major test was against FSU at home. We had to rebound from an early loss for the first time in many seasons—against a significant intersectional opponent. We were attempting to get my 100th win at Auburn against my alma mater on my birthday. But the most significant event of the weekend was finding out from our daughter, Chryssa, and her husband, Tony, that I was going to be a grandfather. Several of our friends have become idiots over their grandchildren. Their conversations always turn to these outstanding babies; our friends' time and focus seem to be warped by the children of their children. I now completely understand. It is hard for me to explain the intensely warm joy that Carolyn and I both experienced at the announcement. Perhaps only other grandparents know the feeling.

Doc Robinson made a free throw with two seconds left in the game to give us a 55-54 victory over Florida State in a defensive struggle. This win helped me become the Auburn coach to win 100 games in the shortest time. It was a great 54th birthday present. Doc Robinson scored 17 of our 55 points.

The next week was final exams at Auburn, and while the players studied for and took their tests, I prepared for what I knew would be a challenge from the University of Pennsylvania. They had won 20 games the year before, won the Ivy League championship, and played in the NCAA Tournament. They repeated this year, led by Michael Jordan, a different but very good Michael Jordan. David Hamilton was able to return to the lineup in the game. Paced by Doc Robinson's and Scott Pohlman's 16 points each and by Mamadou N'Diaye's inside double-double, we were able to secure a quality win against a worthy opponent.

Our next opponent was another frequent NCAA Tournament participant—Coppin State—coached by a man who has the most interesting nickname around, Ron "Fang" Mitchell. Fang is always happy-go-lucky, but when the games begin, he and his team are intense. This team was not one of Fang's better teams, and we won fairly easily.

Next was our Christmas holiday road trip that started in Mobile and ended in San Juan, Puerto Rico.

I've always enjoyed Mobile and the friends we made there when I coached at South Alabama. This trip to the place where my Division I career began was emotional. We played at the Mitchell Center, South Alabama's new on-campus facility, a dream I had had 20 years before. It is named for Mayer Mitchell, one of my best supporters—even though he is an ardent University of Alabama fan. The Mitchell Center is a beautiful arena, a model, a fashion statement for college arenas.

In the Mitchell Center, we dedicated the John Counts Scholarship Room prior to the games of the Coors Classic. Many friends and South Alabama supporters were there to dedicate this beautiful room to the memory of a man who was an early and diligent supporter of Jaguar basketball, a man who was one of my best friends. I helped Alyce, his widow, and Jac and Bradley, his sons, unveil a portrait that decorates the room.

Seeing Ben Nolan among the media there was great; he is the epitome of the professional journalist, a responsible newsman, not just an entertainer.

In our game, we prevailed over Bradley University 78-64, topping off a moving evening.

The San Juan Shootout always has a great field. This year's was typical, including Miami, a Sweet Sixteen participant in the NCAA tournament; Pepperdine, which beat Indiana by 20 points in the opening round; and the University of Louisiana–Lafayette, another 2000 NCAA Tournament participant.

We ended up playing Pepperdine for the championship after defeating Puerto Rico–Mayaguez and Virginia Tech. Mamadou led the way for us, playing inspired and confident ball. He had 18 points and 10 rebounds in the championship game and was named the Most Valuable Player of the tournament, the first MVP award he had ever received. For a young man who had traveled thousands of miles to play the game for the first time only five years before, it was an amazing accomplishment. Seeing him develop, observing his action and reaction both on the floor and off make coaching and teaching a great profession.

The Shootout provides a valuable preconference experience for basketball teams. There is always good competition in a relaxed atmosphere. Attendance is rarely big enough to create a home-court advantage for any team. But this year a nice happenstance put Alabama Gov. Don Seigelman and his beautiful family in the stands for every game. They were visiting their good friends, the governor of Puerto Rico and his family, and the team appreciated their coming to cheer for us.

The usual site of our annual Christmas party is our house. In 1999, we missed the coziness of home, but there were some nice aspects of partying together in a hotel dining room in San Juan: others of our AU family and some members of the media were able to experience the fun and joy.

A tradition of this get-together is that all attendees sing Christmas carols in front of the others–everybody in a group except for freshmen, who conclude the evening singing solos. Marquis Daniels and Jamison Brewer entered the lineup for the Puerto Rico trip, just in time to be able to experience this initiation into the team. Some freshmen have said singing a solo in front of their teammates is worse than shooting free throws in front of thousands of screaming fans.

That Christmas was the last one for four wonderful young men. Listening to Doc, Dou, Chris, and Daymeon, who really have very good voices, was poignant. This was the first of many last times with these seniors who had made Auburn basketball so much fun over the last four years.

We all left Puerto Rico for a short Christmas break. It was our family's first Christmas without Carolyn's brother, John Alan, and without my dad. The writer of Ecclesiastes had much insight into the human condition—into our condition. We all took time to remember and to grieve the loss of good times with our brother and father. We also celebrated and anticipated the new life—Chryssa and Tony's expected baby. Life goes on, waxing and waning, with times for everything under heaven.

After Christmas, we completed our preconference schedule with wins over Stony Brook and Southern Mississippi, a daunting defensive team. In all of our preconference games, there were not a lot of blowouts. Some people were asking, "What is wrong with the Auburn Tigers?"—even though we were entering conference play with a 12-1 record and ranked fourth in the country. I felt honestly that we had played one of our toughest preconference schedules and were prepared by it for SEC play.

We began our defense of the SEC title with a win over the Georgia Bulldogs. That game was Daymeon Fishback's first test in Bryant Smith's role as defender of an opponent's best perimeter player. Daymeon held D.A. Layne, who came in averaging 18 points per game, to 12 points on 4-of-13 shooting. I was happy for Daymeon because he was under a lot of pressure to fill the defensive void left by Bryant's graduation. Our half-court defense became our team's biggest strength. For most of the season Auburn led the nation in field-goal percentage defense, an indicator of the effectiveness of our half-court defense.

Next on our schedule was Kentucky at Beard-Eaves. Auburn had not beaten Kentucky at basketball in 10 years. For the first time in the season, the feeling of the year before returned. Kentucky was a hurdle that had not been jumped. The players were loose, not having the burden of being hunted. The coliseum was at a fever pitch, filled with fans who wanted a win, but were not necessarily expecting one. The nationally televised game was the first that Dick Vitale had called from Auburn. He left, expressing to the nation that the Auburn team was one of the best in the country and that the Cliff Dwellers were one of the most impressive student sections he had ever seen. In fact, the Cliff Dwellers have been named by *ESPN The Magazine* one the four best student sections in the United States with Duke, Stanford, and Michigan State, a great statement for a basketball program that had drawn only 1,000 people in its season opener six years before.

The Kentucky game was a major win in a great atmosphere. Doc Robinson hit a tie-breaking three-pointer with 28 seconds to play, Scott Pohlman added two free throws, and Chris Porter had his fifth double-double (22 points and 13 rebounds) in one of the best games of the 2000 NCAA basketball season. That win marked the first time Auburn had beaten a ranked team it was expected to beat. Auburn had beaten ranked teams before, but always as upsets.

Our first SEC road trip was to Mississippi State University. We won a low-scoring affair, keyed by an unexpected 3 pointer from Chris Porter. For the second game in a row, Doc Robinson hit a tie-breaking three-pointer late in the game.

The trip to Starkville was the beginning of a four-game series in nine days, three of them on the road. Any road win is a good one, especially since we were seeing how rough the road in the SEC was going to be in the 2000 season. Teams we played would have their biggest, rowdiest crowds; their players would be as excited and rowdy. It was actually very exciting for us, too.

From Starkville, we returned to Beard-Eaves for the only home game in this tough stretch. The University of South Carolina was coming in, just off an overtime loss to a very good Syracuse team. Led by Pohlman's nineteen points and Robinson's twelve points, eight assists and only *one* turnover, we won our fourth SEC game.

For whatever reason, the AU-Ole Miss game has always been a very competitive contest. The next game, at Oxford, was typical. The close battle was one of the best games of the SEC season. Players from both teams made wonderful plays. Doc made shots, countered by those of Marcus Hicks. Every player on both sides gave the game his best effort. The game went into overtime, and Ole Miss handed us our first conference loss, 79-77. In the loss, I felt the players had been true to all of the worn-out adages we coaches use—"giving all they had," "leaving nothing on the court." It is true, they played well.

We would then be faced with the toughest task thus far— our going to the University of Tennessee with little time to prepare and Tennessee's having had a week to prepare after a confidence-building win at Florida. In Knoxville, about 20,000 fans, the biggest crowd for men's basketball that season, were hungry. We were beginning to get a taste of what teams with a strong basketball tradition, such as Kentucky, Duke, and

North Carolina, experience every game of every year. In that game, unfortunately, we had no legs, and Tennessee had a great team. We lost.

We were then 4-2 in conference play and facing a critical three-game home stand. It was obvious that the SEC champion was going to have to win at home and hope to try to steal wins on the road.

We faced Mississippi State in the first of these critical home games; it was our second time to play each other in less than two weeks. Chris Porter scored a game-high 20 points, and the bench, especially Reggie Sharp, Mack McGadney, and David Hamilton, demonstrated its strength. We shot well from three-point range and had 22 points off MSU turnovers in our eighth straight win over the Mississippi State Bulldogs.

The next big home game was against our arch rival, the University of Alabama. Behind a 21-2 run with about 15 minutes to go in the game, we won our fourth game in a row against the Crimson Tide. Our fans seemed a little flat for this game—I think because we had beaten 'Bama by an average of over 30 points in the three games we had played the year before. Alabama was a vastly improved team, and our game was a tight contest for the first half. It was still a satisfying win, even though it was not a 40- or 50-point win and was only a 14-point win!

David Hamilton's decision to leave the team because of his grandfather's death came after the Alabama game. David's dealing with this fourth death in his family in one year was affecting his performance and his ability to focus on the game and to respond to the desires I had for him. I don't know of an individual who has been through more: breaking his leg; losing his mother to a stroke; losing two cousins in a senseless murder; and then losing his mother's father. He grew a lot in his year and a half at Auburn, but he faced more than any mature person should have to deal with. There are many people in Auburn who loved David and wanted to be family for him and who now wish him well, including me. Of much less importance was that his leaving diminished our depth in the post position.

When the Razorbacks come to Auburn, it always creates a high level of interest. The 2000 Arkansas game was no different, especially as it relates to me personally. It brought in many friends and family from the past. The Daughtry cousins, my dad's sister's children, came from parts of Florida and Alabama. Friends came from South Carolina; Jack, Jason, and Susan Green from Myrtle Beach; and Dwight Rainey, associate athletic director at Clemson University. Morgan Ashurst, who had been the team physician for South Alabama, and his son came from Mobile.

After the game, we invited everybody over for some good seafood, including Apalachicola oysters that Carolyn's sister and brother-in-law, Mary Beth and Harry Frank, had brought from the Florida coast.

Every one of the 40 or 50 people at the house was a friend of ours from the past, but not necessarily known by each other. We have at least one crazy friend, Ben Main, who had come with Ginger, his wife, and other good friends, the Jimmy Weatherses, to visit after the game before heading home to Union Springs, Alabama, and Niceville, Florida. Ben made himself comfortable, filled his plate with crab and oyster appetizers, and joined Harry and Jack and Jason, whom he did not know, in the living room. There were some moments of discomfort when nobody introduced himself, and then Ben nonchalantly said, "This is great food the Smiths are serving, isn't it?" Harry and Jack looked at each other and experienced another moment of discomfort but didn't know what to say. Again, Ben, without cracking a smile, said, "This is a great home the Smiths have, isn't it?" Finally Harry, protectively, said, "This is not the Smiths' house!" About that time, Ginger walked in and told Ben to "quit bothering these folks," and finally introduced everybody. For a long time, we will laugh about how Ben caused some extra excitement that day.

The University of Arkansas had already caused its own kind of excitement. With its usual flashing three-point barrage, Arkansas gave a fine performance against our half-court defense. They were virtually unstoppable in the first half and went into halftime leading by five points. At halftime we discussed how Arkansas would have a difficult time continuing this barrage—if we extended our defense two steps beyond the three-point line and committed ourselves to very little help on defense; essentially, each man would play one-on-one basketball. In the second half, spurred by the emotion of the crowd, we held Arkansas to an amazing 16-point scoring effort. It was our best half of defense this year.

The Arkansas win (73-55) finalized that home stand, and we opened the second half of the conference season with a record of 7-2.

LSU had added two guards to their staring lineup of Stromile Swift, Jabari Smith, and Brian Beshara and had already demonstrated their improvement by decisively defeating Oklahoma State and Arizona. The Bayou Bengals were posing the biggest threat to our repeating as West Division SEC champions. These LSU starters scored all but six points in an 83-68 victory before a sold-out, wild and crazy crowd of

14,986 in the Maravich Assembly Center. Chris Porter was plagued by fouls, but Mack McGadney came off the bench to score 19 points, and Doc Robinson scored 17.

Each conference team had two open dates in the 2000 season. Our first open date occurred before the season started; therefore, our first real break came after the LSU game while we were preparing for Vanderbilt. We would have this time to gather our legs and plan for the game.

Vanderbilt is always one of the toughest places to play, and the Commodores were having a surprisingly good season and were ranked No. 24 in the nation. We did have lots of bounce and were very active. We had the best offensive game of the year and outscored an offensive-minded team. This was a huge win against a ranked opponent and helped us keep even with the four other SEC leaders.

At 8-3 in conference play, we then faced rugged Ole Miss. In a close battle, Reggie Sharp, a native of Shannon, Mississippi, scored five points in the final minute and a half of the game to help give us a hard-fought 75-72 victory. There were 12 ties and 14 lead changes; no fan, player, or coach had a chance to relax in that game.

As we prepared for our trip to Tuscaloosa to play the University of Alabama again, doctors discovered a meniscus cyst on the knee of Daymeon Fishback and judged him doubtful for the game. He was not able to practice and spent Tuesday morning before the game having the cyst drained by our medical team in Birmingham. At game time, Daymeon wanted to try to play; according to doctors he was at about 50-60 percent of playing condition.

Nine minutes into the Alabama game, Mamadou N'Diaye sprained the medial collateral ligament in his left knee. He was out for the rest of the game and would need 10 to 14 days to recover. Despite Dou's being out and Fishback's being limited, the heart of our team refused to die. Scott Pohlman hit a layup for a 64-63 lead with a minute left. Rod Grizzard, who scored 25 points in the game, hit a three-pointer with 52 seconds left. Scott and Doc missed from three-point range, and we lost to Alabama after four straight victories. Their fans showed their joy at beating us by storming the court and cutting the nets down.

Now 9-4, we headed to Gainesville, Florida, for a Sunday CBS-televised game against the Gators. With the events of the week, we were knotted with four other teams at the top of the conference. We had three games left and felt we controlled our own destiny.

On Saturday I was blindsided by hearing that Chris Porter had had illegal contact with a so-called agent. I felt as though a bucket of iced Gatorade had been dumped on me—but it certainly did not feel like a victory celebration. The Auburn Athletic Department and SEC representatives requested that Chris be taken out of the Florida game and flown back to Auburn.

At the pregame breakfast the next morning, I told the team of Chris' departure. With no practice time without Chris Porter, we took the floor for a noon contest. We were drilled by Florida.

We had to then go back to Auburn to prepare for our last home game—against LSU. Instead of focusing on the SEC lead, we were forced to focus on the change in Chris Porter's status. Monday's practice was filled with reporters and photographers. I did not have the players' total attention, understandably, but I was aggressive in my approach to fighting to try to win the SEC West. Our staff made practices strenuous to try to get the players' minds on LSU and off Chris Porter.

Having only two days of practice to create a change in the chemistry of our offense, we moved toward a perimeter offense. Mack McGadney played Chris' position, but we allowed him to move outside more. We had to virtually eliminate the press from our defense because of our lack of depth.

That last home game was Senior Night. The three seniors in uniform and Chris Porter were honored in an emotional ceremony that included these players and their families, Governor Seigelman, and an overflow crowd. The Auburn Athletic Department staff, particularly Alan Thomas, Chuck Gallina, and Jacob Ridenhour, orchestrated a beautiful audio-visual tribute to these players. Auburn fans in attendance and not, recognized and appreciated what these seniors had accomplished for Auburn University's basketball program. When these seniors entered the program, Auburn basketball was not rich in tradition, was not high profile. Attendance was meager. Yet, in the end, this senior class would become the winningest class in school history with 85 wins in their four years of play. They won the Southeastern Conference championship for only the second time in school history. They were ranked in the top 25 for every week of their last two conference seasons. In their final season, Auburn sold out all of its 10,500 basketball season tickets for the first time in history. Most important, these seniors were on target to graduate by the end of the summer after their last semester of eligibility. This was a tremendous group of young men who took a blue-collar approach to becoming a highly acclaimed Auburn basketball team. They showed much character: they wanted success on the court, in the classroom, in life.

In this SEC showdown with LSU, we had a battle that could have gone either way. In the end, LSU prevailed 55-53, claimed the West title, and ended our 30-game home winning streak.

With the loss of Chris Porter, many people gave up hope for this team. But I could see a chemistry developing and felt a new team could be successful, even though the schedule was tough. With just two days' practice, the team had improved immensely, going from a devastating loss at Florida to a two-point loss to LSU. I was proud of the team and hopeful.

The last game of the 2000 season was another challenging game—Senior Day at Arkansas—the third year in a row that we had faced Arkansas on their Senior Day. Arkansas won this tight game, handing us our third loss in a row without Chris.

Instead of being discouraged, I was encouraged. I told the team after the Arkansas game, "We are very close. In spite of what people are writing about how the season is over, in spite of the criticism, we must continue to do what we are doing because we are very close to having something positive happen to us." Again, I emphasized for them and for me that they were winners—outscored by their opponent, but not losers—winners in the best sense of that word.

Our opening-round opponent in the SEC Tournament was Florida, which had beaten us by about 30 points less than two weeks before. On Monday before the game, Chris was ruled ineligible by the NCAA. The appeals process would conclude on Friday, three hours before the Florida game.

After the Monday ruling of Chris' ineligibility, we began on Tuesday preparing for the SEC Tournament. We had three excellent practices before leaving for Atlanta on Thursday. At three o'clock on Friday afternoon, Chris Porter's appeal hearing was held and his appeal was denied.

Chris Porter's chapter as an Auburn player was closed, ending unhappily, almost tragically. The unhappiness is in direct proportion to the level of play and excitement he brought to Auburn basketball. He chose to come to Auburn because he loves the school, and chose to return to Auburn for his senior year because he wanted to continue to improve his play, because he loves Auburn, and because he wanted to get as close to graduating as he could. He never lost a game in Beard-Eaves Memorial Coliseum. He represented Auburn well as 1999 SEC Player of the Year. The joy he had skying for rebounds, making monster dunks that were on everybody's highlight features, running the court with arms raised in exhilaration or defense, stealing balls on defense—this joy is what I want to remember and emphasize.

Without Chris Porter, no one expected the result against Florida to be positive—except this Auburn team and a few AU fans. This team took on the highly regarded Florida Gators and, in an emotionally charged game, was led by Daymeon Fishback, who had the best game of his career. He scored the first double-double of his college career with a season-high 21 points and career-high 14 rebounds. We believed from start to finish that we could beat the Gators, and we did, 78-70.

Our next round's opponent was the University of South Carolina, which had barely lost to us at Auburn, had finished the regular season strong, and had upset Tennessee the night before. In a game that had 16 lead changes and that was forced into overtime, Auburn won, led by Mamadou's eighth double-double of the season (14 points and 10 rebounds) and Doc's 14 points.

In an unlikely SEC Tournament final round, we faced Arkansas, which had soundly defeated Georgia, Kentucky, and LSU to get to the Sunday game. The Razorback fans are always in force at the SEC Tournament. The Auburn faithful cruised up I-85 in force also. Approximately 20,000 fans in the Georgia Dome watched one of the hardest-fought finals games ever played. Both teams had played a lot of basketball, but they played this game with little sign of fatigue.

In another seesaw battle for us, Arkansas, led by freshman sensation Joe Johnson and the backcourt duo of Ted Gibson and Brandon Dean, offset the tremendous play of Mack McGadney, Mamadou N'Diaye, and Jay Heard—and the entire Auburn team—to win the SEC Tournament championship.

This Auburn team demonstrated their resiliency, determination, and grit by rebounding from the loss of Chris Porter to advance to the SEC Tournament final round for the first time since 1985. I am extremely proud of this group and especially for the seniors.

Following the game, we took the short trip back to Auburn to watch the NCAA Tournament selection show. We found out that we opened against Creighton, champion of the Missouri Valley Conference, in Minneapolis in the Midwest Regionals. This bracket was the toughest of them all, in my opinion.

Having played one of the last games of conference tournament play and needing to prepare for one of the first games of the NCAA Tournament, we took Monday for the players to rest their legs and for the coaches to watch film. We practiced and traveled on Tuesday. On Wednesday we had a short practice and many media interviews at the Metrodome in Minneapolis. I announced that Jimbo Tolbert, a manager for the team, would dress for the NCAA Tournament as a player. Jimbo had practiced with us at times when we needed him—before Marquis and Jamison joined the team and when Fish and Dou were injured. I wanted to reward his contribution.

In our 11:30 a.m. game on Thursday, I felt that we would have the advantage of having played several noon games through the season and that we needed to wield that advantage in the first half. Creighton had played their tournament the week before the SEC Tournament and had the advantage of that extra rest. They would probably wield that advantage in the second half.

Our first half against Creighton was our best overall (offensive and defensive) first half all season. We hit a majority of our shots and held the No. 2 three-point shooting team in the nation to just 25 points. We held a 40-25 advantage at halftime.

Creighton mounted a furious comeback in the second half. But behind the play of Fishback, N'Diaye, and McGadney, we were able to secure a seemingly adequate lead of nine points with 12 seconds left in the game. I was about to learn the truth of Yogi Berra's saying, "It ain't over 'til it's over." In a move to reward Jimbo Tolbert for his contributions, I inserted him into the game. Creighton inbounded the ball and hit a trey with seven seconds left to cut the lead to six points. Jimbo bounced the inbounds pass off Doc Robinson's leg, and the ball went out of bounds. I pulled Jimbo, and Creighton made another three-pointer with three seconds left. Fishback then overthrew a full court pass to N'Diaye, who missed the ball in order to avoid crashing into a photographer on the end line. Creighton got the ball under their own basket with three seconds to play.

Their last second three point try was blocked by N'Diaye.

Much has been made about Jimbo's contribution to Creighton's near win. But two treys were scored over our defense, and Fishback and Mamadou's fumbled pass contributed to the events. I'm glad we won, because I would have been considered a goat for giving a wonderful reward to a wonderful young man.

The No. 2 seed, Iowa State, led by Marcus Fizer (considered by many to be the best collegiate player), was our next opponent. Also, we faced them three and a half hours from their campus. Five hundred staunch Auburn supporters faced about 20,000 Iowa State Cyclones.

The key for us was to devise a plan to stop Marcus Fizer. Our plan was to alternate defenses with constant double teams on Fizer coming from different directions. It worked to perfection in the first half and for eight minutes in the second half. We were double-teaming many times off Jamaal Tinsley, their point guard, who had come into the game shooting 18 percent from the three point arc. At the twelve-minute mark, he hit the first of two straight three-point shots that we didn't answer. Those shots gave ISU their biggest lead, and we never recovered. ISU broke open a close game and advanced to the Sweet Sixteen.

The collegiate careers of our seniors had come to a close. As the team approached the dressing room, I asked everyone else to let the seniors and me go in together, alone. I told them that, even in the disappointment of the moment, Auburn University and I appreciated the wonderful way they had been Auburn Tigers. We hugged, cried, and realized that we had all been blessed by the experience of the last four years.

CHAPTER TWENTY

Dealing With Agents

Chris Porter's last season at Auburn ended unhappily. He and all of us associated with Auburn basketball were hoping that the 2000 season would be not just good, but great. Chris wanted to demonstrate his abilities for NBA scouts and help Auburn attain even greater heights than had been reached in 1999. And the NBA scouts who attended our games were impressed with his athletic skills. I was particularly impressed with Chris' determination to overcome obstacles with class. He entered team practice with energy and enthusiasm. He spent many extra hours working on his own offensive skills. He responded to double teams with patience. He handled taunts from other teams with good humor. Chris Porter was and is an asset to Auburn basketball.

About two weeks before our game against Florida, Chris called me when I was in Montgomery to film our weekly television show, asking to meet with me. I knew something must be askew for him to chase me down while I was out of Auburn. He told me then that his mother needed money to be able to stay in the house that had belonged to her mother.

My first reaction was that I wanted to help. I would have loved to just give him the money that he needed or help him arrange a loan. A coach in many ways functions as a father for his players, but responding to financial need is not an option for the coach/father figure. The consequence of helping someone you really care about in this situation is that the program is jeopardized.

My advice to Chris was to try to handle the situation within his family. I told him that he would be soon free of this kind of problem. In two months he would have had few worries about money. I suggested that he go to his family and investigate appropriate ways to handle the problem—arrange a loan or get legal advice. In a few days, Chris seemed to be free of the worry.

On the Saturday before the Florida game, I found out how he had handled the problem, why he seemed to be free of worry. It seems so illogical and foolish to many people that Chris would have made this decision. There were so many other options open to him, not to mention the fact that in just weeks he was probably going to be able to build his mother a new house. The dilemma is that very rarely do people use logic and wisdom in stressful situations, especially when there is force working to tempt a person to take an easy way out. The stressful situation for Chris was that he felt he needed money for his family. The temptation came in the offer of money from a person who said he was a coach.

When Chris and I discussed the allegations, I asked him to tell the truth. In these circumstances, Chris could have put the burden of proof on the investigators. I encouraged him to cooperate. Chris met with Auburn and SEC officials and was pronounced ineligible for accepting $2,500 from a person who was associated with an agent. Auburn worked through an appeals process, requesting that Chris be reinstated after four games, the number of games since he had received the money. Chris would never play for Auburn again.

In this situation, the NCAA was faced with the task of solving the problem of agents by either insisting on zero tolerance of player-agent contact or offering leniency to someone who aided the investigation.

There are currently three major issues facing NCAA institutions that relate to players' amateur status and the purity of athletic competition. Those issues involve agents, gambling, and AAU basketball. Virtually all players come into our programs having played AAU basketball, traveling all over the United States in spring and summer while college and professional coaches evaluate their performance. With recent rulings involving gifts from AAU coaches to players, every Division I team is probably playing with ineligible players—technically.

The pervasive penchant Americans have for gambling on college athletic events is another danger facing NCAA institutions. If we think we do not have to be diligent in preventing our players from betting on games and shaving points, all we have to do is look at the situation at Northwestern. If it can happen at an institution like Northwestern, it can happen anywhere.

Not all agents are unethical. In fact, agents are necessary for athletes who do not have the legal or business acumen to negotiate contracts. They know the market and they know the language of agreements. I have an agent because I need help when it comes to discussing something other than x's and o's.

Most agents are very honorable and effective. But for as long as I have been a Division I coach, I have had to battle overeager and shady sports agents beginning at South Alabama, continuing at Clemson, and now at Auburn.

On the first day of classes one year at Clemson, one of my players who is a current NBA player was rooming with a player who eventually played NBA ball also. He called from a secluded telephone to whisper that an agent had gotten into their room! I told him to arrange a meeting with this agent in the parking lot of the athletic office complex. The athletic director and I watched from our offices as the meeting developed. I, as emphatically as I could, confronted the agent and told him to stay off our campus forever.

Our staff has an ongoing strategy for helping our players avoid contact with agents before their amateur status expires. I meet personally with each player and discuss the implications and dangers. We hold seminars for all athletes, and they are led by experts. We change players' names on hotel rosters. At LSU in the 2000 season, because of concern over agents, we had managers and administrative staff posted outside of players' rooms.

All of these issues are problems that can best be handled with the cooperation of players—players whose financial needs may be great. I encouraged Chris to be as candid and honest as he could be in order to give SEC and NCAA investigators an enhanced understanding of some of the methods of the leeches who prey on athletes they think will eventually make money, much money, for them. These spurious "agents," unlike the authentic agents, do not have the best interests of the athlete as their motivation. They are selfish and self-serving and work surreptitiously, ignoring rules.

We in collegiate athletics need the information that the victimized student-athlete can give us. The NCAA, on the other hand, feels that giving too many breaks to these affected athletes will void the deterrence that law and punishment are supposed to create. Chris did need to be punished for his mistake. The national headlines were excruciatingly painful. Watching his teammates lose three games in a row was enough to make him cry. I was hoping that that much punishment and his cooperation would warrant some leniency on the part of NCAA officials. I know that it will be difficult to elicit cooperation from the next victim. We are faced with a daunting problem. Meshing intolerance with appreciation of cooperation is a challenge.

Chapter Twenty-One

Doing It My Way

I've always been the underdog. I was raised an underdog. I had to work watermelon fields. I had to work to earn spending money. I didn't belong to the country club, but I would play golf anyway. Maybe that's why I seem to have been drawn to basketball programs that are underdogs.

Going through grade school, there always seemed to be a bully. There would always be that guy who would test me. I can remember Mama giving me recess money. There was one guy who was a couple of years older. He said, "How much recess money you got?" It might have been 15 cents, and he tried to take it. If I'd given it to him, he would have kept coming back for more. He got it that first day and whipped my rear end, but he didn't come back for my recess money anymore. That ol' boy whipped my fanny, but he didn't get my 15 cents without having a scrap. I lost, but in a sense I won. He didn't come back to me for money, because he knew he was going to have to scrap. This was a part of growing up. I was not going to go down easy as an underdog.

I was an underdog, and I've always liked taking over the underdog basketball program. To succeed, I had to get players to play hard and believe in themselves. They also had to have support, so I had to get the fans behind the program.

I've always said that if I have the greatest band, the best popcorn, the prettiest cheerleaders, and play the game of basketball in a slow style, I won't get the fans. It's like being on stage. You can have the look, you can have the flair, you can have all that; but if the song isn't right, people aren't coming back. If I had developed a slowdown philosophy at home, I don't think it would have brought fans.

From the start of my career, I wanted an up-tempo game. There are three things a player can do with the basketball: he can dribble it, pass it, or shoot it. I wanted my team to learn to execute those fundamentals as quickly as they possibly could.

Stressing those fundamentals, I want an up-tempo, fast-breaking-style game on offense trying to beat the opponent down the floor for a score. On defense, I want the press to create havoc for the opponent. This style enables us to be up-tempo on both ends of the floor. I like it. Players like it. Fans like it.

When I started coaching in junior high school, I pressed on defense and ran on offense. I have pressed and run the fast break from day one, and 31 years later I'm still pressing. By the 1973-74 season, Charles Fishback's team at Cumberland led the nation in scoring, averaging 105 points a game without the three-point shot and without the shot clock with this run-and-press philosophy.

I want players who are quick, players who are athletic but who can execute fundamentals. I will allow them freedom on offense as long as they are protecting the ball and taking good shots. On defense they must play hard. Every team member can play hard. I do these things and make it fun for the players. I have always been considered a player's coach.

I want the players to feel free. I want them to have confidence. Their God-given ability is there. If it were out of control, I'd rather tone it down than have to rev it up!

One of the things I'm proudest of in my career is the way our players have performed in the classroom.

At Cumberland, Carolyn would bring players over to our house for tutoring sessions. She continued this practice during the South Alabama years, and my other coaches would also try to provide tutorial help. At Cumberland, it worked efficiently. It didn't work in all cases at South Alabama. By the time we arrived at Clemson, an academic tutoring program was in place. Clemson had the finances to support tutoring.

When I took the Auburn job, the one point I tried to emphasize academically was to encourage every athlete who had ever played here to return to work on completing a degree.

When I entered coaching, I felt that a lot of players were being used. Players had to travel and miss classes for their school. Many colleges could not afford tutors, so players were on their own time to play ball and miss classes on road trips, yet they were expected to make good grades.

I can tell you that my proudest achievement at Auburn has been that all the players who have stayed through this program, even the ones I inherited, have graduated. There have been some dismissals and some have left, but the players who have stayed here have all graduated. Plus, players from the past have come back and graduated.

For instance, Myles Patrick, who was an NBA player, came back, but he thought trying to make it through school would put him in financial straits. I asked a bank to lend him the money to see him through the rough times. The day he graduated, I paid the note off personally. I was proud of him. That was my gift to him for graduating.

Earl Banks came back and graduated. Bobby Cattage has done the same. These were proud moments. Chuck Person, who has millions of dollars, has come back to school. Chuck is one of the finest people I've ever known; he's a guy everyone likes to see make it. He loves Auburn. In the summertime, he's the one athlete who comes back and plays with our players, continually showing them how an NBA player plays.

Another proud moment for me has been to watch the elements of the game outside the court blossom at each institution, especially connecting students with their team. I love seeing the band perform at games with enthusiasm. I have enjoyed reaching out to fraternities to get them involved, going to see them personally, then seeing them come out and rally behind us. I have enjoyed the entertainment of the dance teams, the yells from the cheerleaders trying to encourage our fans to support our team.

Students are special, and I have always had the philosophy that if I reach out to them, they will support us. For example, for one game at South Alabama, I had fliers placed on every car on campus with my signature. The flier stated, "Our team needs you at tonight's game versus (whoever the opponent was). Please come. Your Coach, Cliff Ellis." It worked.

I have always enjoyed relating to students. When I wondered where I could meet the most of them, I decided to find out where they ate lunch. I took a microphone, asked them to come to the game, and told them we needed them. If a coach ever shakes their hands, they'll remember it, and they will come. It multiplies, and the coach has made them a part. They've bought into the program.

Once they come to the game, they need to know they are going to have a good time. It needs to become the thing to do on campus. The team needs to win. That's the most important thing of all, but, again, the extra-game aspects must be exciting and fun.

Like any other coach, I want to win a national championship, but I am not going to allow myself to obsess about it. Only a select few can ever attain this ultimate goal, as there is only one championship per year. And the champion team not only has to be talented, it has to be fortunate. Each year the national champion has been crowned, fortune has looked favorably on it. For example, Jim Valvano's team earned a championship by tapping in an air ball at the buzzer.

In our drive in 1999 for a national championship, in the late stages, our best player had a rebound, with Bryant Smith ahead for an open layup. However, the ball was fumbled, Ohio State got the ball, was fouled, and scored. It was the play of the game. Fortune was not with us in this game.

I felt that in the 1999 championship game, Duke was the better team, not UConn. However, in that one game, UConn put it all together and did everything right; Duke seemingly had misfortune all the way.

What is important when our team plays that final game and when I feel the proudest is when I know that the team has given everything it has in the season and has been the best it could be and has had fun doing it.

Basketball players are a part of my family. I teach them to be the best they can be on the court and off the court. I want that 17- or 18-year-old young man who enters my program to be an adult when he leaves, which is usually around the age of 22. What I teach my own children, I teach my players. At the end of each season, national championship or not, I want my players to have grown physically, mentally, emotionally, socially, and spiritually.

My basketball team is an extension of my family. Therefore, my own family plays a major role in not only my success, but also the success of these young men.

I adore my wife and children. Carolyn and I were married in 1969 after my first year of coaching. In 30 years of coaching, she has seen the thrill of victory and the agony of defeat. Carolyn has been most supportive, and without her support, I would not have achieved the successes that have come my way. Every time we have had to move to another school and uproot our family, she has never wavered, and with every move, she has acknowledged it was the right thing for us to do. If my team loses a tough game, she'll be the first to console me.

Carolyn has raised our children, teaching them values that are everlasting. The coaching profession has uprooted our family from Florida to Tennessee to Mobile to Clemson and to Auburn. She has made sure the moves went smoothly for each of us, especially helping our kids make their new adjustments.

Carolyn is a teacher not only with family, but in the classroom as well. Students love her classes. She enjoys teaching more than anything, and her students are the luckiest in the world to have her. Her teaching spans from local schools to Sunday school at First Baptist Church. She also serves as deacon. You will not find many women deacons in Baptist churches, but her teachings and witnessing have been profound; she has been accepted in spite of her sex. Carolyn has traveled abroad on mission trips to teach in countries such as Albania and Honduras—countries that have been through much suffering and pain in recent years.

Carolyn spreads her teaching to the community, joining clubs like Rotary and the Junior League and gives these clubs her time and energy.

Carolyn is the ultimate coach's wife: radiant, beautiful, caring, consoling, cheering, understanding, sharing, and loving. I am glad that she has ridden shotgun with me the last 30 years of my coaching.

Though I had guilt about uprooting family and being gone a lot through travels to games, recruiting, or speaking, I have always tried to manage quality time with my kids. Quality time is at least as important as quantity. Each day that we are together at home, even if it's a short period, I try to spend some quality time with each member of the family, focusing on them and asking how each of them is doing. I will try to say something positive to them each day. I want to hear about their day and the events that took place and hopefully be able to praise them.

Throughout my coaching career, our family has been loving and caring with each other. As I tell my basketball team, we can't be successful unless we are together; my family has been together. I thank God for this. I have been blessed.

There's no question that recruiting is the backbone of any successful college program. Coaches just have to approach it differently at different schools.

If a coach is at a traditional school like Duke, he will get certain players who automatically want to go there. I have always coached and recruited at the nontraditional schools. I have to be realistic enough to know I am not going to get the top 50 player when I first arrive. I have to find the guy who wants to be top 50 and is close to being top 50. I find this type and get them to play like they are possessed. I have to demand it. I have to get them to believe that they can be successful and can be champions. Talent usually takes over in a game, but upsets can be pulled. The kid who wants to get there, the kid who wasn't a *Parade* All-American and wants to bust his butt and achieve is what I call a blue-collar player.

When I put the blue-collar kid on the floor and have success, then that top 50, *Parade* All-American-type will see this, and I hopefully can convince him that, with his ability, the highest accomplishments can be achieved if he wears our uniform.

In my first year at Auburn, our group of blue-collar workers upset No. 4 Arkansas. Games like this opened the eyes of people like Doc Robinson and Daymeon Fishback, who were top 50 players.

Recruiting is the backbone, but those first teams I put on the floor paved the way to further successful recruiting. When a recruit sees an up-tempo game, young men playing hard, and a team having some degree of success, it opens up many doors.

Another thing that is important is convincing the media to buy into the program. I've always, for the most part, enjoyed the media. Having written a couple of books, having a wife who is an English teacher, I can appreciate journalism to a degree. Through the years, I have seen good coaches and bad coaches, and I have seen good press and bad press. I usually have had a good relationship with most of them.

In Mobile, Ben Nolan, sportswriter for the *Mobile Press-Register,* was one of my best friends. When I went to Mobile, South Alabama basketball was third or fourth sports-page news. I had to get it to the front page. It took me a while to get Dennis Smitherman, sports editor, to buy in. He didn't believe the University of South Alabama could thrive in basketball. Ben Nolan did. I needed the Mobile paper. This paper was my best market. People weren't coming from Birmingham or Montgomery to see South Alabama play—Mobilians were.

In going from Mobile to ACC territory, I met wonderful people from the media. Dan Foster of *The Greenville News* is an excellent writer and good friend. Bill Brill and Ron Green from Charlotte, and John Feinstein from the *Washington Post* are all good writers whom I consider friends. I remember one night John was coming to my house with Lefty Driesell, who was doing TV. Carolyn and I sat down with them, and we all told a lot of tales that night. John has become one of my favorite authors.

There are a lot of great writers who cover Auburn. Unlike the situation at South Alabama, Auburn is going to be front-page news. I have tried to be open and honest with the media.

In judging media, I believe in responsible journalism, and the key word is *fair*. Through the years, the people in the media I have respected the most are the ones who have been responsible and fair in their reporting.

I have always had an appreciation for most of the media. There have been some who I have not been comfortable with, but that's part of the business.

I have to sell my program, and it's virtually impossible without good media coverage. For the most part, the coverage and support have been great.

I've done a lot of things some people seem to find interesting—music, of course being one. Cooking is another.

I've always said the next book I write will be about cooking. I have recipes that go back, I don't know how many years. It all started with my mama, grandma, and my family. What great cooks they were! Mama and Big Mama could just flat cook. I learned to love their food because they were always doing such special things in the kitchen. Their cooking was always a big part of what we did on Thanksgiving, birthdays, Christmas, Sunday dinner, and any special event. We didn't have much money, but when we sat down at the table, it was an event. I loved it.

Cooking has been a getaway for me during my years in coaching. It has helped me cope with the pressures. At the same time it was an escape from coaching, allowing me to forget for a while plays and players, it also involved some of the same skills—creating, learning from others, and entertaining. I started with the simple grilling of steaks, chicken, and seafood, but soon progressed to investigating foods I enjoyed in restaurants or I saw prepared on cooking shows by people like

Justin Wilson or Emeril Lagasse. I love sharing what I prepare with friends, turning a meal into an event.

One recipe that was suggested to me by a cooking show has been a hit at many get-togethers. In fact, I prepared this for about 50 people who had helped us prepare for Chryssa's wedding in Clemson.

Shrimp with Sweet Potatoes and
Red Pepper Sauce (serves six)

Season two pounds of peeled shrimp with salt and pepper. Sautée the shrimp in butter, without overcooking.

Prepare the sauce. Bring to boil 1 1/2 cups diced sweet red pepper, 1/2 cup sugar, 1/2 cup water, 1/2 cup white vinegar. Blend this sauce in blender, adding 2 tsp. Dijon mustard, 1/4 tsp. white pepper, salt. As blender runs, add one cup of olive oil.

Prepare the potatoes. Deep-fry three large julienned sweet potatoes at 350 degrees. When the potatoes float, they are done.

To serve, place 8-10 shrimp on a stack of potatoes. Drizzle the sauce around the potatoes and shrimp.

A family I would grow to love in Mobile had a seafood business. Mr. and Mrs. J. P. Bosarge taught me to love things I'd never thought I would taste—like crawfish. Mrs. Bosarge could make special Cajun sauces, and I would study her techniques. The couple became like family to me. They have both passed away now, and I do miss them, but their cooking legacy continues as I still try to cook like Mr. and Mrs. Bosarge when it comes to what I call "Cajun" recipes.

Crawfish Cliff

Wilt in butter 3 large chopped onions, 1 chopped green bell pepper, 1 chopped red bell pepper, and 1 stalk chopped celery. After this has wilted, sprinkle garlic powder liberally. Add 2 sixteen-ounce cans of tomatoes and 1 can of Ro-tel tomatoes and green chilies. Bring this to a boil and then simmer for about 5 minutes.

Add 2 lbs. cooked and cleaned crawfish tails. Add 1 cup white wine. Simmer for about an hour.

This may be served over rice or by itself.

Corn and Crab Bisque

Wilt in butter 2 chopped onions, 1 chopped green bell pepper, 1 stalk chopped celery, and 1/2 chopped red bell pepper. Add 2 cups water from cooking corn, 1 tsp. salt, 1 cup white wine, 2 cups shrimp stock, 1/2 tsp. thyme, 2 dashes Tabasco. Bring to a boil and then reduce to simmer.

While this is simmering, whisk in a white roux (1/4 cup oil, 1/4 cup flour). Continue simmering for five minutes. Add 3 1/2 cups whipping cream, 1 1/2 cups cooked corn millets, and 1 pound jumbo crabmeat. Just before serving, garnish with chopped green onion and parsley. Eat with French bread.

Some of my favorite recipes grow out of my love for hunting and fishing. The first time I knew cooking was truly fun and creative was when I came home from cast fishing with more mullet than I could fry or smoke and concocted a mullet stew that the family loved. Hunting for deer, dove, quail, turkey, or duck is great sport that I don't have a lot of time for, but when I do bag any of that game, I love to find good ways to cook it and share it with friends. This recipe is one that I got from Fred Chason, a friend from Port St. Joe, Florida, who loved to hunt in the panhandle of Florida, as well as in South Carolina, where we both ended up spending part of our lives.

Chason Venison

Cut 2 or 3 pounds of cubed venison into bite-sized pieces. Soak this in buttermilk for one hour. Drain the buttermilk off and season to taste with salt and pepper. Season liberally with garlic powder and Greek seasoning. Coat the meat with 2-3 heaping tablespoons of prepared mustard. Dredge the meat in flour and fry it. Do not simmer in gravy.

I cook for the team on some special occasions. I also have an annual dinner in the fall for the media who cover our program. A favorite of both these groups is deep fried turkey.

Deep Fried Turkey

Gather these ingredients: Lawrey's Seasoning Salt, garlic powder, onion salt, Worcestershire sauce, and Louisiana hot sauce. Rub all of this on a 12-15-pound turkey. Apply generously because when you cook it, a lot will wash off. Refrigerate the turkey with seasoning applied 24 hours before cooking.

Use enough peanut oil to cover the turkey, approximately four gallons. Cook in a deep pot 3 minutes per pound at 350 degrees.

Coaching is so intense and so demanding, I have to find ways to get away from it a little bit, and cooking helps. Another favorite pastime is going to the beach. This is the place I find most interesting.

In 1977, I bought our family a beach home in Panama City Beach, Florida. It has become a haven for me. I can relieve all tensions and stress at the beach. It is a place where I can totally relax. Each summer before a new season begins, this is the place I go to rejuvenate myself.

I love the white sands and emerald waters of the Gulf Coast. It feels wonderful to breathe the salt air in and go on a peaceful morning walk.

A great day for me is to get up in the morning and walk this beautiful beach, come in for a few minutes of rest, then go check the crab traps I have placed in the bay waters near my home. It is usually quiet and peaceful there, with an occasional mullet jumping through the sparkling water. I love to watch the seagulls and herons that fly above. I will bring the catch of crabs home for cooking. I love cooking crabs, boiling them or making delicious crab cakes with them. By this time, it is lunchtime; if tomato juice and mayonnaise don't drip down my arm while I eat, then it wasn't the ideal BLT. It's nap time by now, and Frank Sinatra is the music I usually choose to sleep by. After my nap, it's time to hit a bucket of range balls to keep my golf game from getting too rusty. As the sun sets, I will watch the breathtaking beauty of the sunset beyond the horizon like a crystal ball dropping into the water. Now it's time to cook a meal for family and friends; rarely are there fewer than 10 folks around the table. We eat and laugh and share our lives. Ten days of this, and I start to rejuvenate.

Sometimes I take the family to Mexico Beach and snorkel for scallops with my friend Al Cathey and his wife, Carol. This is our family's favorite outing. These succulent creatures from the sea are the sweetest little morsels to eat. I may also choose to fish in the fresh river waters with my friend Jimmy Weathers, Uncle Bill, Clay, or Randy. Occasionally a saltwater fishing trip with Gary Walsingham, Weathers, Terry Dubose, or other friends for red snapper and grouper will be on the docket. I would also be remiss if I did not mention that on many days, as the sun sets, I will be in the bay waters with the locals pitching my cast net for mullet. If caught and eaten on the same day, there is not a better fish to take from the gulf waters.

People find it interesting that I once raised ostriches. Really, it was just a hobby. Robert Trammell got me interested in it. Where I was raised is truly a farming community. Most people have cattle and horses, but I thought it would be interesting to have ostriches. It was something unique.

I could go to the ostrich farm. I could talk to the birds and they wouldn't talk back. They wouldn't tell me how bad a move it was that I made the night before. There is something about going to a farm. Those ostriches never asked me why we had so many turnovers or why we couldn't shoot or why I called some stupid play. It was relaxing, talking to those ostriches. Eventually, the novelty of it ran out, and we sold them.

Most people have probably never tried to eat ostrich meat. Grilled ostrich is very good meat with very low cholesterol and very low fat.

One true pleasure that I've enjoyed in recent years is going to Alaska to fish with Jimmy Rane and his brother Greg—Auburn alumni. They take the coaches of schools that their business supports to Alaska each year to fish.

Gene Stallings, Wimp Sanderson, Vince Dooley, Ray Goff, Larry Blakeney, Danny Ford, and Pat Dye are usually there. Greg is usually my fishing partner. Greg used to be a musician like me, so we like to get off on our boat and listen to good old rock-n-roll.

A lot of great stories have come from these fishing expeditions. To see a 200-pound halibut come out of those Alaskan waters is something I won't ever forget. I helped Greg pull a 210 lb. halibut into the boat once. I am glad that thing didn't strike my line, or it would probably have pulled me overboard.

Fishing the Alaskan waters offers a spectacular view. The waters are aglow, sparkling from the sunshine. The backdrop of the mountains with snow still on them is majestic. On a June day, high temperature around 70, eagles glide through the air. Fishing the waters with special people has built lasting friendships.

CHAPTER TWENTY-TWO

Adapting to the Game

Over the years, we've developed something of a reputation for turning out top-notch big men. It's something I've worked hard on. We've sent a number of them on to the NBA and to play professionally in Europe.

When I began coaching, I did not understand the big-man game. I understood the basics of defense. I understood the perimeter game. The area I felt the weakest at when I started coaching was teaching big men. I made it a point to overcome my deficiencies in this area. I read and studied everything I could.

In my studies, I found out how different coaches and people worked with their big men. In the public school and at Cumberland, there were no rules on practice, so I took our young men who were willing to work and tinkered with new ideas and began to develop my own philosophy of post play.

I would usually let my assistants work with the perimeter players, and I would work with the forwards and centers. Like anything else, the more you work at it, the better you get at it.

I've had big men who were willing to work hard and pay the price to improve. It's all come together.

I now have instructional videos for coaches that show our techniques of coaching big men. The videos have been very successful. They include *From Paint to the Pros* and *The Attitude of Rebounding.*

The first big guy I coached was on that junior varsity team at Niceville High School, a gangly 6'6" kid named Pat Lang. He had not played in junior high school.

Pat ended up receiving a scholarship to a small school in Florida. We went 19-1 in that junior varsity year, and he just got better and better as a post player. My confidence in coaching post play was growing.

Inside play has changed a lot in college basketball since I entered coaching. The biggest change is the advent of the three-point shot. Without the three-point shot, what a coach would do is try to find two shooters and play with as much power as he could get inside. If teams pressed, a coach would use his one and two guards to break the press.

Now, with the three-point shot, there are more three-guard offenses. Before the three-point shot, if a team shot 50 percent from the field, that team would usually win. With the advent of the three-point shot, if a teams hits a third of its three-point shots, that team is going to score as much as if it hit 50 percent of its two-pointers. That's why the third guard is much more frequently used now.

I see power forwards now who can make that shot. Horace Grant didn't shoot the three-point shot a lot, but he was capable of hitting it. Pretty much everybody but Mamadou N'diaye, our seven-foot center, had the green light at Auburn when we won the SEC championship.

Big guys are getting better and better every day. Big men are shooting the ball better and with range. The further out that a big man can shoot from, the bigger advantage he has.

I am extremely proud of my craft and the results of our efforts in the past with our big men. But they are the ones who have taken their God-given ability and allowed it to flourish. I have tried to be the vehicle to help them along the way.

Some people feel the basket should be raised because post players are getting taller. I never want to see the basket go to 12 feet, but realistically, the basket was placed at 10 feet when people weren't as big as they are today. The game was set up for someone 6-1, 6-2, 6-3 in the paint. That used to be a big man. Today, 6-8 is, by most standards, a small big man.

I think that soon we will see the lane widened in college basketball, as it is in the international game. Players have become so proficient near the basket on offense, and with the growing sizes over the years, they are able to get the ball in too close to the rim with too much ease.

Widening the lane would keep those 6-10, 6-11, 7-foot guys from just camping out under the basket. I don't know if the lane will be widened during my coaching tenure, but I do think if I live to be as old as my dad, I will see one day a three-point shot that is further out, a raised basket, and a widened lane.

The game is in a great state. Considering the three major sports, there is no sport that has grown in popularity like basketball has in the last 20 years. It's headed straight to the top because it's a great game. It's a great spectator sport.

Basketball, unlike all other sports, has become an international sport. Football is not going to make it internationally. It's never going to overtake soccer. Baseball is a great sport, but it hasn't become truly international, because it is just now being recognized as an Olympic sport. Basketball is popular worldwide. I think it's the best game there is.

The game is also in a constant state of change. The most successful coaches are those who adapt to the times. I've learned from many people, and I'm still learning.

I've been fortunate enough to go into other countries and participate against international teams. I've especially learned a lot as a coach playing against European teams.

I've always felt that European teams blocked out better than other international teams. It's been interesting to exchange ideas with their coaches. Learning from them has changed the way I teach and approach rebounding. For instance, I had always taught my players to pick and roll to set up for a rebound so that my player had his back to his opponent and his face to the basket. I noticed that European players execute a side block-out so that they end up with one arm on the opponent and a view of the basket. This move does decrease stability of position, but it also significantly increases the player's vision of the court. I have incorporated this method of rebounding into my own coaching style.

As the game has changed with time, I have changed. When I entered coaching, the college game was dominated by the power game. But when the three-point shot came in, I, as well as all coaches, had to adapt our thinking and make changes to incorporate this new wrinkle. If I had not been willing to change, the game would have passed me by. Coaches must change.

In the past, basketball coaches had football duties before basketball began. These days, basketball coaches must work year round. Even in the off-season, I work on my game—in addition to recruiting, promoting, running clinics and camps, I reflect. I take a look at where we are at that time. I ask what I have done in the past that can be incorporated with this next group. What can we do to get better? How can we go about it? My system has been evolving over the years, changing as I analyze and adapt. This daydreaming, talking to myself, has helped our teams.

Another reason to change is that other coaches watch our team play on television, and if we don't change even within the season, they will pretty much have us scouted. I have to throw something new in at times. I constantly go back to my files. Fortunately, I'm like a pastor who has been preaching for 30 years and has a lot of sermons. I can pull out an offense from 25 years ago that people haven't seen, and I know it will work. In coaching, change is necessary and fun.

Growing up in the South before integration, I never went to school with any African-Americans. The music business helped my coaching career in a lot of ways, and relating with various artists who happened to be African-American showed me how warm, caring, and talented all people can be. The color of a person's skin does not reflect his heart or character.

In the music business, I was a minority. At Fame Recording, I don't remember any other white groups. I do remember recording and sitting in sessions with African-Americans. I can remember relationships I had with rhythm-and-blues singers.

In the music business, different races were in studios together, we performed together, we talked, and we interacted. It was the first time I saw that these were some beautiful people. It wasn't what some people had depicted in the South. I made a lot of friends. When I went into coaching because of those interactions, I was able to communicate in a positive, caring way with people of other races.

But racial interaction was a relatively new experience—not just for me, but sometimes for the athlete also. He, too, had to get accustomed to a white man coaching him. Through the years of coaching, I have had young men of color become like sons to me. I will never judge a person by the color of his skin.

In 1984, I made what many people considered a bold move at the time. Even some of my African-American friends were concerned about the move at that time. I was the first head coach at a major school to hire all African-Americans on my full-time staff. One of those on my staff, Rudy Washington, became the leader and one of the founders of the Black Coaches Association. He currently serves as a commissioner of the Southwest Athletic Conference.

This move helped enable us to become runner-up in the ACC in 1987, due mostly to this staff's recruiting efforts.

When I took the job at Vanguard, Ocala had had racial problems. They'd had a major walkout the year before. I took the job with open arms; I listened and communicated. I made practice fun, like playing my favorite soul singer, James Brown, at practice. I wanted it to be a place they didn't want to walk out of but wanted to walk into. Also, I made sure that I took my team to their homes personally after practice. I took each player directly to his doorstep.

We became a close-knit group. I still adore that group of young men. They helped knock down racial barriers forever at Ocala Vanguard. They would win 20 games and unite the school and community through their character and skills.

CHAPTER TWENTY-THREE

The Winning Edge

Life has been a wonderful and exciting adventure for me. I have been fortunate enough to find the path to success. In paving the way for my journey as a basketball coach, musician, businessman, student-athlete, and husband and father, I have allowed myself to dream large dreams. I have determined that if it's going to happen, I've got to *make* it happen. Instead of asking, "What's happening?" I want to make it happen. It is called *efficacy*, the causative power to make something happen.

Through my walk in life, I have defined my 10 steps to success. Before I list these steps, I think it is important to understand my definition of success. Success is doing that thing you most want to do and doing it your absolute best. I believe 75 percent of success is mental, forming the right frame of mind. If a person wants to become a doctor, lawyer, or school teacher, it's not up to anyone else. If I am not the person I want to be, I can meet with the guy who is keeping me back. I feed this person, brush his teeth, and look at him in the mirror.

Step 1 of my 10 steps to success begins with the God-given talent that I have been allowed to use. I knew in the eighth grade I was going to coach. I felt I was given good hand-eye coordination to participate in sports such as golf, baseball, and basketball. It is important for everyone to recognize his or her talents. Every individual is different, and each individual is given a talent. It is not arrogant to claim to be talented. It is realistic to look for the areas of talent.

Step 2 involves taking that talent and skill and showing tremendous *desire, dedication*, and *determination*. One of the greatest events I have ever watched involved Cal Ripken, baseball player for the Baltimore Orioles. It was a televised event for the world to see. Cal Ripken was about to break what I think is one of the most fascinating records in sports history—Lou Gehrig's consecutive-game streak of 2,131. Cal Ripken broke this seemingly impossible streak. He had not missed one day of work for 12 years. Four thousand players have been on the disabled list since Gehrig's streak. What an example for all of us. It shows tremendous desire, dedication, and determination. By the way, on the night he broke the record, Cal Ripken homered and played a great game. It was exhilarating for me to watch. I cried.

Step 3 involves courage. Courage is the fertilizer that grows champions. Courage involves risk. People must be willing to take risks if they are going to be successful. A great story of courage to me involves Heather Whitestone, an Alabamian. She was born deaf, but despite her handicap, she became Miss America in 1994. What a great story of courage. She spelled American with its last four letters—I CAN.

Another step involves developing good friends. Association brings assimilation. So often we become a part of what we associate with. If I associate with winners, I am more likely to become a winner; if I associate with losers, I can become a loser. My good friend Gene Stallings, former football coach at Alabama, shared this poem with me one day, and I have never forgotten it. It is powerful.

Portrait of a Friend

When things don't come out right
  He comes right in;
He never looks for your money
  Except when you've lost it;
He never gets in your way
  Except to clear it for you;
Nothing is more important to him
  Than making you important;
He is in your corner
  When you get cornered;
He turns up
  When you get turned down;
All he wants in return for his helping hand
  Is your handshake;
He never insists on seeing you
  Except when no one else wants to;
The only time he sponges off of you
  Is to absorb some of your trouble;
When you are taking bows
  He is bowing out;

You can do anything with his friendship—anything!
    Except buy it and sell it;
He makes you realize that having a best friend
    Is like having an extra life;
All he asks of your friendship
    Is the privilege of deserving it.

Step 5 involves *pride.* I have always felt that you should be proud of who you are and whom you represent. I tell all of my student-athletes to be somebody and not just a social security number. "You hold on to your steering wheel of life—take pride in yourself and control this steering wheel." The story I so often relate to pride is the Sammy Jacobs story. Sammy Jacobs was a young man who grew up in the '50s in a small town similar to where I was raised. In these towns there were corner drugstores with the stools to sit on and eat ice cream sundaes and talk about the upcoming game, as well as other things. Sammy walked into the local drugstore one day and put a dime in the pay phone. A lady answered the call, and Sammy stated, "Ma'am, I am Sammy Jacobs and I need a job. I'll cut your grass for $5." The lady replied, "Sammy, I already have someone to cut my grass." Sammy said, "Ma'am, I'll take your garbage out also and still do it for $5." Again she replied, "Sorry, I already have someone." Sammy made another attempt. "Ma'am, I am Sammy Jacobs and I really need a job. I'll cut your grass, take out your garbage, and I'll go to the supermarket and do all your grocery shopping and I will do all this for $5." Again she replied, "I am sorry, I already have somebody." He hung up the phone and the pharmacist said to Sammy, "I could not help but overhear your conversation, and I am so impressed with your attitude and energy that I will give you a job." Sammy replied, "Sir, I am not really Sammy Jacobs. I am the person who cuts her grass, and I just wanted to find out what kind of job I was doing." This young man had tremendous pride in who he was, what he was doing, and how he was doing it.

Step 6 is *discipline*. This can be a person's breaking point. It is so important to have self-discipline. Each of us must build resiliency. We must say no when we need to. Lack of discipline can take a family down.

Step 7 involves *overcoming adversity*. Life is not always fair. In basketball we will not win every game, nor will things always go my way. This is true in life as well. I have found in my vocation that I have to stare adversity down. I like to meet adversity face to face, smile, and say, "Have a nice day." I can't please everyone, but I can work hard and care about others. If I do this, I believe I will meet adversity face to face and overcome it.

Step 8 involves *dependability*. I must be dependable. Be as good as my word. If I say I am going to do something, I will do it. A person should never leave room for doubt of words or actions.

Goal setting and affirming those goals is a vital step— step 9. It is important to set goals. I learned several years ago from a great teacher, Lou Tice, to write these goals down, to be broad with my goal setting, to set goals for work, goals for friendships, family goals, and any goal that is important to me. A person should be reasonable with goals and write goals in the present tense. An example of one of my goals is written like this and adopted because of my propensity to gain weight during the season—I love to eat. "I am glad that I weigh only 180 pounds, as it makes me look good and feel good while our team performs on television in front of millions of people." Through the years, this has helped me keep my weight stable. Today I weigh 178 pounds.

Another goal is written: "I am excited about the young men on our team and their ability to defend, rebound, take charges, practice free throws, and take good shots, as it will propel us to Auburn's first SEC Western Division championship." As has been documented, this team ended up going even beyond this. I believe in writing these goals down in the present tense and then reading these goals every day, preferably in the morning as I start my day, and in the evening when I go to bed. If I believe in my goals, I will self-regulate. When people set goals, they start to buy into themselves. Every day can be like Christmas. Life becomes an adventure.

The 10th and final step may be the most important, for without it, people will struggle to succeed. *Positive attitude*— thinking positively. We are born thinking negatively. After all, our first life experience is a spanking from our mom's doctor. Newspapers are more negative than positive. Headlines are not usually about something good, but rather something devastating that has happened. It always amused me back in the '60s, watching the network news on CBS, ABC, or NBC, that commercials following the news were aspirin commercials. No wonder we needed an aspirin. We had a headache after hearing all the bad events of the day.

The human mind is like the ground. Whatever is planted in the mind is what the body sows. If a farmer plants corn in the ground, he gets corn. If we plant positive thoughts, we get positive results.

Failure is never final; it is only temporary. Ernest Hemingway wrote the last chapter to *Farewell to Arms* 39 times before he got it right; *Love Story* was written 23 times before it was gotten right.

I love hearing the story about the paralyzed man who swam the English Channel. What an effort, and what an attitude.

A positive attitude can carry a person a long way. Without it, life can become a pain in the butt, and a person's life becomes stagnant.

Without these 10 steps, I would not have achieved. These steps, along with strong family values and ties from my parents to my wife and children, have been my anchors.

As you can tell, I love to tell stories. My favorite success story is a story Paul Harvey told about a man named Al. Al was useless, utterly useless. In a letter to his sister, he wrote, "I am nothing but a burden to my family. It would be better if I never was born." As a youngster, he was taken out of school and considered retarded. At 22, Al hit rock bottom. His parents were impoverished. He couldn't get a job. He appealed to an old school friend whose class notes he used to copy, who had governmental connections. He needed work badly. His friend's father worked for the federal patent office. His name was Fred Haller, and he was the director. Director Haller interviewed Al, and he needed someone to evaluate requests for patents. "What do you know about patents?" Haller asked. Al replied, "Nothing." He did not know what to say. After all, he had flunked out of high school, couldn't get into college, and couldn't pass the entrance exam into technical school. Al had finally gone to another high school and graduated, but he had "loser" written all over him. And now he was asking for a job for which he was not even qualified. Haller amazingly kept on with the interview and wanted to hear why he should hire Al. After 2 1/2 hours of personally interviewing Al, Haller decided he was not stupid, was not retarded, he was simply a failure who needed a dose of confidence. Fred Haller gave Al a break. He gave him a probationary job as technical expert, third class. Paul Harvey concluded the story in his inimitable way: "Al was not inexorably destined to guide lesser minds through these intricacies of space and time. In fact, at 22, he stood at the brink of utter uselessness, until Fred Haller gave him a chance at the Swiss Federal Patent Office. Inspired by that first success, he learned to live up to his potential. From that beginning came the incomparable genius, *Albert Einstein*."

I can never rest in this game. My goal when I came here was to build a program that could consistently compete on a championship level. There are things we still need to do. We have to continue to recruit, continue to upgrade our facilities, continue to make it a show people want to come to see.

We have to continue to graduate our players and do things in the right way. There will always be new players and new challenges, but those things are what I love about the game. They are the reasons I wanted to be a coach in the first place back in Chipley, Florida.

I signed a new eight-year contract after we won the championship. If things go as they should, I think I will finish my career at Auburn. It's a wonderful place. It's a great town with great people.

My coaching career has been more rewarding than I ever even imagined. I've known so many great people and made so many friends. I've had the opportunity to compete on the highest level, to be a part of big games when the atmosphere is electric. I have relationships with players that will last a lifetime.

I've been blessed.

Coach Ellis's Lettermen

Cumberland College (1973-1975)

Allen Anglea, 1974
Thomas Ayers, 1974
Walt Bellamy, 1973
James Britt, 1973, 74
Gary Burdsell, 1975
Sandy Burnett, 1973
Lee Carter, 1974, 75
Keith Dean, 1975
Joe Eskew, 1973
Johnny Farmer, 1975
Charles Fishback, 1973, 74
Ed Follins, 1974, 1975
John Garnett, 1973
Harris Gholson, 1973
Gary Gilley, 1973, 74

Barry Hamilton, 1975
Willie Hamilton, 1974
Jerry Kamis, 1973
Tinker Kelley, 1973
Danny Kng, 1975
Thomas Ledford, 1975
Plato Mathis, 1975
James McClellan, 1975
Mitch Moss, 1975
Norman Pace, 1975
Steve Payne, 1973
Willie Pickett Smith, 1973, 74
Craig Sullivan, 1974, 75
Randy Vanatta, 1973, 74

South Alabama (1975-76 to 1983-84)

Bill Anderson, 1979
Herb Andrew, 1980, 81
Rick Baker, 1976
Anthony Barge 1982, 83, 84
John Bennett 1979, 80
Kelly Blaine 1982, 83, 84
Greg Bouyer 1977
John Brown 1977
Damon Bryant 1981, 82
Hank Carter 1982, 83, 84
Terry Catledge 1982, 83, 84
Percy Cooper 1982
Kevin Courtney 1976, 77, 78

Billy Culbertson 1980
Ronnie Davis 1978, 79, 80
Keith Dean 1977
John Farmer 1976, 77, 78
Albert Gardner 1975, 76
King Gaskins 1977
Michael Gerren 1983, 84
Kenny Gibson 1983, 84
Phil Green 1982, 83
David Grube 1976
Joe Hampton 1979
Randy Hampton 1979
Reggie Hannah 1982

Don Hogan 1977, 78, 79, 80
Willie Jackson 1982, 83, 84
Michael Jones 1982
Olan Johnson 1976
Joe Karr 1983
George Kearse 1983
Alonzo Lambert 1976
Hal Langston 1983, 84
Thomas Ledford 1976, 77, 78
Lonnie Leggette 1978, 79
John Mallard 1977, 78
John May 1978, 79, 80, 81
Dale Osbourne 1983, 84
Ed Rains 1978, 79, 80, 81
Bubba Raymond 1981
Garry Reese 1977, 78

Jay Rich 1981, 82
Ric Scott 1980, 81, 82, 83
Rick Sinclair 1975, 76
Dennis Still 1979, 80
Jerry Sypkens 1982, 83
Jimmy Tate 1976, 77
Troy Taylor 1980
George Torres 1978
Jose Waitman 1983, 84
Benny Washington 1981
Emory Wells 1981
George White 1976
Rory White 1978, 79, 81, 82
Willie White 1976
Scott Williams 1978, 79, 80, 81

Clemson (1984-85 to 1993-94)

Ryan Amestoy 1992
Rudy Antoncik 1964, 66
Michael Best 1986
Anthony Blackman 1985
Jeff Brown 1993
Michael Brown 1987
Donnell Bruce 1988, 89, 90, 91
Wayne Buckingham 1990, 92, 93, 94
Eric Burks 1991
Ed Bynum 1985
Elden Campbell 1987, 88, 89, 90
Marion Cash 1989, 90
Merl Code 1994
Gary Cooper 1988
Glenn Corbit 1985, 86
Chris Couch 1986, 87
Dale Davis 1988, 89, 90, 91
Derrick Forrest 1989, 90
Harlan Graham 1985
Harvey Grant 1985

Horace Grant 1985, 86, 87
Devin Gray 1992, 93, 94
Vincent Hamilton 1985
Steve Harris 1991, 92
Kevin Hines 1992, 93
Jeff Holstein 1986, 87
Kirkland Howling 1989, 90
Anthony Jenkins 1986, 87
Ricky Jones 1988, 89, 90, 91
George Kelada 1992
Andy Kelly 1993
Tim Kincaid 1987, 88, 89
Shawn Lastinger 1990, 91
Todd Logue 1992
Glen McCants 1985, 86
Grayson Marshall 1985, 86, 87, 88
Bruce Martin 1992
Jimmy Mason 1991
Chris Michael 1985, 86

Larry Middleton 1986, 87
Rod Mitchell 1988, 89
Byron Morris 1993, 94
Tyrone Paul 1991
Rayfield Ragland 1994
Michael Tait 1986, 87

Frank Tomera 1993, 94
Sean Tyson 1988, 90, 91
Corey Wallace 1992, 93, 94
Chris Whitney 1992, 93
Sharone Wright 1992, 93, 94
David Young 1989, 90, 91

Auburn (1994-95 to 1998-99)

Charlton Barker 1999
Earnest Brown 1996
Pat Burke 1995, 96, 97
Derek Caldwell 1996, 97, 98
Adrian Chilliest 1996, 97, 98, 99
Reid Clark 1995, 96
Jim Costner 1995
Chris Davis 1995
Leroy Davis 1995
Ray Donald 1995, 96
Daymeon Fishback 1997, 98
Wes Flanigan 1995, 96, 97
John Gomillion 1998
David Hamilton 1999
Jay Heard 1999
Randy Hughes 1998
Andre Jasquith 1995
Alvin Jefferson 1996
Kendell Mack 1998

Mack McGadney 1999
Mamadou N'diaye 1997, 98, 99
Moochie Norris 1995
Adrian Person 1999
Scott Pohlman 1998, 99
Chris Porter 1999
Clifton Robinson 1998
Doc Robinson 1997, 98, 99
Reggie Sharp 1999
Abe Smith 1999
Bryant Smith 1996, 97, 98, 99
Dudley Smith 1998
Mike Springfield 1995, 96
Phillip Thomas 1996
Corey Watkins 1999
Lance Weems 1995, 1996
Franklin Williams 1995, 96, 97, 98

Cliff Ellis' Coaching Record

Year	School	Record	Pct.	Conf. (Finish)	Postseason
1972-73	Cumberland College*	20- 5	.800	*	*
1973-74	Cumberland College*	34- 2	.944	*	*
1974-75	Cumberland College*	24- 5	.828	*	*
1975-76	South Alabama	18- 9	.667	*	*
1976-77	South Alabama	17-10	.630	3-3	(3rd)
1977-78	South Alabama	18-10	.630	3-7	(4th)
1978-79	South Alabama	20- 7	.740	10-0	(Champions)
NCAA Midwest Regional (first round)					
1979-80	South Alabama	23- 6	.793	12-2	(Champions)
NCAA Midwest Regional (first round)					
1980-81	South Alabama	25- 6	.806	9-3	(Champions)
NIT (quarterfinals)					
1981-82	South Alabama	12-16	.429	2-8	(6th)
1982-83	South Alabama	16-12	.571	6-8	(5th)
1983-84	South Alabama	22- 8	.733	9-5	(2nd)
NIT (second round)					
1984-85	Clemson	16-13	.552	5-9	(t-6th)
NIT (first round)					
1985-86	Clemson	19-15	.559	3-11	(7th)
NIT (quarterfinals)					
1986-87	Clemson	25- 6	.806	10-4	(2nd)
NCAA Southeast Regional (first round)					
1987-88	Clemson	14-15	.483	4-10	(7th)
NIT (first round)					
1988-89	Clemson	19-11	.633	7-7	(6th)
NCAA West Regional (second round)					
1989-90	Clemson	24- 8	.750	10-4	(Champions)
NCAA East Regional (Sweet 16)					
1990-91	Clemson	11-17	.392	2-12	(7th)
1991-92	Clemson	14-14	.500	4-12	(9th)
1992-93	Clemson	17-13	.567	5-11	(7th)
NIT (second round)					
1993-94	Clemson	18-16	.592	6-10	(t-7th)
NIT (quarterfinals)					
1994-95	Auburn	16-13	.552	7-9	(4th-Western)
NIT (first round)					

1995-96	Auburn	19-13	.452	6-10 (t4th-Western)
NIT (first round)				
1996-97	Auburn	16-15	.516	6-10 (t3rd-Western)
1997-98	Auburn	16-14	.533	7-9 (3rd-Western)
NIT (second round)				
1998-99	Auburn	29-4	.879	14-2 (Champions)
NCAA South Regional (Sweet 16)				
1999-2000	Auburn	24-10	.706	9-7 (2nd-Western)
NCAA Midwest Regional (second round)				

*Cumberland College (J.C.) Totals (three years): 78-12 (.867)
South Alabama Totals (nine years): 171-84 (.671)
Clemson Totals (10 years): 177-128 (.580)
Auburn Totals (five years): 120-69 (.635)
Overall Collegiate Head Coaching Record (27 years): 546-293(.651)
Division I Head Coaching Record (24 years): 468-281 (.625)

Numbers in parentheses below indicate (Clemson's/Auburn's rank, Opponent's rank) heading into the game. Not all rankings are known prior to each game.

1975-76

South Alabama (18-9)

(W/L)	SA		OPP
L	68	Centenary	82
W	86	at South Dakota	79
W	79	at Jacksonville	68
W	74	at Centenary	72
L	82	at UNLV	122
L	81	(1) Northeast La.	84
W	82	(1) Hardin-Simmons	77
W	112	(2) Rice	64
W	70	(2) Ole Miss	54
W	88	St. Bernard	69
L	62	Jacksonville	68
W	87	McNeese State	79
W	102	Samford	70
W	99	Baptist	77
L	81	Southwestern La.	82
W	97	Mercer	84
L	84	South Florida	95
W	87	at B'ham Southern	78
W	88	at Samford	81

L	70	at Northeast Louisiana	87
W	83	at Mercer	70
W	78	at Georgia State	77
W	117	at Baptist	74
L	71	Georgia State	78
W	109	at SW Louisiana	89
L	76	at McNeese State	85
W	74	at Stetson	61

(1) Indian Holiday Classic
(2) Senior Bowl

1976-77

South Alabama (17-10, 3-3 Sun Belt)

(W/L)	SA		OPP
W	83	Oglethorpe	53
L	65	Stetson	66
W	102	(1) Rider	80
W	80	(1) James Madison	77
L	74	at McNeese State	75
L	71	(2) Cal. St.-Fullerton	89
L	64	(2) Pepperdine	73
W	85	(3) New Mexico State	83
W	58	(3) Army	54
W	81	(4) Samford	67
W	76	(4) Texas Tech	67
L	57	McNeese State	59
W	113	Hardin-Simmons	86
W	96	Texas-Arlington	71
W	106	Missouri-St. Louis	89
L	86	at Florida State	115
W	91	Northwestern State	73
W	77	at Robert Morris	74
W	77	B'ham Southern	66
L	81	at Northwestern State	89
W	74	Spring Hill	72
W	78	VCU	76
W	96	at Hardin-Simmons	89
L	82	at Illinois State	107
W	100	Robert Morris	80
L	70	at VCU	85
L	81	(5) Georgia State	82

(1) James Madison Invitational
(2) Malibu Classic
(3) Birmingham Classic
(4) Senior Bowl
(5) Sun Belt Tournament

1977-78

South Alabama (18-10, 3-7 Sun Belt)

(W/L)	SA		OPP
W	101	Oakland	78
L	62	Campbell	66
L	58	at Texas Tech	60
W	55	at Houston Baptist	49
W	43	Louisiana Tech	39
W	87	at Texas-Arlington	79
W	94	(1) Bucknell	68
W	82	(1) Pepperdine	64
W	82	Missouri-Kansas City	74
L	47	New Orleans	50
L	53	UNC-Charlotte	54
W	81	at Georgia Southern	66
W	82	at South Florida	68
L	82	at Jacksonville	85
W	77	UNC-Wilmington	66
W	70	South Florida	61
L	81	at New Orleans	92
W	71	Georgia State	58
W	58	at Florida State	56
L	60	at Georgia State	62
W	99	Georgia State	79
L	72	Jacksonville	83
W	67	at Louisiana Tech	65
L	78	at UNC-Charlotte	105
W	80	South Florida	75
W	66	(2) UNC-Charlotte	56
L	20	(2) New Orleans	22
W	83	Spring Hill	69

(1) Senior Bowl
(2) Sun Belt Tournament

1978-79

South Alabama (20-7, 10-0 Sun Belt)

(W/L)	SA		OPP
W	111	SIU-Edwardsville	78
L	78	at Mississippi State	86
W	79	at Northwestern State	66
L	91	Georgia Southern	93
W	75	North Park	68
L	72	at UAB	75
W	96	(1) Austin Peay	67
W	71	(1) Louisiana Tech	69
W	111	Wisconsin-Whitewater	90
W	97	Houston Baptist	74
L	63	at UNC-Wilmington	65
W	71	UNC-Charlotte	60
W	84	Georgia State	70
W	80	at New Orleans	73
W	72	Jacksonville	61
W	101	New Orleans	65
W	89	at Georgia State	71
W	114	South Florida	83
W	78	Florida State	61
W	71	UAB	69
W	72	at Jacksonville	71
W	73	at South Florida	61
L	70	Illinois State	77
W	66	at UNC-Charlotte	63
L	77	(2) Jacksonville	85
W	97	Northwestern State	91
L	66	Louisville (NCAA)	69

(1) Senior Bowl
(2) Sun Belt Tournament

1979-80

South Alabama (23-6, 12-2 Sun Belt)

(W/L)	SA		OPP
L	73	at Louisville	75
W	61	McNeese State	58
W	97	at Tennessee Tech	68

W	55	at Middle Tenn. State	49
W	81	at Hardin-Simmons	63
W	98	Oregon Tech	62
W	60	at Va. Commonwealth	56
W	65	at New Orleans	54
W	101	(1) Rider	72
L	77	(1) Alcorn State	82
W	105	Missouri Baptist	47
L	74	Va. Commonwealth	87
W	70	at Georgia State	61
W	64	at Jacksonville	63
W	84	South Florida	55
W	70	Georgia State	59
W	74	New Orleans	56
L	62	UAB	70
W	80	at UNC-Charlotte	69
W	88	at South Florida	72
W	66	UNC-Charlotte	65
W	65	Jacksonville	58
W	94	at Georgia Southern	79
W	89	Georgia Southern	61
W	76	Hardin-Simmons	64
W	66	at UAB	65
W	86	(2) South Florida	57
L	72	(2) Va. Commonwealth	74
L	61	Alcorn State (NCAA)	70

(1) Senior Bowl
(2) Sun Belt Tournament

1980-81

South Alabama (25-6, 9-3 Sun Belt)

(W/L)	SA		OPP
W	86	Wisconsin-Parkside	58
L	79	Middle Tenn. State	80
W	77	(1) Texas-El Paso	66
W	77	(1) Holy Cross	53
W	67	Tennessee Tech	48
W	101	Prairie View A&M	53
W	76	at Ohio State	67
W	52	at Akron	49
W	65	(2) Navy	47
W	79	(2) Fordham	61

W	98	Miss. Valley State	67
W	76	at Va. Commonwealth	62
W	92	at UNC-Charlotte	61
W	74	Georgia State	54
W	80	UNC-Charlotte	63
W	95	Nicholls State	62
L	70	Va. Commonwealth	86
W	64	at McNeese State	60
W	55	at Jacksonville	48
L	70	at UAB	73
W	54	South Florida	50
W	86	Jacksonville	65
W	82	at Georgia State	49
L	52	at South Florida	70
W	77	UAB	57
W	50	at Illinois State	44
W	79	(3) Georgia State	41
L	59	(3) UAB	86
W	74	Texas-Arlington(NIT)	71
W	73	at Georgia (NIT)	72
L	68	at Tulsa (NIT)	69

(1) Worcester County Classic
(2) Senior Bowl
(3) Sun Belt Tournament

1981-82

South Alabama (12-16, 2-8 Sun Belt)

(W/L)	SA		OPP
W	103	Illinois-Benedictine	61
L	69	at Middle Tenn. State	71
W	83	Prairie View A&M	73
L	64	at Va. Commonwealth	90
L	58	Ohio State	68
W	72	California St.-Chico	50
W	91	(1) Grambling	66
L	66	(1) American	70
L	56	UNC-Charlotte	58
W	72	St. Xavier	45
L	72	at Oklahoma	79
L	59	at UAB	78
W	65	Akron	55
L	68	Louisville	75

W/L	SA		OPP
L	67	Va. Commonwealth	74
W	81	South Florida	57
L	91	Jacksonville (OT)	95
L	62	South Florida (OT)	74
W	55	at Georgia State	50
L	59	at West Virginia	65
L	82	UAB	86
L	72	at Jacksonville (OT)	75
W	70	Georgia State	40
W	78	Nicholls State	58
W	73	at UNC-Charlotte	68
L	73	at Southern Miss	86
L	75	(2) Jacksonville (OT)	77
W	68	(2) Va. Commonwealth	66

(1) Senior Bowl
(2) Sun Belt Tournament

1982-83

South Alabama (16-12, 6-8 Sun Belt)

(W/L)	SA		OPP
W	74	Prairie View A&M	62
W	94	Middle Tenn. State	91
W	120	Florida International	73
W	82	Texas Southern	74
W	85	Miss. Valley State	65
L	77	at Louisville	94
W	86	Illinois Wesleyan	66
W	101	Roosevelt	62
W	95	(1) Baltimore	82
W	87	(1) Northeastern	61
L	74	at Ohio State	79
L	73	Chicago State	88
W	84	UNC-Charlotte	72
L	67	at UAB	73
L	59	at Old Dominion	62
L	77	at Va. Commonwealth	89
W	88	Jacksonville	73
L	76	Va. Commonwealth (OT)	79
W	74	South Florida	73
L	75	at UNC-Charlotte	77
W	81	Western Kentucky	77
W	92	at Jacksonville	82

L	83	at South Florida	94
W	65	at Western Kentucky	64
L	76	Old Dominion	77
L	80	Ala.-Birmingham	85
W	86	Bethune-Cookman	75
L	59	(2) South Florida	66

(1) Senior Bowl
(2) Sun Belt Tournament

1983-84

South Alabama (22-8, 9-5 Sun Belt)

(W/L)	SA		OPP
L	70	Illinois State	84
W	84	Prairie View A&M	55
W	91	Miss. Valley State	71
W	81	(1) Florida A&M	70
W	95	(1) Auburn	73
W	72	at New Orleans	68
W	86	Texas Southern	72
W	73	Southern Miss	71
W	89	(2) at Florida Int'l.	48
W	78	(2) Oklahoma State	72
W	106	Roosevelt	57
W	97	Va. Commonwealth	73
W	59	South Florida	58
L	75	at Old Dominion	88
L	55	at Va. Commonwealth	84
L	79	UAB	80
W	87	Old Dominion	82
W	82	UNC-Charlotte	77
W	91	Jacksonville	76
W	66	at Western Kentucky	65
W	81	New Orleans	74
L	50	at UAB	51
W	73	Western Kentucky	71
W	67	at South Florida	57
L	58	at Jacksonville	63
W	101	at UNC-Charlotte	91
W	110	Bethune-Cookman	75
L	68	(3) at UAB	76
W	88	(4)Florida	87
L	66	(4)Virginia Tech	68

(1) Colonial Classic
(2) Orange Bowl Classic
(3) Sun Belt Tournament
(4) National Invitation Tournament

1984-85

Clemson (16-13, 5-9 ACC)

(W/L)	C		OPP
L	67	Tennessee Tech (OT)	68
W	90	(1) Campbell	55
W	79	(1) South Alabama	69
L	66	at South Carolina	71
W	89	Augusta	62
W	81	Middle Tenn. State	75
W	55	at Furman (OT)	53
W	86	(2) Massachusetts	72
W	81	(2) at Vanderbilt	74
W	84	Appalachian State	77
W	90	at Georgia Tech (NR,8)	81
L	68	North Carolina State	71
L	61	at Wake Forest	83
L	84	at Maryland	94
W	82	Virginia	62
L	59	Georgia Tech (NR,15)	64
L	83	Duke (NR,5)	100
W	52	North Carolina (NR,11)	50
W	96	Delaware State	65
L	57	at North Carolina State	69
W	98	South Carolina	81
W	80	Wake Forest	65
W	71	Maryland (NR,19)	64
L	66	at Virginia	69
L	50	at North Carolina (NR,13)	84
L	73	at Duke (NR,5)	90
W	100	Winthrop	55
L	63	(3) North Carolina State	70
L	65	(4) at UT-Chattanooga	67

(1) IPTAY Tournament (Clemson, SC)
(2) Music City Tourney (Nashville, TN)
(3) ACC Tournament (Atlanta, GA)
(4) National Invitation Tournament

1985-86

Clemson (19-15, 3-11 ACC)

(W/L)	C		OPP
W	83	Maryland-Eastern Shore	57
W	92	(1) East Tennessee State	67
W	70	(1) South Florida	60
W	101	Rider	63
W	79	Morgan State	36
W	73	South Carolina (OT)	66
W	87	Bethune-Cookman	60
W	89	Baptist	63
W	100	Georgia State	60
W	65	at Texas Tech	64
W	81	(2) Bradley	76
L	64	(2) Missouri	69
W	69	(2) Seton Hall	62
W	91	Wake Forest	64
L	81	Virginia	83
L	57	at North Carolina State	60
L	71	Georgia Tech (NR,5)	83
L	64	at South Carolina	65
W	46	at Wake Forest	43
L	78	at Duke (NR,5)	89
L	67	at North Carolina (NR,1)	85
L	69	N.C. State (OT) (NR,19)	73
L	69	at Maryland	78
L	64	North Carolina (NR,1)	79
W	96	Florida A&M	52
W	70	Maryland	60
W	75	Furman	57
L	69	at Virginia	82
L	69	Duke (NR,1)	77
L	63	at Georgia Tech	74
L	61	(3) Georgia Tech	79
W	99	(4) Middle Tenn. State	81
W	77	(4) at Georgia	65
L	57	(4) at Wyoming	62

(1) IPTAY Tournament (Clemson, SC)
(2) Rainbow Classic (Honolulu, HI)
(3) ACC Tourney (Greensboro, NC)
(4) National Invitation Tournament

1986-87

Clemson (25-6, 10-4 ACC)

(W/L)	C		OPP
W	108	(1) Georgia State	91
W	92	(1) Boston University	77
W	89	UNC-Asheville	58
W	86	Texas Tech	72
W	71	at South Carolina	65
W	103	Prairie View A&M	45
W	112	Armstrong State	39
W	95	(2) Delaware State	42
W	76	(2) Ark.-Little Rock	44
W	90	(3) Fordham	86
W	93	(3) Hawaii Pacific	74
W	73	N.C. State (20,18)	69
W	91	at W. Forest (OT) (20,NR)	88
W	108	Fla. International	55
W	94	Furman (12,NR)	77
W	72	Maryland (12,NR)	64
W	67	at Ga. Tech (10,NR)	66
L	103	Duke (OT) (10,12)	105
W	96	Winthrop (14,NR)	69
L	99	North Carolina (14,1)	108
W	89	Virginia (14,NR)	83
W	80	at Maryland (12,NR)	79
W	74	South Carolina (12,NR)	52
W	78	at N.C. State (12,NR)	75
W	94	at Virginia (OT) (12,NR)	90
W	87	Wake Forest (10,NR)	71
L	80	at North Carolina (10,3)	96
W	88	Georgia Tech (13,NR)	77
L	59	at Duke (13,15)	65
L	62	Wake Forest (13,NR)	69
L	60	(5) SW MO State(13,NR)	65

(1) IPTAY Tournament (Clemson, SC)
(2) TCBY Arkansas-Little Rock Classic
(3) Hawaii Pacific Tourney
(4) ACC Tourney (Landover, MD)
(5) NCAA Southeast Regional (Atlanta, GA)

1987-88

Clemson (14-15, 4-10 ACC)

(W/L)	C		OPP
W	69	(1) Oregon State	54
W	81	Baptist	60
W	71	Towson State	61
W	103	Mercer	68
W	76	Coastal Carolina	57
L	85	Southern Miss	88
W	91	Augusta	45
L	88	(2) Michigan (NR,11)	93
W	98	(2) Fla. International	47
L	61	at North Carolina State	70
L	53	at Maryland	68
L	75	at Virginia	77
W	83	Rider	48
W	75	Wake Forest	62
W	76	Furman	65
W	69	South Carolina	65
L	76	at Georgia Tech	85
L	63	at Duke (NR,5)	101
L	64	North Carolina (NR,8)	88
L	63	at South Carolina	75
L	66	Maryland	70
L	63	North Carolina State	88
W	65	Virginia	62
L	73	(3) Wake Forest	79
L	52	at North Carolina (NR,9)	88
W	79	Duke (NR,9)	77
W	97	Ga. Tech (2OT) (NR,13)	94
L	72	(3) N.C. State (NR,11)	79
L	69	(4) Southern Miss 74	

(1) Taiwan
(2) South Florida Invitational
(3) ACC Tourney (Greensboro, NC)
(4) National Invitation Tournament

1988-89

Clemson (19-11, 7-7 ACC)

(W/L)	C		OPP
W	96	The Citadel	82
W	79	at Furman	64
L	70	at South Carolina	90
W	79	Wagner	36
W	93	South Carolina State	70
W	77	at Hofstra	63
W	81	(1) Middle Tenn. State	77
W	74	(1) Oregon	61
L	58	(1) Oregon State	72
L	65	N.C. State (NR,16)	73
W	75	Maryland	58
W	88	Virginia	70
W	75	at Wake Forest	71
W	104	Youngstown State	74
W	77	Western Carolina	60
L	74	at Georgia Tech (NR,22)	75
L	62	at Duke (NR,8)	92
W	85	North Carolina (NR,8)	82
W	78	South Carolina	65
L	87	at Maryland	98
W	96	Liberty	71
L	75	at N.C. State (NR,19)	90
L	83	at Virginia	85
W	94	Wake Forest	83
L	86	at North Carolina (NR,5)	100
W	79	Duke (NR,9)	74
W	81	Ga. Tech (OT)(NR,25)	79
L	73	(2) Virginia	90
W	83	(3) St. Mary's (NR,22)	70
L	68	(3) Arizona (NR,1)	94

(1) Far West Classic
(2) ACC Tournament (Atlanta, GA)
(3) NCAA West Regional (Boise, ID)

1989-90

Clemson (24-8, 10-4 ACC)

(W/L)	C		OPP
W	87	(1) American Univ.-PR	73
W	74	(1) Stetson	61
L	48	(1) Alabama	57
W	71	at The Citadel	54
W	72	(2) Providence	71
W	114	Radford	76
W	104	at UNC-Charlotte	79
L	71	(3) Villanova	73
W	85	(3) Niagara	65
L	77	at N.C. State (NR,13)	79
W	82	Maryland	77
W	76	at Virginia	70
W	78	UNC-Asheville	54
W	76	Wake Forest	57
W	117	Georgia State	59
W	97	Western Carolina	61
W	91	Hofstra	58
W	91	at Georgia Tech (NR,13)	90
L	60	at North Carolina	83
L	80	Duke (NR,5)	94
W	83	South Carolina	65
W	75	at Maryland	73
W	74	Virginia	63
W	89	North Carolina State	81
W	85	Furman	74
W	89	at Wake Forest	75
W	69	North Carolina (23,NR)	61
W	97	Duke (20,5)	93
L	69	at Ga. Tech (20,10)	85
L	53	at So. Carolina (17,NR)	54
W	79	(4) Wake Forest (17,NR)	70
L	66	(4) Virginia (17,NR)	69
W	49	(5)BYU* (17,NR) 47	
W	79	(5)LaSalle* (17,12)	75
L	70	(6) Connecticut* (17,3)	71

(1) San Juan Shootout (San Juan, PR)

(2) ACC-Big East Challenge
     (Greensboro, NC)

(3) Texaco Classic (San Diego, CA)

(4) ACC Tourney (Charlotte, NC)

(5) East Regional (Hartford, CT)

(6) East Regional (E. Rutherford, NJ)

* NCAA Participation vacated

1990-91

Clemson (11-17, 2-12 ACC)

(W/L)	C		OPP
W	90	Md.-Baltimore County	73
W	96	Samford	56
W	91	The Citadel	77
W	68	Furman	66
L	62	(1) Seton Hall	78
W	75	Wisconsin-Green Bay	68
L	100	UNC-Charlotte	108
W	103	South Carolina State	83
W	71	(2) Coppin State	70
W	99	(2) Florida Atlantic	89
L	70	at North Carolina State	74
L	65	at Maryland	81
L	78	Virginia (NR,13)	82
L	88	Wake Forest (OT)	93
W	103	Western Carolina	82
L	52	Temple	71
L	68	at Ga. Tech (NR,25)	89
L	70	Duke (NR,7)	99
L	77	North Carolina (NR,9)	90
L	53	at South Carolina	58
W	73	Maryland	69
L	62	North Carolina State	72
L	47	at Virginia	57
L	57	at North Carolina	73
L	55	at Wake Forest	81
L	62	at Duke (NR,8)	79
W	69	Georgia Tech	62
L	59	(3) No. Carolina (NR,8)	67

(1) ACC-Big East Challenge (Syracuse, NY)
(2) Florida Int'l. Tourney (Miami, FL)
(3) ACC Tournament (Charlotte, NC)

1991-92

Clemson (14-14, 4-12 ACC)

(W/L)	C		OPP
W	114	Morehead State	69
W	96	Oral Roberts	76
W	87	Charleston Southern	67
W	85	Tennessee State	60
W	87	Furman	83
L	87	(1) Texas	95
W	63	(1) Northern Iowa	60
L	58	Wake Forest (NR,20)	73
L	69	at No. Carolina (NR,8)	103
W	94	UNC-Asheville	54
W	79	Wofford	59
L	75	North Carolina State	78
W	51	Virginia	48
L	71	at Maryland	84
L	73	at Duke (NR,1)	112
W	81	at Western Carolina	71
W	55	South Carolina	52
W	95	Ga. Tech (OT) (NR,24)	78
L	90	at Florida State (NR,23)	102
L	48	at Wake Forest	60
L	72	North Carolina (NR,6)	80
W	68	Florida State (NR,16)	67
W	82	Maryland	70
L	61	at North Carolina State	63
L	49	at Virginia	69
L	97	Duke (NR,1)	98
L	82	at Georgia Tech	101
L	75	(2) Maryland	81

(1) Sun Bowl Carnival (El Paso, TX)
(2) ACC Tourney (Charlotte, NC)

1992-93

Clemson (17-13, 5-11 ACC)

(W/L)	C		OPP
W	93	Liberty	68
W	89	Howard	70
W	88	UNC-Greensboro	62

W	82	at Furman	59
W	76	The Citadel	54
W	93	Davidson	77
W	91	(1) Appalachian State	73
W	87	Mercer	69
W	80	Furman	72
L	67	at Duke (NR,1)	110
L	82	at Virginia (NR,14)	100
L	72	North Carolina (NR,5)	82
L	71	Florida State (NR,22)	89
L	56	at Wake Forest	74
W	82	Maryland	72
L	70	at North Carolina State	72
W	83	at Ga. Tech (NR,22)	80
W	89	at South Carolina (OT)	84
L	84	Duke (NR,3)	93
L	78	Virginia (NR,24)	83
L	67	at N. Carolina (NR,3)	80
L	92	at Florida State (NR,9)	102
W	76	Wake Forest (NR,12)	74
W	81	at Maryland	73
W	92	North Carolina State	82
L	59	Georgia Tech	66
W	87	(2) Florida State (NR,12)	75
L	61	(2) Georgia Tech	69
W	84	(3) Auburn	72
L	64	(3) at UAB	65

(1) Charlotte, NC
(2) ACC Tourney (Charlotte, NC)
(3) National Invitation Tournament

1993-94

Clemson (18-16, 6-10 ACC)

(W/L)	C		OPP
W	86	Texas-Arlington	55
W	120	at Charleston Southern	103
W	85	Furman	70
L	54	at Minnesota (NR,15)	73
W	76	The Citadel	64
L	79	(1) Davidson	82

L	80	(2) Evansville	81
W	72	(2) Army	48
W	68	(2) Okla. State (NR,20)	65
L	65	Duke (NR,3)	71
W	67	UNC-Charlotte	63
W	88	at Mercer	71
L	57	Virginia	64
L	62	at N. Carolina (NR,1)	106
L	57	at Florida State	60
W	75	Wake Forest	68
W	66	Appalachian State	56
L	53	at Maryland (NR,18)	73
W	95	North Carolina State	73
W	88	Georgia Tech	69
L	74	at Duke (NR,1)	78
L	88	South Carolina	91
L	44	at Virginia	52
W	77	North Carolina (NR,2)	69
L	71	Florida State	79
L	69	at Wake Forest	80
W	73	Maryland	67
W	82	at North Carolina State	63
L	79	at Georgia Tech	90
W	76	(3) North Carolina State	63
L	64	(3) Duke	77
W	96	Southern Miss (NIT)	85
W	96	at West Virginia (NIT)	79
L	74	at Vanderbilt (NIT)	89

(1) Charlotte, NC
(2) Rainbow Classic (Honolulu, HI)
(3) ACC Tourney (Charlotte, NC)

1994-95

Auburn (16-13, 7-9 SEC)

(W/L)	AU		OPP
W	78	Lynn	70
W	60	at UAB	54
W	77	(1) Georgia Southern	45
L	74	(1) at Ball State	82
W	96	West Florida	59
W	95	Troy State	71

W	102	Alabama State	62
W	83	(2) at Florida A&M	70
L	75	(2) Kansas State	78
L	64	at Kentucky (NR,6)	98
W	88	Ole Miss	74
L	73	LSU	76
W	104	Arkansas (NR,4)	90
W	61	Tennessee	57
L	77	at Georgia	83
W	77	Florida (NR,23)	71
L	63	at Alabama (NR,20)	65
L	75	at Ole Miss	77
L	59	Vanderbilt	77
W	70	at Miss. State (NR,21)	69
W	80	at South Carolina	78
L	73	Alabama (NR,18)	86
W	81	at Southern Miss	79
L	78	at LSU	89
W	76	Miss. State (NR,14)	69
L	66	at Arkansas (NR,7)	68
W	81	(3) South Carolina	66
L	81	(3) Kentucky (NR,3)	93
L	61	Marquette (NIT)	68

(1) Cardinal Varsity Club Classic (Muncie, IN)
(2) Capital City Classic (Tallahassee, FL)
(3) SEC Tournament (Atlanta, GA)

1995-96

Auburn (19-13, 6-10 SEC)

(W/L)	AU		OPP
W	70	(1) La Salle	60
W	82	(1) James Madison	71
W	82	(1) Louisville (NR,13)	78
L	54	UAB	66
W	63	(2) Liberty	58
W	83	(2) at Baylor	64
W	59	at South Alabama	50
W	80	Northeast Louisiana	71
W	82	Coastal Carolina	66
W	73	Wofford	56
W	92	(3) Norfolk State	56

W	84	(3) at Florida A&M	54
L	62	at Tennessee	66
W	101	Arkansas	76
L	65	at Alabama	72
W	89	Georgia (NR,17)	86
W	95	LSU (23,NR)	87
L	69	at Ole Miss (21,NR)	82
L	62	at Vanderbilt (22,NR)	76
L	75	Miss. State (22,NR) (ot)	78
W	84	South Carolina (22,NR)	73
W	73	at Florida (22,NR)	70
L	72	Alabama	75
L	77	at Arkansas	87
W	69	Ole Miss	62
L	67	at LSU	93
L	73	Kentucky (NR,1)	88
L	51	at Mississippi State	67
W	68	(4) Vanderbilt	65
L	58	(4) Miss. State (NR,25)	69
L	73	(5) Tulane (ot)	87

(1) Puerto Rico Shootout (Bayamon, PR)
(2) Dr. Pepper Invit. (Waco, TX)
(3) Capital City Classic (Tallahassee, FL)
(4) SEC Tourney (New Orleans, LA)
(5) National Invitation Tournament

1996-97

Auburn (16-15, 6-10 SEC)

(W/L)	AU		OPP
L	57	at UAB	64
W	89	Arkansas-Pine Bluff	56
L	72	(1) Colorado (ot)	78
W	98	(1) at Hawaii-Hilo (ot)	92
L	66	(1) TCU	86
W	75	Arkansas-Little Rock	63
W	66	Georgia State	48
L	63	Baylor	68
W	80	Western Carolina	55
W	60	South Alabama	51
W	86	(2) Murray State	72
W	95	at Florida A&M	57

W	80	Winthrop	55
L	56	at South Carolina	66
L	55	Arkansas	56
W	79	Florida	65
W	43	Tennessee	35
L	53	at Kentucky (NR,4)	77
L	59	at LSU	75
L	48	at Georgia	55
W	72	Alabama	62
L	46	at Ole Miss	57
W	81	Mississippi State	68
W	76	LSU	72
L	42	at Arkansas	75
L	61	Vanderbilt	75
L	50	at Alabama	55
W	68	at Mississippi State	64
L	63	Ole Miss	71
W	67	(3) Tennessee	54
L	50	(3) Kentucky (NR,6)	92

(1) Island Island Invitatonal (Hilo, HI)
(2) Mulligan Hiliday Hoopfest (Birmingham, AL)
(3) SEC Tournament (Memphis, TN)

1997-98

Auburn (16-14, 7-9 SEC)

(W/L)	AU		OPP
L	42	(1) Temple (NR,24)	68
W	70	at Central Florida	63
W	96	Nicholls State	75
W	83	Southern Miss	70
W	68	Wofford	51
W	79	Florida A&M	69
L	55	(2) Pepperdine	62
W	63	(2) Weber State	58
W	89	Jacksonville State	61
L	65	(3) UAB	71
W	70	Navy	54
W	73	Georgia	62
W	74	at Tennessee	69
L	54	at LSU	59
W	94	Alabama	40

L	65	Arkansas (NR,18)	79
L	56	South Carolina (NR,14)	61
W	69	at Mississippi State	66
W	68	Ole Miss (NR,12)	67
L	62	at Alabama	76
W	68	Mississippi State (ot)	66
L	64	at Florida	81
W	66	LSU	44
L	66	at Vanderbilt	82
L	83	at Arkansas (NR,16)	107
L	58	Kentucky (NR,7)	83
L	67	at Ole Miss (NR,13)	74
L	64	(4) Florida	68
W	77	(5) Southern Miss	62
L	60	(5) at Marquette (ot)	75

(1) NABC Classic (Albuquerque, NM)
(2) Cougar Classic (Provo, UT)
(3) Holiday Hardwood Classic (Birmingham, AL)
(4) SEC Tournament (Atlanta, GA)
(5) National Invitation Tournament

1998-99

Auburn (29-4, 14-2 SEC)

(W/L)	AU		OPP
W	114	Southeastern Louisiana	60
W	94	Florida A&M	47
W	77	Central Florida	42
W	62	BYU	43
W	70	(1) Rutgers	55
W	84	(1) at Hawaii	57
W	91	UNC-Asheville	60
W	80	at Florida State	68
W	77	at UAB (24,NR)	64
W	79	Wofford (18,NR)	51
W	88	at Navy (18,NR)	70
W	99	Bethune-Cook.(15,NR)	46
W	90	Tennessee (15,NR)	62
W	83	Arkansas (14,18)	66
W	73	at LSU (14,NR)	70
W	74	at Ole Miss (8,NR)	59
W	88	Florida (8,NR)	69

L	62	at Kentucky (6,7)	72
W	73	at Alabama (6,NR)	58
W	64	Mississippi State (7,NR)	54
W	85	at Georgia (7,NR)	74
W	76	at So. Carolina (6,NR)y C	48
W	80	LSU (6,NR)	54
W	95	Ole Miss (3,NR)	66
W	102	Alabama (3,NR)	61
W	81	Vanderbilt (3,NR)	63
L	88	at Arkansas (2,NR)	104
W	76	at Miss. State (2,NR)	73
W	93	(3) Alabama (4,NR)	61
L	57	(3) Kentucky (4,14)	69
W	80	(4) Winthrop	41
W	81	(4) Oklahoma State (4,NR)	74
L	64	(5) Ohio State (4,14)	72

(1) United Airlines Tipoff Classic   (Honolulu, HI)
(2) Arby's Hardwood Classic (Birmingham, AL)
(3) SEC Tournament (Atlanta, GA)
(4) NCAA South 1st/2nd Rounds (Indianapolis, IN)
(5) NCAA South Region Semifinals (Knoxville, TN)

1999-2000

Auburn (24-10, 9-7 SEC West)

W/L	AU		OPP.
W	100	Arkansas-Pine Bluff	44
L	58	(1) vs. Stanford (2, 7)	67
W	65	Belmont	56
W	55	Florida State	54
W	77	(2) vs. Penn	70
W	63	Coppin State	35
W	78	(3) vs. Bradley	64
W	109	at Puerto Rico-Mayaguez	52
W	73	(4) vs. Virginia Tech	63
W	87	(4) Pepperdine	76
W	56	Southern Miss	50
W	100	Stony Brook	45
W	67	Georgia	52
W	66	Kentucky (4, 20)	63
W	73	at Mississippi State	67

W	65	South Carolina	61
L	77	at Ole Miss (ot)	79
L	76	at Tennessee (7/11)	105
W	73	Mississippi State	57
W	77	Alabama	63
W	73	Arkansas	55
L	68	at LSU (8, 25)	83
W	86	at Vanderbilt (11/24)	80
W	75	Ole Miss	72
L	64	at Alabama	68
L	59	at Florida (8, 9)	88
L	53	LSU (13, 12)	55
L	55	at Arkansas	64
W	78	(5) vs. Florida (23, 10)	70
W	77	(5) vs. South Carolina (ot)	72
L	75	(5) vs. Arkansas	67
W	72	(6) vs. Creighton	69
L	79	(6) vs. Iowa State (22, 6)	60

(1) Wooden Classic (Anaheim, CA)

(2) Hardwood Classic (Birmingham, AL)

(3) Coor's Classic (Mobile, AL)

(4) San Juan Shootout (San Juan, PR)

(5) SEC Tournament (Fayetteville, AR)

(6) NCAA Midwest Regional (Minneapolis, MN)

Numbers in parentheses indicate (Clemson's/Auburn's rank, Opponent's rank) heading into the game. Not all rankings are known prior to each game.

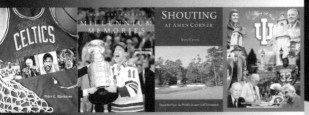